DATE DUE

GAYLORD

PRINTED IN U.S.A.

Dangerous Convictions

Dangerous Convictions

What's Really Wrong with

the U.S. Congress

TOM ALLEN

Oxford University Press is a department of the University of Oxford.
It furthers the University's objective of excellence in research,
scholarship, and education by publishing worldwide.

Oxford   New York
Auckland   Cape Town   Dar es Salaam   Hong Kong   Karachi
Kuala Lumpur   Madrid   Melbourne   Mexico City   Nairobi
New Delhi   Shanghai   Taipei   Toronto

With offices in
Argentina   Austria   Brazil   Chile   Czech Republic   France   Greece
Guatemala   Hungary   Italy   Japan   Poland   Portugal   Singapore
South Korea   Switzerland   Thailand   Turkey   Ukraine   Vietnam

Oxford is a registered trademark of Oxford University Press
in the UK and certain other countries.

Published in the United States of America by
Oxford University Press
198 Madison Avenue, New York, NY 10016

© Oxford University Press 2013

Library of Congress Cataloging-in-Publication Data
Allen, Thomas H. (Thomas Hodge), 1945–
Dangerous convictions : what's really wrong with the U.S. Congress / Tom Allen.
p. cm.
Includes bibliographical references and index.
ISBN 978-0-19-993198-9 (hardback)
1. United States—Politics and government—2009–
2. United States—Economic policy—2009–
3. United States. Congress—History—21st century. I. Title.
JK275.A55   2013
328.73—dc23   2012028783

Excerpt from "Kindness" from *Words Under the Words: Selected Poems* by Naomi Shihab Nye,
copyright © 1995. Reprinted with the permission of Far Corner Books, Portland, Oregon.

"The Peace of Wild Things" by Wendell Berry. Copyright © 2012 by Wendell Berry from
New Collected Poems. Used by permission of Counterpoint.

9 8 7 6 5 4 3 2 1

Printed in the United States of America
on acid-free paper

For Diana

Convictions are more dangerous enemies of truth than lies.
—FRIEDRICH NIETZSCHE, *Human, All Too Human: Texts in the History of Philosophy*

CONTENTS

ACKNOWLEDGMENTS

A life in Congress depends on teamwork. Writing a book is a more solitary endeavor, in my case for almost four years, but I have benefitted beyond measure from the guidance and suggestions of others.

At the top of the list is Cal Mackenzie, my Bowdoin College friend and classmate, distinguished professor of government at Colby College, noted author, and wise observer of Congress. Cal set me on the track of drawing on my congressional experience (without doing a memoir) to attempt a deeper commentary on our current dysfunctional politics. His encouragement throughout has made this book possible. Janice Cooper, as a member of my congressional team, helped write columns and speeches for years, and brought her insight and editing skills to this book from the beginning. She sharpened my prose and filled gaps in information, which made this book more readable and informative.

Jim O'Toole and Sandy Maisel read earlier drafts of the text and each in his own way advised me that "less is more." The book is sharper and more focused thanks to their suggestions. Others who gave helpful advice on the manuscript were John and Jean Gulliver, Ron Bancroft, Peter Murray, and Todd Stein.

The chapter on budget and taxes is built upon advice and information provided by Bob Greenstein, Jim Horney, and the ongoing data gathering and analysis of the Center for Budget Policy and Priorities. That center's reputation for puncturing inflated political claims about economic policy makes it an essential resource for anyone trying to make sense of controversies about the federal budget.

During the debate over President Bush's plan to invade Iraq, I relied for advice on another Bowdoin friend and classmate, Larry Pope, whose distinguished foreign service career lasted more than thirty years. Larry reviewed and critiqued the chapter on Iraq, which has benefitted from his suggestions for both additions and deletions.

Susan Lexer, my health policy advisor in Congress, clarified and much improved the discussion of health care, as did Chris Jennings in reviewing an early version of the chapter. Their help was invaluable.

The chapter on climate change reflects information and helpful advice from Roger Ballentine, Joe Romm, Julia Roberson, Conrad Schneider, Barney Balch, Ed Maibach, Greg Dotson, Molly Jacobs, and Ellen Bolen. My experience with the Faith and Politics Institute and the discussion of its work and importance owes much to Rev. Doug Tanner and Father Clete Kiley, and Kathy Gille made insightful contributions to the manuscript.

I now understand the value of a great publisher. The Oxford University Press team has been terrific. Dave McBride, my acquisitions editor, believed in this book and encouraged me to revise and reorganize to make it stronger. Mary Sutherland, my copyeditor, scoured the manuscript for errors and missing details, and made the final stages of preparation surprisingly enjoyable. Joellyn Ausanka managed the production process effectively and efficiently. In addition, my agent, Mel Berger, has been a forceful champion of the book, and I am grateful for his support. Despite the assistance of so many, I take full responsibility for any errors that remain.

If I had written more about my work in Congress, I would have highlighted my most satisfying achievement, which was building a team of committed advocates for the people of Maine. My congressional staff worked tirelessly to use the time we had together to make a difference for those who gave us the privilege and the responsibility to work for them. Led successively by Jackie Potter, the late Peter Wiley, and Mark Ouellette, they were passionate public servants. Their work and mine was made possible over the years by our devoted campaign staff and countless volunteers.

Finally, and most important, this book is dedicated to Diana, my life partner, who has shared with me over four decades the highs and lows of caring deeply about the world around us, and who gave her support to my twelve-year career in Congress that created, as all do, pressures on family life. Her love, and her enthusiasm for my work on this book, entitles her now to celebrate its publication knowing that much more of my time on weekends will now be ours. And our time will be more devoted to our grandchildren—for whom recovering a more pragmatic politics matters most.

Dangerous Convictions

Introduction

"Do these guys believe what they are saying?" Sitting in the chamber of the U.S. House of Representatives, listening to a heated debate, we asked each other that question about our Republican colleagues. We usually thought the answer was no but, if so, they were phenomenally good actors. Their arguments made no sense to us.

Such well-worn phrases as "tax cuts pay for themselves," "we'll be welcomed as liberators," "climate change isn't proven," and "government-run health care doesn't work" were repeated over and again. Republican arguments along these lines seemed incomprehensible to Democrats, just as ours seemed misguided to them. The evidence that mattered to us made no difference to them. The free-market principles they took as given conflicted with the information we took every day from our constituents and the economists we consulted.

News media preoccupation with lack of civility missed the point. I traveled with Republican members of Congress to Iraq and Afghanistan and enjoyed their company. We worked out together in the House gym. Still, more time socializing with each other would not have closed the chasm between our competing views of the world and the role of government. It's those world-views and the lack of comprehension on both sides that cripple the capacity of Congress to make bipartisan strategic public policy decisions. This, I came to see, is our greatest institutional weakness, and it defies simplistic cures.

Nietzsche wrote, "Convictions are more dangerous enemies of truth than lies."[1] In Congress I watched settled convictions, some of them deeply cherished by most Americans, overwhelm evidence that pointed to more pragmatic ways to resolve our differences about the federal budget, taxes, health care, energy, climate change, and Iraq. I wrote this book first to understand and then to explain the dysfunctional, polarizing nature of our political arguments.

I believe we cannot solve our country's most difficult problems unless the press and public treat seriously the ideas that motivate politicians. I tell the story from my personal experience in Congress and try to explain why our political debates have become ideologically frozen. To understand our differences one must listen carefully to the language that we use to argue our respective positions. I describe how those debates are driven below the surface by the enduring tension in American politics and culture between individualism and community.

Congress today is deeply divided because, to each side, the opinions of the other make no sense and therefore, each concludes, cannot be honestly held. Interest-group politics is still with us, fueled by unprecedented amounts of money. But it is overlaid and often dominated by what I can only call "worldview politics," a clash of values and convictions much deeper than the competition of interest groups in Washington.

We need a new perspective to visualize congressional polarization. The media and political commentators typically bemoan the wide gap in views between Right and Left. But Republicans and Democrats speak past each other not because they are too far apart on a left-right spectrum, but because they operate on different planes, higher and lower from the ground defined by evidence and expertise. On one hand, Republicans who are determined to cut taxes and shrink the size of government in order to increase personal freedom will reduce federal funds for education. On the other hand, Democrats believe that federal support for education is essential in order to increase individual opportunity and strengthen the American economy. Consequently, those who believe that government spending restricts personal freedom and induces a "culture of dependency" cannot successfully engage with advocates of a federal role in health care, education, and environmental protection.

I see no way to diminish our current political polarization without a sustained public dialogue about individualism and community in American life, because that is the primary source of congressional gridlock. Our businesses, our sports, our military, even our political parties are focused on team building. But our politics and capacity to govern ourselves successfully have been immeasurably weakened by a fierce hostility to government rooted in a radical individualism that denigrates the idea—in the context of government—that helping others strengthens the country.

The ideological struggle intensified during my twelve years in Congress, and with the rise of the Tea Party movement the trend has accelerated. Polarization itself is a second-order problem because the country can continue to survive pitched political battles, as we have in the past. The fundamental problem for Republicans—and for Democrats who would like to work with them—is that "smaller government, lower taxes" provides too little fabric to weave a national strategy for economic competitiveness, health-care reform, energy, or climate change because it denies a significant role for public leadership. Without comprehensive conservative policies to address these challenges, Republicans become unable, and therefore unwilling, to engage Democrats in constructive compromise. That's the primary source of Congress's inability to make long-term decisions without an overwhelming partisan majority.

Chapter 1 covers some of my early experiences in Congress, including those that taught me when bipartisan compromise was possible and when it was not. Gradually I came to understand the power of basic attitudes or worldviews in shaping positions on particular issues. The next four chapters explore areas of political controversy that at first glance appear unlikely to generate the intensity of social issues like abortion or gay rights. In each case I try to explain why Democrats cannot comprehend certain Republican arguments, and to a lesser extent, why Republicans don't understand what we say.

Chapter 2 addresses the budget and tax issues that raised the most baffling question for Democratic members of Congress, "Do these guys believe what they say?" The Republicans' apparent conviction that tax cuts pay for themselves by increasing revenues made no sense to us; it was contradicted by the independent Congressional Budget Office and almost all economists. The Bush tax cuts of 2001 were sold to the public in a "recklessly dishonest fashion."[2] Why did that happen at the very beginning of his administration? Is the conservative view of the benefit of taxes simply faith-based? The tax cuts of 2001 and 2003 reduced revenues, increased deficits, and undermined America's economic strength and resilience. The continuing conflict over the federal budget and taxes is the most fundamental and consequential of our differences, and it can now be compromised, even temporarily, only with enormous difficulty.

Chapter 3 argues that the Bush administration policy on Iraq involved willful avoidance of evidence. "We'll be welcomed as liberators" was a triumph of wishful thinking over hard analysis. Vice President Cheney pressured the CIA to find evidence that fit his established convictions. The State Department planned for post-invasion chaos and was ignored, because Rumsfeld bested Powell in the internal administration debate—to the extent one existed. Rumsfeld's pre-invasion speech about the risks of creating a "dependency" among Iraqis reflected the same conservative attitude of alarm about the risks of helping people in poverty. Neglect of evidence also undermined the institutional integrity of Congress; after the invasion Republican senators refused to hold hearings on the massive waste, fraud, and abuse by private American contractors in Iraq. They chose to protect the president instead of fulfilling their institutional responsibility to conduct oversight of the war and reconstruction. From the marketing of the invasion to the suppression of information about the occupation, why did supporters of the war in Iraq so freely manipulate or deny evidence?

Chapter 4 is about health care, ground zero of the partisan battle over the role of the federal government. The Republican effort to strengthen the private sector role in health care culminated in the Bush Medicare Prescription Drug legislation. Later, even the Obama health-care reform had to be built on a conservative concept of regulated state exchanges through which private insurers would compete for beneficiaries. Since the evidence and expert opinion on health-care reform is diverse, the important question is why Republicans made so little effort to address the dual concerns of people without coverage and businesses overwhelmed with rising insurance costs. Even when almost fifty million Americans lacked health insurance, no comprehensive Republican proposal for near universal coverage was put forth—because there was no free-market model that could accomplish that goal.

Chapter 5 asks why most Republicans deny the scientific consensus that human activity, particularly emissions of fossil fuels, is altering the atmosphere and oceans with potentially alarming consequences. If accepted, that scientific consensus would require engagement by the federal government, since there is no plausible private-sector solution to global warming. Nor is there a national solution independent of action by other countries. Why did the Bush administration feel free to intentionally alter research conclusions of government scientists on climate change and other environmental issues? Was it just to accommodate business supporters? Does lack of respect for scientific knowledge among Republicans have another source?

These four topics—budget/taxes, Iraq, health care, climate change—involve different issues, evidence, and approaches. Yet in Congress they seemed to be part of a whole, as if something not immediately apparent tied them all together. Otherwise, the two parties would not have been so fiercely divided on such disparate matters. Interest-group politics can explain some of the differences; each party appeals to and is supported by different combinations of business, labor, and other organized activists. But interest-group politics is now often overwhelmed by "worldview politics," a widening, hardening conflict between those who believe that the mission of government is to advance the common good and those who believe government is an obstacle to that end. If this is true, at one level all domestic issues merge into one—an unproductive, irreconcilable, ideological conflict about government itself.

Ultimately, however, this conflict is less about the role of government than the enduring tension between individualism and community in American politics and culture, and therefore, as much about the electorate as our representatives. In chapter 6 I explore the deeper sources of our current political polarization and the puzzling rigidity of the Republican Party. We should put on different spectacles to examine those subjects. If we consider how we talk about our lives and politics, Americans are much more comfortable with our "first language" of individualism than our "second language" of community. Conservatives have a message advantage in our political struggles, because they are the more articulate champions of individualism. By research into the "cognitive structures" of Americans, scholars from different disciplines have shed new light on how our basic values, attitudes, or worldviews influence our political preferences. Human beings also appear to be "wired" differently; some people interpret the world through a "single central vision" while others accept, even revel in its complexity, confusion, and contradictions. In short, a combination of forces and ideas are driving Americans into the two parties based on increasingly incompatible worldviews, transforming our politics and making Congress increasingly dysfunctional.

In chapter 7 I ask how we can contain the growing dominance of worldview politics and the public disillusionment that follows in its wake. Although reforming congressional practices and containing the influence of money in politics would help, Americans will not have a Congress we can respect until we find a better accommodation between our competing ideas about what Americans should do together—through their governments— and what individuals should do for themselves. Ideas and values, when integrated into worldviews, drive our political behavior, both in Congress and the country. Our second language of community may be weaker than the language of individualism, but it is still a powerful shared narrative of our experience—more fitted to the interconnected, rapidly changing world of the twenty-first century. We need to recover some portion of what we have lost: respect for evidence, tolerance of ambiguity, and some shared understanding of the common good. The challenges of this new century can be met only with levels of national and global collaboration that American individualism and "free markets" are inadequate to address.

This book is not intended to be another chapter in the partisan wars, to allocate blame for existing polarization between the parties, or to assess the grievances that each side has accumulated against the other. It is about two competing bundles of ideas and attitudes, both of which are deeply rooted in the American experience. Most Americans in varying degrees believe in both individualism/self-reliance on the one hand and community/cooperation on the other. I concentrate primarily on the Republican worldview because it has changed the most in the last twenty years, as its main precept of "smaller government, lower taxes" has calcified into an anti-government orthodoxy that is much less pragmatic than the policies even of the Reagan administration.

After twelve years in Congress I know too well the partisan battle for political power with all the money, organization, and spin that each side can muster against the other. I do not mean to diminish its importance. But I also know that members of Congress on both sides of the aisle have a vision that drives us toward a political life and informs what we seek to accomplish. There is less overlap in our competing visions than there used to be, and we will not escape from our current dysfunctional gridlock without understanding why that has happened.

This book has been shaped by three impressions from my congressional experience. First, I doubted that my Republican colleagues really believed some of their own arguments, but they spoke with great conviction. Second, our debates on the House floor seemed to only skim the surface of the ultimate nature and source of our disagreements. Third, those deeper disagreements were connected in some way to differences in broader perspectives on the world, including religious faith. For example, I wondered why Republicans gravitated toward congressional prayer groups, and the Faith and Politics Institute reflection groups that I attended attracted mostly Democrats. I hope that this view of congressional dysfunction from the inside can illuminate why its deepest source is a split in the American psyche, magnified by our contemporary media and politics.

In both religion and politics, individuals can unite as adherents of specific beliefs or in pursuit of a more general common purpose. In the public square religion has recently been more often invoked on specific issues—abortion, gay marriage, and contraception—than as a reminder of our common humanity. Democratic institutions require mutual respect and reasoned deliberation on matters of common concern, however difficult they may be. Faith and reason we are all given in measure. Perhaps wisdom is knowing the limits of each.

Early Lessons in Congress

Here, Sir, the People Govern.

—ALEXANDER HAMILTON (*Inscription—House
Corridor—United States Capitol*)

I didn't know what to expect. Although I had been involved in politics and
government for most of my life, winning a seat in Congress was not part
of any life plan. After leaving the practice of law after nineteen years to run
for governor of Maine, and losing in the Democratic primary in 1994, I
entered the race for the First Congressional District primarily because a
conservative Republican had been swept into office in 1994 on the Newt
Gingrich tide, and I thought I could help reverse it. It was a second and
probably last chance for major political office. I had never served in the
state legislature; my elected experience was limited to the nonpartisan
Portland City Council.

Ten days after the 1996 election, I traveled to Washington for orientation sessions and organizational meetings. Twenty-six years earlier,
George J. Mitchell, then a young Maine lawyer, had hired me to work for
Sen. Ed Muskie (D-ME); both men remain models for me of the highest
level of public service. In 1970–71 I had spent about eight months in
Washington divided between Ed Muskie's senatorial office and his presidential campaign. That was a different era, one with limited lessons for the

increasingly polarized climate gripping the White House and Congress in the mid-1990s.

During our first freshman orientation meeting, Newt Gingrich, the Speaker of the House, cautioned us not to become jaded or self-satisfied: "If you ever find that you can walk by the Capitol Dome all lit up at night and not be moved, then it's time to leave." Dick Gephardt, the Democratic leader, told us that we had two jobs—one in Washington working on legislation, and the other in our district meeting with constituents, either of which could consume all our waking hours. Our challenge was to perform both well and still carve out some time for our families.

The orientation sessions by the Congressional Research Service, the nonpartisan research arm of the Library of Congress, attracted many Republican and Democratic participants. Along with other programs, the party divisions were already apparent. In fairness, we had come to Washington with different agendas, so it was not that surprising that more Democrats attended the Kennedy School center-left orientation and more Republicans went to the center-right Heritage Foundation program.

New members plunge into a world of constant motion with few pauses for rest or reflection. The tasks seem infinite: setting up offices in DC and the home district, hiring staff in both places, creating systems to respond to mail and phone calls from constituents, learning the legislative ropes, meeting with constituent groups, giving speeches back home to Chambers of Commerce, Rotaries, and other groups, holding forums on the issues of the day, visiting businesses, retirement communities, and so on.

The travel schedule is daunting, but it quickly (for those with manageable commutes) becomes routine. Most members are in DC on the days we vote and back home or on the road the days we don't. In Washington, I would start most days with a 6 a.m. workout in the House gym, attend an 8 a.m. gathering, such as an Aspen Institute breakfast on a current topic, the informal Democratic Budget Group on Wednesday, or my Faith and Politics Reflection Group on Thursday. The rest of the day would be filled with committee hearings, discussions with staff, press calls, meetings with constituents, floor votes throughout the day, brief appearances at receptions in the evening, and more work and reading in the office until about 10 or 10:30 at night.

Democrats and Republicans staked out different territories, physically and philosophically. We saw each other on the floor and in committee hearing rooms but usually sat on opposite sides of the chamber. We shared a small gym in the basement of the Rayburn House Office Building, and once we had more than one television, Democrats watched CNN while Republicans took in Fox News. We talked in office hallways and on the sidewalk or tunnels in hurried sprints to vote in the Capitol, but longer conversations were less common. The more senior members remembered the old days of bipartisan socializing at night and on weekends, but most of us returned to our districts and families as soon as votes were done for the week.

I came to Congress with great hope and little experience. For a freshman in Congress, the big picture is easily lost in the intense swirl of daily decisions: which bills to support, people to see, speeches to give, alliances to build, votes to cast, explanations to present, press releases to send. Decisions had to be made and votes taken—always—with incomplete information about substance and, of course, the future reactions of people back home.

Over time I learned—from Bosnia, the Clinton impeachment, 9/11, Afghanistan, Iraq, and the economic recession—that members of Congress are swept along by forces in the world that they, as individuals, cannot control. The unpredictable forces include foreign and domestic crises, popular movements, and party leadership choices. We react much of the time and have to fight to make space for personal legislative initiatives.

Serving in Congress is breathtakingly complex and all-consuming. Only with experience did I learn to decode much of what I regularly saw and heard, for the daily debates covered layers of largely unexamined attitudes, ideas, and convictions that shape the partisan struggle. Some of the convictions are dangerous because they drive public policy in directions that make little moral or economic sense.

I found that there were two great mysteries in my congressional experience. First, why were the two parties always making the same arguments against each other no matter what the subject? Second, what was the answer to the question we Democrats asked each other, "Do these guys believe what they say?" But, for now, let's look at some areas where common ground was possible, and some where it was not.

Bipartisanship is consistently overvalued by the mainstream media, which too often skims the surface of policy debates, and is consistently trivialized by the most partisan media. By the end of my first three years in Congress I had begun to understand the conflict in congressional worldviews that has led to the crippling polarization in Washington. I found that working across the aisle was possible on campaign reform and oceans policy but very difficult on health care. Everything was harder after the Clinton impeachment further poisoned the congressional well.

CAMPAIGN FINANCE REFORM: FRESHMAN COLLABORATION

Notwithstanding the importance of party affiliation, there is a special bond among freshman members of Congress. We share the experience of learning the ropes in a demanding and very public undertaking. Within our first week in office, the Democratic freshmen elected Jim Davis (D-FL) as our class president. Jim asked me to be the Democratic chair of a bipartisan freshman task force on campaign finance reform. On both sides of the aisle many of us had been appalled by what we then thought was a flood of outside money in our campaigns. Asa Hutchinson (R-AR) was the Republican chair. I liked Asa; he was thoughtful, bright, and easy to work with.

Our task force met frequently and held informal hearings; our staffs developed proposals and consulted with experts. Creating draft legislation involved lengthy back-and-forth negotiations between Asa and me as co-chairs, and between each of us and our colleagues on the task force. At one point Asa told me that House majority leader Tom DeLay seemed fully aware of our task force negotiations, and we realized that there was a leak. We suspected that Sen. Mitch McConnell (R-KY), the most outspoken opponent of campaign finance reform in the Senate, had recruited Rep. Anne Northup (R-KY) on our task force to keep DeLay informed about our confidential discussions. We then had to work around Anne as best we could.

Our class focus on campaign finance reform was somewhat ironic. Asa and I were separately warned by our party leadership that, if successful, we would undermine our party's prospects. I was told that if our effort succeeded, Democrats would never regain the majority because we were dependent on "soft money" contributions from labor organizations. Asa was told that if legislation passed, the Republicans would lose the House majority and never regain it because they would lose the fund-raising advantage they had held for decades.

Asa and I agreed that the Republican and Democratic leaders could not both be right, and we believed that both were wrong. I thought that both parties would adapt to any new rules of the road and figure out how to compete under the new system.

In 1997–98 we struggled to find common ground that would contain the corrupting influence of unfettered campaign spending. After a process that almost fell apart several times, we agreed on a bill to ban unlimited contributions to the national parties from labor and business organizations ("soft money") and to regulate independent expenditures by a vast array of political groups. On the latter subject our bill was somewhat weaker than the leading campaign finance reform bill in the House, introduced by Rep. Chris Shays (R-CT) and Rep. Marty Meehan (D-MA). But we had brought a significant number of freshmen on both sides into the campaign finance reform tent. The Senate counterpart to Shays-Meehan bill was sponsored by Sen. John McCain (R-AZ) and Sen. Russ Feingold (D-WI).

During the August recess in 1998, the Republican leaders took so much public flack for blocking a House vote on campaign finance reform that Speaker Gingrich decided they had to bring a bill to the floor. But he didn't want a bill to pass. Instead of the traditional leadership tactic of blocking amendments by the minority, Gingrich and Tom DeLay decided to weigh the process down by filing and allowing debate on a huge number of amendments, including a number of "poison pills," which if passed would force supporters to back off. When the rule governing debate was announced, the Hutchinson-Allen bill was the base bill. Six substitute bills and more than five hundred amendments were allowed, the most ever allowed on one piece of legislation in the history of the House.

The floor debate consumed more than a month, and the campaign finance reform groups prevailed. In the end, the freshman caucus bill, Hutchinson-Allen, was supplanted by Shays-Meehan. I was content because their bill had stronger restrictions on independent expenditures, but Asa Hutchinson was unhappy with that provision and voted against the final bill.

The freshman task force had done its work. Although our bill did not pass, we had been instrumental in helping Democrats and Republicans find common ground on an important national issue, despite our leaders' opposition, unmistakably conveyed in quiet cloakroom conversations and procedural shenanigans.

At the time, the passage of McCain-Feingold was considered a dramatic success with the potential to contain the growing power of money in American politics. Campaign reformers were proud that they had taken on the leadership of both parties, although by the time of the debate, Democratic leaders had become converts. A decade later, in *Citizens United v. McConnell*, the Supreme Court—without prompting by the parties and virtually on its own initiative—would pull the rug out from under the independent expenditure provisions of McCain-Feingold and almost all legislation to control corporate political spending. Republican support for campaign finance reform has evaporated, and corporate money is more influential than we ever could have imagined in 1998.

MEDICARE PRESCRIPTION DRUG COVERAGE: BIPARTISANSHIP REBUFFED

Leon Currier was a gruff retired firefighter from Sanford, Maine, who had worked on my first campaign for Congress. In February 1998, my second year, I was speaking with a group of seniors in Sanford about the long-term financial woes of Medicare and Social Security. Leon, dismissing my big-picture remarks with a wave of his hand, said, "This is all well and good, but I just got another prescription from my doctor. It costs $100 a month, and I'm not going to take it." I knew that other Medicare beneficiaries must be in the same predicament, because Medicare didn't cover prescription drugs.

After the meeting I called Beth Beausang, my health-care legislative assistant, and asked her to review all House bills designed to help seniors with the high price of prescription drugs. A few days later, she gave me the answer: "There are none." I was surprised.

As we researched the issue, we learned the scale of the problem. When Medicare was created in 1965, prescription drugs were not a significant part of medical care costs. More than thirty years later, Medicare still didn't cover prescription drugs, but the variety, use, and cost of medicines had exploded. Americans with private health insurance often had some coverage for prescription drugs, but soaring out-of-pocket drug costs were taking large chunks from the limited fixed income of most Medicare beneficiaries. Many seniors, who had worked hard all their lives, were forced to choose between food and controlling their blood pressure, diabetes, or other life-threatening aliments.

As a member of the House Government Reform Committee, I worked with the ranking Democrat, Henry Waxman (D-CA), a fearless, smart, progressive leader with a talented professional staff. In April, Phil Schiliro and Phil Barnett of Waxman's committee staff offered to do studies in my district on an issue of my choice. They had several suggestions, but remembering Leon Currier, I asked if we could conduct an investigation on prescription drugs for seniors. Within a few weeks we put together plans for a study of commonly prescribed drugs, comparing the prices paid by Maine seniors with the prices for the same drugs sold to the Veterans Administration, insurance companies, and large hospitals. Our second study would compare prices paid by uninsured Mainers to prices in Canada and Mexico.

In July I released the first report, which showed that elderly Mainers were paying up to twice as much as the drug companies' favored customers.

The report attracted widespread publicity; we led the evening news after our first press conference in Maine. In August Rep. Marion Berry (D-AR) and I created the Prescription Drug Task Force to heighten awareness and share information about the issue with other House members.

Beth Beausang had been working with Representative Waxman's staff to develop three legislative options: (1) a commission to conduct a comprehensive study of the problem; (2) a discount to give all Medicare beneficiaries the lowest price charged to the federal government (Medicaid or the Veterans Administration); or (3) a broad Medicare prescription drug benefit.

I chose the discount option because I wanted Republican support. My experience with campaign finance reform led me to believe that with persistence and flexibility, common ground could be found. The Medicare program would be positioned to use the bargaining power of tens of millions of recipients to get large discounts for beneficiaries. This market-based approach would reduce the price of prescription drugs for seniors at relatively little cost to the federal government, so I thought it would appeal to Republicans.

I introduced H.R. 4627, the Prescription Drug Fairness for Seniors Act in September 1998, and we attracted fifty-three Democratic co-sponsors before the session ended. In October I released our second study, a comparison of drug prices in Maine, Canada, and Mexico. We found that Canadians and Mexicans were paying half as much as uninsured Americans for the same drugs. The public response to the results of our studies grew in intensity.

We had solid data about the nature of the problem, public support, and a low-cost solution, but I had been naïve about attracting Republican support. Not one would co-sponsor my bill and cross the pharmaceutical industry, one of the most powerful lobbies in Congress. I also learned that Republicans would not touch the bill for another, more doctrinaire reason. Although the VA and Medicaid had for years received deep discounts on drug prices to help their beneficiaries, the expansion of any "government program" would almost always meet unyielding Republican resistance. The bill had raised an ideological red flag.

THE PEW BIPARTISAN RETREATS

When I entered Congress in January 1997, two years into the Republican ascendancy, the intensity of the partisan rancor in the House had led the Pew Charitable Trusts to fund three bi-annual "Bipartisan Retreats" for House members in Hershey, Pennsylvania. The retreats had the support and engagement of the leadership of both parties. The first was held in March 1997 and attracted 200 members of Congress, 165 spouses, and 100 children. The second and third retreats were held at the beginning of the next two Congresses—in 1999 and 2001.

The first night of the 1997 retreat we gathered in groups of six to eight members and spouses for dinners. The intimate setting was intended to give us more personal knowledge of our colleagues on the other side—and it did. I was struck by our different reasons for getting into politics. Every Democrat at those dinners said at some point that they got into politics to "help people." Not one Republican used that phrase. They usually said something to the effect that in college they had discovered that they "liked politics." Although it was too small a group for a legitimate survey, the underlying difference in attitude was significant.

Despite that disconcerting observation, I left the bipartisan retreat in 1997 with hope about our capacity to improve the climate in the House. The more senior Democrats, however, seemed skeptical, even cynical, about whether these efforts to improve mutual understanding would matter when we returned to Washington. The effort undoubtedly had some short-term benefit, but the coup de grâce for fundamental change was delivered the following year by the battle over whether President Bill Clinton, my friend from our time together at Oxford, should be impeached.

PARTISAN WARS: THE CLINTON IMPEACHMENT

During my first term senior members in both parties told me that Newt Gingrich was primarily responsible for undermining what had been civil personal relationships among congressional Republicans and Democrats before he arrived in 1978. Nevertheless, I admired his intelligence and thought he was a worthy opponent. When Gingrich and the Democratic leader Dick Gephardt—a much better floor debater than ever credited by the press or public—closed out the debate on a major piece of legislation, I felt I was watching a heavyweight bout.

Gingrich, however, for all his street and book smarts, made major miscalculations as a political leader. One was the campaign to impeach President Clinton. The Independent Counsel Ken Starr and the House Republicans had kept the heat on Clinton throughout the summer and fall of 1998 with hearings and salacious revelations that the media devoured. The investigation had begun based on allegations about the Clintons' financial investments known as Whitewater; it roamed into un- related new areas, including sexual misconduct by the president. The Republican-crafted Articles of Impeachment cast the president's lies about his extramarital affairs with Paula Jones and Monica Lewinsky as perjury and obstruction of justice warranting removal from office.

The effort to impeach President Clinton split the parties in the House and the public, and stoked anger on both sides. Yet by the mid-term elec- tions in November 1998, most Americans agreed with most Democrats in the House: President Clinton's personal conduct was disgraceful but did not constitute the kind of misconduct related to his public duties—a "high crime or misdemeanor"—for which impeachment was designed. His approval ratings as president remained high throughout the process.

The 1998 midterm elections were partly a referendum on impeach- ment. A mid-term election during the second term of a president has usu- ally produced a swing to the opposition, but this time Democrats gained five seats in November 1998. Gingrich, a history professor, understood the context. After the election, he admitted to me in the House gym that they should have picked up a large number of seats. Under pressure from his caucus, he announced he would retire from Congress and step down as Speaker as soon as a replacement was selected.

We had a "lame duck" session during November and December to deal with impeachment and other matters before the new Congress convened in January. It was too late to stop the impeachment train, and Tom DeLay had no desire to slow it down. Given the uneasiness about impeachment expressed to me by some Republicans, I knew that a substantial majority of the House favored a resolution censuring the president for his actions. But DeLay controlled the Rules Committee and used it to block a floor vote on censure to make sure Republican members had no way to avoid a vote on impeachment.

For at least two weeks before the vote, the volume of calls to my DC and Portland offices exceeded anything we would ever see again. In both offices, the phone lines were jammed, and no other work could be done. Each staff member, regardless of other responsibilities, would simply talk with one outraged constituent, put down the phone, and pick it up almost immediately to answer another angry caller. Clinton supporters were outraged, and so were advocates of impeachment. For two weeks all my staff did was answer the phone.

The impeachment debate was set for Saturday, December 19, 1998. Rep. Ray Lahood (R-IL) had been chosen to control the debate from the Speaker's chair. He was regarded on both sides as the fairest and most effective member at managing floor debates. From the beginning, though, the mood in the chamber was surreal. Most Democrats could hardly believe that the Republican leadership continued to demand an up-or-down vote on impeachment charges essentially related to the president's deplorable personal conduct.

Lahood eventually recognized Rep. Bob Livingston (R-LA), who we understood was the Republican choice to replace Gingrich as Speaker. In the week before the vote, press reports indicated that Livingston had been engaged in extramarital affairs of his own. Livingston began by criticizing President Clinton for the damage that he had done to the country and then called on the president to resign. Given our view that the Republican leadership had carried the process beyond the bounds of reason, infuriated Democrats shouted, "You resign, you resign!"

And he did. Livingston said he would not be a candidate for Speaker and would leave the Congress. From our side, cries went up, "No, no!" Bizarre is an inadequate word for the situation. Congressmen and women are flawed human beings, like the voters who select them. The media frenzy over Monica Lewinsky and the impeachment process seemed to have driven the House to turn on itself with an unreasonable personal standard for public service. Acceptance of human frailty and forgiveness for past mistakes was evaporating. Several members have told me it was the strangest moment they experienced in the chamber.

In the end, the Senate acquitted the president on all the articles of impeachment that the House had adopted. Why did the Republican leadership push this initiative so relentlessly? In our view Tom DeLay never felt confined by custom, tradition, or propriety; it was all about power and votes. If he had had the votes, he would have brought the president down. There had been room to compromise—on a censure motion, for example—but Republican leaders refused to consider it.

A conviction of President Clinton would not have advanced the Republican agenda, for Al Gore would have become president and perhaps served for a decade. Nor did pursuing impeachment to its bitter end serve any broader national purpose. As predicted, the work of the highest levels of the federal government had come to a virtual halt for months. At the end, I concluded that impeachment was mostly about feeding and inflaming the Republican base. Still, in the nooks and cracks of our wall of challenges, there were relatively non-ideological places to find common ground.

COLLABORATION ON OCEANS POLICY

Representative Curt Weldon (R-PA) was a passionate, tireless advocate for a robust national missile defense system on the House Armed Services Committee. As a freshman, I joined Rep. John Spratt (D-SC) as an outspoken critic of this multibillion-dollar program. We saw the national missile defense system as a colossal waste of money in search of an unattainable level of security against an unlikely threat. Curt and I argued the subject in committee and on the floor whenever it came up.

That didn't stop us from working together on another subject. In 1999 Curt asked me to join him, Rep. Jim Greenwood (R-PA), and Rep. Sam

Farr (D-CA) in founding a bipartisan House Oceans Caucus to concentrate on vital oceans issues that were not being effectively addressed by Congress. Curt was motivated by the Russian disposal of dangerous nuclear material in the Arctic Ocean, and Jim by the decline of coral reefs he had seen while scuba diving. Sam represented Monterey, home to a world-class oceans research facility, and I wanted to preserve the health of the Gulf of Maine both for the fish and the fishermen. We used the Oceans Caucus to educate other members and their staffs about the economic, environmental, and national security challenges that touched the oceans. We created House Oceans Week, a series of events, panels, and speeches on relevant topics.

Neither Congress nor the executive branch was organized to develop a coherent national oceans policy. Overlapping committee jurisdictions had hobbled effective congressional action for years, and in the executive branch too many government agencies with limited authority had led to neglect of the looming environmental and economic challenges of the world's oceans.

The House Oceans Caucus became a vital forum for sharing information and developing bills on oceans issues. We built on the findings of two national commissions, one funded by the Pew Charitable Trusts and the other by Congress. We developed comprehensive legislation on governance—to create congressional and administration coherence in developing and implementing policy. I wrote legislation to fund a national ocean observing system of integrated buoys and sensors to provide data about oceans comparable to what National Oceanic and Atmospheric Administration (NOAA) satellites provide for the atmosphere. I wrote another bill to fund research to study the most alarming threat to the health of microscopic organisms at the bottom of the ocean food chain—acidification caused by the too-rapid absorption of carbon emissions—the "other carbon" marker of global warming.

Oceans Caucus members were trying to deal with serious evolving threats to the health of the ocean, which could ultimately limit global food supplies and depress global economies. We built bipartisan support for several bills, in part because out on the blue water there were few if any ideological conflicts about federal-state jurisdiction or conflicts between government and the private sector. The Republican leadership, however, was opposed to new money and new programs. Nothing in the core Republican principles of "smaller government, lower taxes" spoke to the critical condition of the ocean. Although we worked some productive changes in the reauthorization of the Magnuson-Stevens Act, which defined the regulatory framework for fisheries, our governance bill and the two bills I had written did not move.

The oceans received substantially more attention after the 2008 election. New legislation and executive branch policies that had been impossible under Republican control were created and implemented by a Democratic administration. I learned that "new spending" and "new programs" were off the table for Republicans, even when needed to deal with pressing new threats.

COLLABORATION DEFENDING LOCAL JOBS — BRAC 2005

Even after the Clinton impeachment hearings, the 2000 election, the Bush tax cuts, and the invasion of Iraq intensified partisanship in Congress, not every issue triggered ideological conflict. When jobs associated with military facilities are threatened, constituents expect us to mount a vigorous defense. That's what Maine and New Hampshire members of Congress did when the Pentagon tried to shut down the Portsmouth Naval Shipyard (PNSY), which has been in existence for two hundred years in one form or another; it is the nation's oldest public shipyard in continuous use. The shipyard is located on Seavey Island in Kittery, Maine, just across the Piscataqua River from Portsmouth, New Hampshire. About half of the yard's 4,500 workers live in Maine and most of the rest in New Hampshire.

The Base Realignment and Closure (BRAC) process provided for the periodic appointment of an independent commission by Congress and the president to review a list of military base closures and "realignments" proposed by the Defense Department. Congress could only accept or reject the commission's report in its entirety, not alter or amend it.

The Maine and New Hampshire delegations knew we were in for a fight. Two years before the BRAC battle, we demanded that the U.S. Navy produce data on future work allocations among the four public shipyards. Grudgingly, the navy complied; it showed a declining workload at Portsmouth and either increases or smaller reductions at the other yards.

On Friday, May 13, 2005 ("BRAC Friday," or "Black Friday" in Maine), the Pentagon released its list of bases to be closed or "realigned," including the Portsmouth Naval Shipyard. In addition, the Brunswick Naval Air Station and a Defense Finance and Accounting Center in northern Maine were targeted.

The next five months involved intense active collaboration on a bipartisan, bicameral, and with respect to Portsmouth, a bi-state basis. Staff members of the senators and congressmen from both states met multiple times each week, the elected officials every two weeks. The BRAC process in 2005 was opaque; no one in the Pentagon or at the facilities in uniform was allowed to provide information without going through channels. We could talk with the BRAC staff and occasionally the commissioners, but the navy was not forthcoming with information. We were convinced they had essentially rigged the data about the Portsmouth facility.

By 2005, after several years of effective labor-management collaboration, Portsmouth had become the best-run and most cost-effective nuclear submarine maintenance and repair facility in the country. Its employees were being sent across the country to provide advice on productivity measures to other yards. The navy that sent these workers, however, was unmoved and oblivious to the value of the yard. We knew that all base closings meant a loss of jobs in the surrounding community, but we had to convince the BRAC commissioners of the facilities' military necessity.

On July 6, 2005, the BRAC Commission held its hearing in Boston on New England facilities. Each member of the two state delegations had a topic to cover as part of the presentation. We were, in fact, disciplined and brief. Yet our most effective witness was the shipyard worker Earl Donnell. He presented data showing that the navy estimates of future workloads consistently understated actual workloads and that closing one of the four public yards would leave zero room for contingencies, work stoppages, or any disruptions caused by hurricanes and other natural disasters. Closing PNSY was dangerously shortsighted, for it would leave the navy without any excess maintenance capacity and without its most productive yard.

A hearing on the Brunswick Naval Air Station was held in the Senate Hart Building in Washington on August 10, 2005. All four members of the Maine delegation rehearsed our remarks in a small room in the basement of the Capitol a day or two before the hearing. Maine's two Republican senators, Olympia Snowe and Susan Collins, and our two Democratic House members, Mike Michaud and I, critiqued and refined each other's statements until we were all satisfied. I am not sure how many other senators would have done the same with House members of the other party.

On August 24, 2005, the BRAC Commission began televised hearings to consider and vote on the Pentagon recommendations. I gathered with my staff in front of the TV, all of us too nervous to speak. The result was out of our hands.

The first Maine facility vote was on Portsmouth. The chair of the commission, Anthony Principi, criticized the navy's analysis and said that the shipyard was the "gold standard" for the country's public yards. In the end, the vote was 7–1 to keep it open.

After the decision, the navy re-allocated work to Portsmouth as we knew they could have earlier. The PNSY effort was a case study in the importance of collaboration and good information. Together, the two state delegations had put together a compelling case to the commission, but the workers at the yard, aware for years of the risk of closure, had made that case possible by dramatically improving their own productivity.

What the Maine and New Hampshire delegations accomplished was unusual. The BRAC issue involved a simple, non-ideological home state jobs issue with the Department of Defense as a common adversary. With BRAC, we also had a decision-making body—the BRAC Commission— that responded to data-driven arguments. Unfortunately, this has not been the case with the issues discussed in the following chapters on the federal budget and taxes, health care, climate change, and Iraq. And our constituents continue to wish we could consistently work together on major issues as we did on BRAC.

VIEWS ACROSS THE AISLE

As I became more and more engaged in debates in committee or on the House floor, I was struck by the eerie similarity of the language used in arguments on very disparate subjects. To be sure, different interest groups were involved with health care, energy, and environmental legislation. A parade of varied industries and organizations came into my office seeking direct federal assistance or targeted tax breaks. Our debates were usually about what the government should do and what it should leave to others; they were conducted with an intensity that indicated that more was at stake than a simple allocation of responsibility. I wondered why it was so hard for each side to understand the other. Here is how I would summarize in fairly general terms the views across the aisle.

First, most Republicans appear to pay less attention to evidence—about the economic consequences of a proposal, education reform, scientific controversies, or nonmilitary aspects of foreign policy. Instead, they appear to be guided by broad principles about the ineffectiveness of government, faith in free markets, and the exercise of power in foreign affairs. In an argument between a Republican who wants federal "spending" for education reduced so "government" will be "smaller" and a Democrat who emphasizes research about the connection between investment in education and economic growth, there is little common ground for understanding or compromise.

Second, Democrats have the impression that Republicans maintain much greater emotional distance from Americans struggling to get ahead and a closer affinity with the successful, those whom Dan Quayle once called the "best people." Republicans have no reservations about favoring tax cuts that primarily benefit the wealthy, because they believe the rich are "job creators." That's also why they can leave tens of millions of Americans without health insurance rather than vote for the Obama reform plan that provided for regulated competition among *private* insurers and would cover more than 30 million people.

Third, Democrats believe most Republicans are obstructionists, the Party of No. Without a serious programmatic agenda of their own on the major issues that matter to Democrats, Republicans in the majority appear to have no coherent plan, and in the minority, they coalesce around stopping Democratic initiatives. When President George W. Bush's plan for creating private accounts in Social Security failed to pass, the Republicans lost interest in simpler and less disruptive reforms. In short, even when both parties understand the long-term fiscal challenges of programs like Social Security or Medicare, our competing proposals cannot be compromised because they are usually polar opposites of each other.

When I listen to Republicans' principal criticisms of the Democratic Party, I can see that Republicans hold onto their belief that Democrats are the party of big government and that government screws up almost everything it touches; it is inefficient, wasteful, and in an attempt to improve people's lives, almost inevitably compromises their personal freedom of action. Since "free markets" are more effective allocators of resources, markets provide the best path to prosperity in almost all circumstances. Republicans also believe that Americans struggle every day with unnecessary government regulations, an ineffective bureaucracy, and burdensome taxation, all of which retard economic growth and diminish personal freedom.

Republicans also believe that a "culture of dependency" is undermining America's strength and future prosperity. They see Democrats as pandering to those who need or want government help. They believe that Democrats seek to redistribute resources from those who have succeeded in the American economy and provide most of the jobs to those who are dependent on government for their needs. Republicans believe that the "confidence" of the business community is vital to the American economy and should be enhanced by periodic tax cuts and relaxed regulations.

In addition, Republicans believe they are the party trying to stop America's decline from its traditional values and historic mission, while Democrats seek change that will undermine these fundamental values. America's central mission is to create opportunity for individual initiative in free markets. It now seems that nothing Republicans can do by legislation is more important than denying President Obama a second term; stopping the Democratic agenda is their first and most important objective, as Mitch McConnell admitted after the 2010 elections.

One consequence of this different mind-set is that Democrats (who want to pass new legislation adapted to a changing world) see the opposition (which doesn't) as interested solely in power for its own sake. During my time in Congress I could not count the times that a Democratic representative said, "All these guys (Republicans) care about is power." Democrats, for the most part, simply cannot comprehend why someone would seek political office in order to dismantle programs and investments that strengthen the capacity of Americans to make more of their lives.

These views across the aisle, simplified as they are, seem unremarkable and not noticeably different from descriptions that might have been written in the past. So the questions remain: Why do our partisan differences seem so intense today, and why is compromise so much more difficult to reach? If we could find answers to those questions, perhaps we could find a path to a less dysfunctional politics. The inquiry should begin by searching for the most fundamental of our differences and exploring cases where rigid adherence to "principle" leads to rejection of otherwise compelling evidence and expertise.

INDIVIDUALISM AND COMMUNITY—A FIRST TAKE

I gradually realized that the major partisan differences between Democrats and Republicans grow out of the enduring tension in American politics and culture between individualism on the one hand and community engagement on the other. What should we do together and what should we do alone? Of those things we should do together, which should be addressed by governments and which by other institutions, groups, or the market?

Self-reliance is the quintessential American virtue. We celebrate those who have climbed to success from difficult beginnings. We tell our children that if they work hard, they can do anything they want.

Individual effort is how we explain success, and its absence is the usual explanation for failure. But we also place great value on family, on team-work, community service, and responsibility for the less fortunate. Well-run companies create shared missions and motivate employees to pull in the same direction. These competing values find constant expression in our politics.

AYN RAND: A MOTHER OF IDEOLOGICAL INDIVIDUALISM

Ayn Rand was a compelling proponent of a radical individualism that saw little value in caring for others or for government regulation of markets. She was born in Russia, grew to detest Bolshevik collectivism, and immigrated to the United States in 1926, shortly after her twenty-first birthday. Rand's two major novels, *The Fountainhead* (1943) and *Atlas Shrugged* (1957), both paeans to her philosophy of individualism, have sold more than 13 million copies in America. One biographer states that although Rand is "rarely taught in universities, new readers, most in their teens and early twenties, have always found their way to her books . . . [which has made her] a potent influence on three genera-tions of Americans."[1]

Alan Greenspan, former head of the Federal Reserve, is her best-known follower. Others include Rep. Paul Ryan, chair of the House Budget Com-mittee; Chris Cox, former head of the SEC; Rep. Ron Paul, frequent Lib-ertarian or Republican candidate for president; and John Hospers, a founder of the Libertarian Party. Greenspan was a friend and advocate for Rand's ideas. Ryan requires all of his congressional staff to read *Atlas Shrugged* and has said that she was a primary reason for his being in poli-tics. As Mitt Romney's choice for his running mate, Paul Ryan's libertarian philosophy and his proposals to dismantle the existing Medicare and Medicaid programs have been contentious issues in the 2012 campaign.

Rand was a confirmed atheist. The author of *The Virtue of Selfishness* understood that her attacks on altruism conflicted with the teachings of

Christianity and the world's other great religions. In her journal she wrote that Christianity "is the best kindergarten of communism."[2] Nevertheless, her fierce commitment to individualism and the "Objectivist" philosophy she built on that foundation left her no doubt about the correctness of her ideas. She wrote:

> If a life can have a theme song, and I believe every worthwhile one has, mine is a religion, an obsession, or a mania or all of these expressed in one word: individualism.[3]

When Bennett Cerf, her publisher at Random House, told her that John Galt's speech in *Atlas Shrugged* needed to be cut, Rand responded, "Would you cut the Bible?" The speech was left alone. Rand's unshakeable convictions about rational selfishness, egoism, and unregulated capitalism led her to drive from her circle of admirers those who disagreed. Her novels, however, have great power to move readers, especially the young. Anne Heller says that with *Atlas Shrugged* Rand "was retailing her philosophy of strict rationality through a primal emotional appeal by characters in a fable."[4] A fable for sure, but one with great resonance for Americans.

Ludwig von Mises, an economist favored by libertarians, told Rand that she was right in that novel "to tell the masses [that they] are inferior and all the improvements in [their] conditions" are due to "men who are better than you [the masses]."[5] Another of her biographers, Jennifer Burns, comments on Rand's "Nietzschean fixation on the superior individual."[6] Those who attribute almost all progress to exceptional individuals can easily neglect the great majority of human beings who don't fit that category. I see elements of that attitude in the preference of conservatives for the wealthy ("job creators") and their lack of concern for millions of Americans living on the financial edge without health insurance.

To understand the impact of Ayn Rand's ideas on conservative politicians, consider Mark Sanford's description of her influence on his worldview. In a November 2009 *Newsweek* review of two books on Ayn Rand, Sanford (R-SC), a former congressman and South Carolina governor, says he was "blown away" by Rand's portrayal of "the power of the free individual" when he first read *The Fountainhead* and *Atlas Shrugged* in the 1980s." Sanford continues:

> *The Fountainhead* is a stunning evocation of the individual and what he can achieve when unhindered by government or society. Howard Roark is an architect who cares nothing about the world's approval; his only concerns are his integrity and the perfection of his designs. What strikes me as still relevant is its central insight—that it isn't "collective action" that makes this nation prosperous and secure; it's the initiative and creativity of the individual.[7]

This "central insight"—to one not caught up in radical individualism—seems both unnecessary and wrong. Why are prosperity and security the product of *either* collective action *or* individual initiative? If forced to choose between these opposites, everything we know about team sports, scientific progress, military training, or current corporate best practices stresses the importance of working with other people to build an effective team.

Rand's character, Howard Roark, goes on trial for dynamiting a building he had designed because "some bureaucrats" altered the structure. Sanford quotes Roark's statement at trial:

> "I do not recognize anyone's right to one minute of my life. Nor to any part of my energy. Nor to any achievement of mine. No matter who makes the claim, how large their number or how great their need . . . I recognize no obligations toward men except one: to respect their freedom and to take no part in a slave society."

Sanford admits that these words "sound cold," but says they contain "two basic truths . . . an individual can achieve great things without government benevolence . . . and one man has no right to another's achievement."[8] To me the first truth makes sense and the second is absurd. The latter ignores the fact that most of what we accomplish depends directly or indirectly on contributions of others, including whatever we achieve through action by governments. Warren Buffett, taking a dramatically different view of individual achievement, has said that if he had been raised in Bangladesh, a country without a stock market, he would not have been successful.

The shelves of virtually every bookstore in the country are packed with books on corporate team-building advice. Listen to players and coaches on successful professional sports teams and you will hear a steady mantra of how the team comes first. In a competitive, complicated environment, building the best possible team is usually the first step. Given the importance of uniting individuals in a common endeavor, why does Mark Sanford approve Ayn Rand's "central insight—that it isn't 'collective action' that makes this country prosperous and secure; it is the initiative and creativity of the individual?" In any event, why do we have to choose one part of our brain or psyche over another?

HABITS OF THE HEART

Robert Bellah et al.'s *Habits of the Heart: Individualism and Commitment in American Life* is a study of individualism and civic engagement (what I call community) in our culture and politics. The book's several authors interviewed white, middle-class Americans about how they think and talk about their private and public lives. They found that in their private lives "however much Americans extol the autonomy and the self-reliance of the individual, they do not imagine that a good life can be lived alone. Those we interviewed would almost all agree that connectedness to others in work, love, and community is essential to happiness, self-esteem, and moral worth."[9]

The authors of *Habits of the Heart* make the case that American culture is characterized by a "first language" of individualism with which we find it relatively easy to make sense of our personal and public lives. "Individualism, the first language in which Americans tend to think about their lives, values independence and self-reliance above all else."[10] We explain our own successes, and others' failures, in language about what we as individuals have done or not done, rather than larger social and economic forces.

For most Americans, independence and self-reliance are primary virtues. Yet when they are taken to mean freedom from the demands of others, how do we find a vocabulary that values working with others toward a common purpose? In short, how can we speak coherently about our need to be independent of others and still work together for the good of all?

Habits of the Heart also argues that Americans share a "second language" rooted in our understanding of community. But our second language is so much weaker that many of their subjects had great difficulty describing the ties that bind them to family, friends, neighbors, fellow workers, and to society at large. Most of those interviewed "emphasized that they attained their present status in life through their own hard work, seldom mentioning the part played by their family, schooling, or . . . [other] advantages."[11]

We may be less fluent in this second language, but it is indeed deeply ingrained in religious traditions that draw people together through a relationship to a transcendent being and also in our public tradition of "civic republicanism." Both traditions guided the nation's founders to conclude that the purpose of our experiment in democracy was to serve the common good.

The contrasting messages of the two congressional parties are derived from Americans' more accessible first language of individualism and our less familiar second language of community. Democrats have message envy about the simplicity of the Republican mantras of "smaller government, lower taxes" and "freedom, faith, and family." In our Democratic Party retreats and meetings, political discussions often devolved into complaints that we needed to better articulate our so-called values. "We have values, too," said one Democratic leader to me in some frustration. But when we spoke on the floor, clarity about values often eluded us. We reviewed polls, debated slogans, and struggled to flesh out compelling ways to talk less about programs and more about motivating the public in support of the middle class, working families, community, or the common good—which in America have far less resonance than "individual freedom."

BUILDING COMMUNITY

Ayn Rand may have inspired Paul Ryan to get into politics, but I took my inspiration from other sources. My parents were both heavily involved in community activities, my mother for the League of Women Voters and my father on the Portland City Council. Eight years on football and track teams in high school and college taught me the profound satisfaction of working with others for a common purpose. The political movements of the 1960s were exciting examples of citizen participation in our democracy that opened doors of opportunity to racial minorities and women, and ushered in comprehensive legislation to control pollution. The campaign to stop the Viet Nam War created a domestic firestorm, but it also spawned a level of public engagement needed for a democracy to function well.

The Republican worldview emphasizes personal liberty and free markets; the Democratic worldview focuses on equality of opportunity and the common good. Republicans in Congress tend to believe that government diminishes individual freedom; Democrats believe it can help expand opportunity for many people. Both parties value personal liberty, but one of them is much more likely to see it threatened by our government.

Democrats treasure movements for progressive change. The combined actions of thousands or millions of people working toward a common purpose stir our passions. And that is why in the last century it was the New Deal, Social Security, Medicare, civil rights, the women's movement, and environmental causes that breathed life into Democratic politics. The labor union movement is a primary place of "all for one, one for all" activity.

Although I have described these political movements as inspirational for Democrats, they were in many respects far more bipartisan than political controversies today. Opposition to the Viet Nam War was much less partisan than opposition to the conflict in Iraq. In the 1960s and 1970s Republicans were involved in civil rights, women's rights, and environmental causes. What has changed? I argue that Americans have sorted themselves into the two parties more by attitude or worldview and less by specific public issues. The resulting cleavage is deeper, more intense, and harder to bridge. Yet failure to overcome our differences produces dysfunctional government and public distrust and cynicism.

In *Bowling Alone: The Collapse and Revival of American Community,* Robert Putnam argued that America is witnessing a decline in "social capital," a measure of trust, engagement in community activities, and personal relationships, all of which are vital for a healthy democratic society.[12] The title was taken from Putnam's observation that Americans are still bowling in large numbers but more often alone than as members of bowling clubs. He found that similar declines in regular social interaction with friends, family, and others on common projects have been accompanied by a pervasive loss of trust and mutual support. Since *Bowling Alone*'s publication, Putnam has found signs of a revival in social capital, but nothing on a scale to compensate for the public collapse in confidence with American politicians and our government.

I have seen widespread examples of enthusiastic participation in local nonprofit projects of all kinds, from soup kitchens to coastal conservation projects. But overall, it seems as if many of us cannot imagine being part of a national movement for progressive change, however differently we might define that term.

In March 2001 my wife, Diana, and I went on a pilgrimage with other members of Congress and their spouses to Selma, Birmingham, and Montgomery, Alabama, to visit the sites and talk with participants in the demonstrations and marches that defined the civil rights movement. We rode chartered buses between the cities, watched the documentary *Eyes on the Prize,* talked with Fred Shuttlesworth and other living leaders of the movement, and visited the Sixteenth Street Baptist Church in Birmingham where four Negro girls died when the church was bombed in 1963.

This pilgrimage is organized every other year by the Faith and Politics Institute, created more than twenty years ago by Rev. Doug Tanner Jr. Its purpose was to offer opportunities for spiritual community and moral reflection to members of Congress and others on Capitol Hill, and to cultivate effective public leadership for racial justice and reconciliation. Former

Rep. Amo Houghton (R-NY) and Rep. John Lewis (D-GA) for years chaired the Alabama pilgrimage. In 1965 Lewis had led the march over the Edmund Pettus Bridge in Selma on what became known as "Bloody Sunday." At that time, Alabama State Police on foot and horseback waded into the marchers and beat them back—while the television cameras rolled. Those images so shocked the nation that President Lyndon Johnson asked Congress to pass the Voting Rights Act and by August 1965 it was law.

Immersed for three days in the history of a transformative chapter of the nation's public life, we had a lesson in the power of conscience, courage, and community. The civil rights activists in Alabama were trained in non-violent tactics, committed to the cause, and truly cared for each other. They followed the vision of Martin Luther King Jr. and John Lewis of a "beloved community" without racial or ethnic barriers. Stepping back into that moment in time, I could feel the power of their faith and commitment.

We cannot expect members of Congress to demonstrate that same shared vision and cooperation in the face of controversy, but we may be able to find ways of stepping off the roller coaster long enough to recover our bearings and make sure that we are acting for the greater good. The Faith and Politics Institute runs weekly reflection group meetings for members, which were particularly helpful to me. Those members in my group remain close friends—we have shared personal tragedies of illness and death of loved ones, frustrations about not being able to meet the expectations of the people who elected us, and our hopes and fears about the political system of which we were a part and of the country we will be leaving for our children.

Our Thursday morning group was run by Fr. Clete Kiley or Rev. Doug Tanner. The weekly meetings took place in Rep. Jim McDermott's wood-paneled office in the Longworth House Office Building. Jim's desk over-flowed with papers, the shelves with books, and the walls with photos of Jim's family and political colleagues. We sat in the same chairs, as we might have sat in the same pew for years. I started coming to these gatherings ever since Rep. Earl Pomeroy (D-ND) told me, "It's the best hour of the week." We began each session with a reading, followed with a discussion, and closed with a prayer.

The concept of the Institute is grounded in Thomas Merton's advocacy of a contemplative life as a path to spiritual awareness. Members of Congress have no chance of a contemplative life, but the reflection groups provide some contemplative moments. On the House floor we would ask each other, "Are you going to church tomorrow?" We are not a Bible study or prayer group, although our session closed with a nondenominational prayer. We reflected together on our lives and work in search of the inner strength and understanding to provide effective public leadership. One reading from Thomas Merton was perhaps the defining expression of our weekly gatherings:

> But the world of politics is not the only world, and unless political decisions rest on a foundation of something better and higher than politics, they can never do any real good for men. . . . There must be a new force, the power of love, the power of understanding and human compassion, the strength of selflessness and cooperation and the creative dynamism of the will to live and build, and the will to forgive. The will for reconciliation.[13]

In Congress the consuming "world of politics" can often seem the "only world." We struggled over how we could help make "this place" (as we called the Congress) mesh with our inner values and outer responsibilities to the people back home. The reflection groups offer an opportunity for members of Congress to stay grounded in our deepest questions, concerns, and insights, and become more open to those of others. Political life is so frenetic that it is otherwise easy to lose touch with one's own core wisdom and values.

We have, I believe, a basic human drive to live with and care for each other. But that sentiment was hard to detect during debates in committee or on the House floor. For instance, the Bush administration pursued ideological battles that left those on both sides cynical about the integrity and motives of the other: the Democratic minority believed the Republican domestic and foreign policies were taking America down a road to ruin; the Republicans believed they were finally setting the country on a stronger path.

Politics is part of American life, and Congress tests the inner compass of those who are elected. The job requires a desire to serve others and a willingness to engage in self-promotion. We owe the public our independent judgment and a deep concern for the preferences of our constituents. We are faced with conflicting demands from business and labor, consumers and producers, environmental and economic interests, seniors and families, and other myriad conflicting interests of a large population. We are asked to work across the aisle but not to compromise our principles. How should we make hard choices about what to say and how to vote in the swirl of intense daily activity? When do we have enough information to make a decision?

The next four chapters explore the disconnected worldviews of congressional Republicans and Democrats on the budget and taxes, health care, climate change, and the Iraq war. I try to address the question of why Republicans are so insistent that "tax cuts pay for themselves," "we'll be welcomed as liberators," "government-run health care doesn't work," and "climate science isn't proven." Across a wide spectrum of issues, doctrine overwhelms contrary evidence and makes difficult, if not impossible, the collaboration across party lines required to make progress on twenty-first-century challenges.

I loved serving in Congress because of the pressure, complexity, competition, risks, and relevance of the job. I had the opportunity to fight for what I believed and for the people who had elected me to make decisions that would affect their lives. It was an experience of unmatched intensity, winning and losing, struggle and frustration. Nevertheless, I went to Congress with hope. I left—after twelve years of direct experience—alarmed at America's increasingly dysfunctional politics.

2
—

The Federal Budget

Faith-Based Economics

Ideologies separate us. Dreams and anguish bring us together.
—EugÈne Ionesco

I was standing outdoors in front of a bank of microphones in Fort Lauder-dale, Florida. About twenty reporters were huddled behind the mikes, many kneeling, with a half-moon of perhaps eighty to one hundred screaming demonstrators behind them. Although they were only a few feet away, the reporters could hear us only because their earphones were connected to our microphones. The noise was deafening.

I had answered the call of the House Democratic leadership to go to Florida in November 2000 to help give the press our side of the debate about the recount in the presidential election. The Republican demonstrators were getting 24/7 coverage, and our story wasn't getting through.

With a few other Democratic House Members that day I did three press conferences in the Florida counties—Palm Beach, Broward, and Dade—that were dealing with the most contentious ballot disputes. The protesters didn't look like a cross-section of local residents or of America. They were almost all white, mostly young, and well dressed. Later, we learned that many were staffers of Republican congressmen shipped to Florida to create public pressure to stop the recounts that if continued, might put Al Gore in the White House.

The explosion in Florida followed an unusually bland campaign. During President Clinton's second term, the expanding economy had turned annual federal deficits into surpluses for the first time in decades. Al Gore promised to continue the administration's successful economic policies. George W. Bush spoke and debated in generalities and claimed to be a different kind of Republican, a "compassionate conservative." The media focused on the "personal qualities" of the candidates and brushed over their policy differences; they asked which candidate voters would rather "have a beer with." Many people seemed to believe the differences between the two candidates were minor.

There were, in fact, profound differences. The clash of the party agendas had been masked by the division in control of the presidency and Congress. President Clinton had blocked the Republican passion for lower taxes by urging Congress to "Save Social Security First." The Clinton years were marked by significant but relatively incremental changes in policy, a growing economy, and intensifying partisanship.

The Supreme Court's decision in *Bush v. Gore* was a shock. Five justices of the Court who had previously been the most deferential to state control of elections set aside their prior judicial philosophy to stop the Florida recount with George Bush in the lead. Apparently recognizing the conflict with their prior position, the justices in the majority wrote that their decision should have no precedential value. Despite losing the popular vote, George W. Bush became the forty-third president of the United States.

In hindsight, the 2000 election was a sea change, the most consequential since Ronald Reagan replaced Jimmy Carter. It is almost certain that Al Gore would neither have signed anything like the massive 2001–2003 tax cuts nor invaded Iraq, the two Bush administration initiatives that had the most profound effect on America's prosperity and world standing. With control of the House, Senate, and presidency for five of the next six years, Republicans were largely free to carry out domestic and foreign policy priorities that had been stymied by the Clinton administration.

In contrast to the internal Clinton administration debate that led to the 1993 deficit reduction package of tax increases and spending cuts, the

Bush tax cuts of 2001 and 2003 were promoted with a surprising lack of attention to economic evidence and expertise. The Bush administration's aggressive approach and disingenuous supporting arguments heightened the wall of disrespect between the parties.

Democrats had historically and with some justification been accused of overspending, especially when President Johnson was fighting one war in Viet Nam and another on poverty at home. Although Republicans had been consistent supporters of lower taxes for decades, they had also expressed concern about federal deficits. President Reagan's 1981 tax cut, contrary to predictions of his supply-side economic advisors, produced significantly higher deficits. Bruce Bartlett, a Treasury Department official at the time, noted that Reagan signed eleven tax increases during the rest of his term in office to contain the damage.[1] It had not been enough. In 1990 President George H. W. Bush raised taxes—in spite of his now-famous "Read my lips: no new taxes" speech in 1988—including the top income tax rate, which generated much anger and frustration on the right. But that still wasn't enough.

In 1993 President Clinton abandoned his campaign promise of a middle-class tax cut in order to deal with expanding annual deficits, and pushed a deficit reduction plan through Congress with both tax increases and spending cuts. Not one Republican in the House or Senate supported his plan. In 1997 Clinton adopted a balanced budget policy and reached agreement with Republicans on another bill to contain the risks of future deficits. The budget surpluses of the next four years convinced many House Democrats that disciplined budgeting was sound economic policy. Three administrations in a row, despite their differences over particular expenditures and taxes, had treated the existence and risks of deficits as a serious matter. And that was why what happened next was such a jarring change.

THE BUSH TAX CUTS: STARVE THE BEAST OR INCREASE REVENUE?

Despite his razor-thin victory, President Bush pushed for all he could get in his first legislative battle. His signature domestic proposal was a $1.6 trillion tax cut over ten years, which he developed in response to his

Republican primary rival Steven Forbes's campaign for tax cuts of that size. It was the largest tax cut in American history and an abrupt reversal of the Clinton administration's balanced budget policy.

President Bush's push for the initiative changed the nature of political debate; although the stated reason was to return the existing budget surplus to the taxpayers, the underlying rationale was obscure. Was the Republican objective "to starve the beast," that is, to dry up funds for the federal government in order to increase deficits and thereby the pressure to cut spending? Although that was the position of right-wing activists like Grover Norquist, the head of Americans for Tax Reform, it was not at the time a viable political argument, even if it was the ultimate goal. Still, Democrats listened in puzzlement and disbelief as conservatives argued in 2001 that tax cuts would reduce revenues by returning to taxpayers "their own money," and exactly the opposite in 2003: that "tax cuts pay for themselves" by stimulating economic growth and increasing tax revenue. But that tired old supply-side argument was not supported by the Congressional Budget Office (CBO) or mainstream economists.

David Stockman, President Reagan's director of the Office of Management and Budget, explained in *The Triumph of Politics: Why the Reagan Revolution Failed* that although the president had initially been persuaded that tax increases reduce revenues and tax cuts increase them, "the supply-siders, including me, were wrong from the very beginning."[2] That's why the administration repeatedly raised taxes before Reagan left office.

Why was an economic theory, discredited for more than fifteen years, still alive during the Republican ascendancy? The belief in a free lunch, that we could cut taxes and gain revenue—or at least experience insignificant reductions—appeared almost universal among my Republican colleagues. The honest conservative argument was that government spends too much and we should reduce spending for entitlements, defense, education, transportation, and other federal priorities. But that was an argument leading straight into discussions of specific programs and taxes, which Republicans tended to avoid. So from the start, truth was sacrificed in the campaign to pass the 2001 tax cuts. On March 23, 2001, two months after George W. Bush was inaugurated, I heard the president himself make a case for his tax cuts that went well beyond spin.

That morning I had flown on Air Force One to Portland, Maine, to attend the new president's speech at the Merrill Auditorium next to City Hall. It was the brief moment of bipartisanship in the early days of Bush's first term, and he was inviting members of Congress of both parties to ride on Air Force One when he traveled to their states. Senators Olympia Snowe and Susan Collins of Maine were on board; in fact, they disappeared into the president's enclosed office in the front of the plane shortly after take-off.

I sat with the Ari Fleischer, the president's press secretary, and Karl Rove, his notorious political advisor. Rove noted that Collins, up for reelection in 2002, would get to announce a steady stream of grants and other financial assistance for Maine over the next two years. He was trying to discourage me from making a Senate race in 2002 (which in fact I had no intention of doing because of the advanced age of my parents). Snowe and Collins, captive in the president's compartment for the duration of the flight, later told the press how "persuasive" he was on the subject of his $1.6 trillion tax cut.

The crowd in Portland was enthusiastic and welcoming. Our Independent governor, Angus King, introduced the president by saying, "Another reason that I am glad to welcome the president is that I believe in tax cuts." I remember thinking that he would not like the reduction of federal revenues to Maine that would inevitably follow the president's tax cuts, as 50 percent of the Maine government's revenues come from federal sources.

The president was gracious to all of us, but what he said about his tax and budget proposals was startling. Before the crowd in Portland, he proclaimed:

Now, I know these numbers sound like a lot, but this is reality I'm talking about. We've increased discretionary spending by 4 percent, we pay down $2 trillion worth of debt, we set aside $1 trillion in the budget over a 10-year period for contingencies, and guess what? There's still money left over. And that's the debate. The fundamental question is, what to do with it.[3]

Bush was in fact not talking about "reality," because *none of it was true.* The 4 percent increase did not include the Department of Defense budget, which was widely expected to, and eventually did, get a much greater increase. The $2 trillion pay down of debt ("the biggest debt repayment in the history of the world," according to the president) was built on wholly unrealistic expectations about the decade to come. There was no $1 trillion set aside for contingencies.

In Portland, Bush used the "it's your money" line to great applause. Most people don't need to be urged to pursue individual self-interest. They do need to be encouraged to consider the interests of others and the common good. The president didn't take that approach; he told the crowd to think of themselves first.

In the early months of the Bush administration, I was struck by the disengagement, even passivity, of the mainstream media that had been so critical of President Clinton. The press coverage of the debate over President Bush's proposed $1.6 trillion tax cut was usually the "he said, she said" argument without rigorous examination of the claims of either side. Preposterous and well-grounded claims got equal play. For many of us, only the *New York Times* columnist Paul Krugman was telling the truth: the numbers were being fixed and the bill was riddled with gimmicks.

Krugman rushed a book, *Fuzzy Math,* into print to make his case. He began by saying that the administration's "arguments made for tax cuts have been startling in their intellectual dishonesty," and continued "What has happened since Bush moved to Washington—the deliberate misstatements and suppression of the facts—is, as far as I know, unprecedented in the history of American economic policy."[4] Krugman detailed how the Bush administration grossly understated the cost of its plan, falsely sold it as a middle-class tax cut, and misrepresented it as providing a short-term stimulus to the economy.

Krugman also noted that the shift in party control changed the information available to the public. Before the 1994 elections, the House Ways and Means Committee calculated the effects of proposed tax law changes on different income groups so that members of Congress would understand the impact of a proposal on their constituents. Before the

2000 election, the Department of the Treasury did the same. But after Republicans won control of the House and later the presidency, the Ways and Means Committee and the Treasury both stopped providing that information.

Two think tanks, the Urban Institute–Brookings Institution Tax Policy Center and Citizens for Tax Justice, periodically produced the same calculations. But the press was less likely to use nongovernmental reports than those of the Treasury. Data about income distribution tended to undermine the case for Republican tax cuts because it exposed the disproportionate benefits that would flow to wealthy Americans.[5] So the Republicans simply stopped producing the data.

The nominal "cost" of the tax cuts (the amount by which they would reduce revenues) was $1.35 trillion over ten years; the real cost would be much higher. In order to get such an enormous tax cut through the Senate, the Republican leadership used the "reconciliation" process, which took only fifty-one votes because it barred the use of the filibuster. "Reconciliation" had been designed as a legislative vehicle to reduce deficits, but in 2001 it was used for the first time to increase federal deficits.

The response to Bush's 2001 tax cut by the chair of the Federal Reserve, Alan Greenspan, was inconsistent with his advice to the prior administration. Greenspan, together with Bob Rubin, had persuaded Bill Clinton of the importance of tax increases and spending reductions to cope with the deficits Clinton had inherited from the first President Bush. At a Senate Budget Committee hearing on January 25, 2001, Greenspan endorsed the proposed tax cuts on the ground that large surpluses are bad for the economy. Two months later we were into a recession that would combine with the tax cuts to turn prior CBO projections of future surpluses into fantasy.

The administration and Republican congressional leaders had been able to get a Senate majority for a Budget Resolution with tax cuts of $1.35 trillion over ten years. But they wanted a lot more. They phased in some tax cuts so that the revenue loss would be for less than the full ten years; they gradually reduced the estate tax and then specified the complete reinstatement of the higher 2001 rates in year ten. In addition, the cost of the bill was deliberately understated by ignoring the long-term impact of the Alternative Minimum Tax that without an annual, bipartisan "fix" would increase taxes on even middle-income Americans. All three gimmicks helped to keep the ten-year cost at $1.35 trillion while maximizing the long-term reduction in revenue. The estimated cost in the second decade was more than $4 trillion. The Republican chair of the House Ways and Means Committee, Bill Thomas, compared the problem of squeezing a $1.6 trillion tax cut into a $1.35 trillion budget resolution as a need to get "a pound and a half of sugar into a one pound bag."[6] The bill's sunset provisions and accounting gimmicks hid the true cost of the cuts, and the ruse worked remarkably well. There was little consideration by the Bush administration of the consequences of its policy.

Five years after the 2001 tax cut vote, the respected congressional scholars Norm Ornstein and Tom Mann wrote in their aptly named book on Congress, *The Broken Branch*, "Whatever one's ideological disposition on these matters, there is no avoiding the conclusion that this bill was enacted in a recklessly dishonest fashion and was itself a dishonest product."[7] They added: "In 2001, Congress with the encouragement of President Bush set a new standard for accounting chicanery."[8] Clive Crook of the *National Journal* wrote that the bill was "filled with a whole series of outright frauds and outrageous lies."[9] The Center on Budget and Policy Priorities (CBPP), a nonpartisan think tank, reported that the true cost of the $1.35 trillion tax cut was more likely $1.8 trillion in the first ten years and $4.1 trillion in the second decade.[10] It is hard not to conclude that the 2001 bill was the most fiscally irresponsible act in the history of the Congress.

Two years later, after the commitment to waging war in Afghanistan and Iraq, it happened again.

I was crossing Independence Avenue in DC with Rep. Ander Crenshaw (R-FL), to vote on the Bush 2003 tax cut. The measure would greatly benefit the wealthy by reducing dividend income and capital gains rates. The total cost was estimated to be $350 billion over ten years; in other words, it would reduce net federal revenues by that amount over the next decade. By then, federal budget surpluses had disappeared, replaced by rapidly rising annual deficits. The rationale for the tax cuts had been reversed, from "it's your money," (which doesn't work when the budget is already in deficit) to "tax cuts are needed to stimulate a sagging economy." I was as upset by this latest fiscal irresponsibility as I had been during the Clinton impeachment and the authorization to invade Iraq. "Aren't you worried about the deficits this bill will create?" I asked Ander. He responded: "Perhaps there will be more money in a few years."

How do you work with people who don't believe their votes have consequences? There wasn't going to be "more money" in a few years because Congress had passed a gimmick-riddled $1.35 trillion dollar tax cut in 2001, had authorized invasions of Afghanistan and Iraq that would cost hundreds of billions of dollars, and at that moment was about to vote for another huge tax cut likely to drive the country into a fiscal hole from which it might never recover. We had alarming deficit projections from respected sources. But the Republicans chose not to believe them. Ander Crenshaw came to Congress from the financial services industry. He was smart enough to understand the risks we were taking, but like most Republican members of the House, he wanted to believe that tax cuts pay for themselves; he wanted to believe in a free lunch.

We didn't know then that the 2003 tax cuts had been the subject of intense debate within the administration before and after the midterm elections. On September 4, 2002, Treasury Secretary Paul O'Neill met with President Bush to warn him about the administration's proposal for another major tax cut. O'Neill explained that the proposed tax cuts would do little to stimulate the economy and would increase deficits by nearly $400 billion over ten years. He continued: "Mr. President, if you start pushing through a second, major stimulus plan, you run out of money. You won't have any money to do anything you want to do, such as changing Social Security or fundamental tax reform, for the rest of your term."[11]

Two months later the Republicans maintained control of Congress in the 2002 elections, and the planning for the 2003 tax cut intensified. O'Neill again objected, telling Vice President Cheney "what rising deficits will mean to our economic and fiscal soundness." Cheney cut him off. "Reagan proved deficits don't matter. . . . We won the midterms. This is our due."[12] In fact, Reagan proved that deficits did matter; he raised taxes eleven times after his initial tax cut in 1981 drove deficits higher.

On December 5th, Cheney called O'Neill to tell him that the president wanted changes in his economic team and he, O'Neill, was part of the change. Paul O'Neill left the Bush administration concluding that both preemptive war and deep tax cuts had proved to be ideologies that "were impenetrable by facts."[13]

In the end, the 2003 tax cuts passed the Senate by one vote, including Senator Collins, but without the support of Snowe or McCain. Its effect was, as opponents predicted, to increase the national debt and widen the expanding gap between the very wealthy and the rest of America.

THE HOUSE BUDGET COMMITTEE: THE LANGUAGE OF ECONOMIC IDEOLOGY

If you listen carefully to the language that advocates use, you can sometimes hear the underlying rationale for their positions. My two terms on the House Budget Committee provided that opportunity. Instead of facing the public as in many other committee rooms, members of the Budget Committee sit across from the other party in a horseshoe-shaped arrangement, which heightens the adversarial atmosphere. Most of the Republican members are drawn largely from the right wing of their caucus; the Democratic members reflect a broader range of views within our caucus.

The House Budget Committee is charged with reporting a Budget Resolution within the first few months of each congressional session, after which the committee is largely dormant. The Budget Resolution sets the parameters of tax and spending authority for Congress. It can be an effective device for tax and budget policy, but without a resolution, appropriations bills can still be debated and enacted. Each spring, the debate over the Budget Resolution is intense because it goes to the heart of the differences between the two parties. Democrats fight for services; Republicans fight for tax cuts. Democrats don't express much concern for the most fortunate; Republicans don't express much concern for the poor. We bring a different set of values, worldviews, and rationales to the table, and the resolution does not by itself change law, spending, or taxes.

I served on the House Budget Committee during my last four years in Congress, from 2005 to 2008. In 2007–8, when Democrats were in the majority, we met to identify which members would lead the response to the Republican amendments designed to highlight their perceptions of weaknesses of the Democratic budget proposal. Almost every vote on amendments and the final budget resolution was a straight party-line vote.

Since we all knew that compromise on the Budget Resolution with the other side was impossible, arguments in the committee debates had a ritualistic feel; they barely changed over the years. For example, take the classic debate over "cuts" in the federal budget to domestic programs. On February 8, 2005, Chairman Jim Nussle of Iowa convened a budget hearing with Josh Bolten, then the director of the Office of Management and Budget, and later George W. Bush's chief of staff. Nussle in his opening statement said:

[R]eading the newspaper today has been kind of an interesting experience. Almost all of the headlines talked about the Bush budget: cutting, spending, cutting, gouging, and eliminating. Well, you look through the budget and precious little is in the area of actual cuts.

What we see in Washington is the definition of cuts that we have got to be real about. A cut in Washington is often a decrease of an anticipated increase.[14]

My response came later in the hearing when I had a chance to speak:

The Chairman said at the beginning that a reduction, a cut, in Washington is sometimes a reduction in an anticipated increase. Well, back home people have a real simple idea: If they can't provide the same services year to year, they know that services are being reduced. It doesn't matter what the number on some piece of paper in Washington is. If they can't provide the same services, they are losing ground.[15]

During my years in Congress this argument about spending "cuts had eternal life. We talked past each other, and the debate never changed: Republicans were talking numbers on a page, and Democrats were talking services delivered to people. Since the costs of almost all federal programs rise with inflation, services to the public cannot be sustained with flat funding. Neither side could persuade the other about the differences between numbers and services because we were fighting a larger battle over the role and responsibility of the federal government. Democrats tended to concentrate on funds needed for specific activities; Republicans had a broader interest in simply getting the government to do less. In general, the public didn't have time to sort out these differences, and the media just reported whatever we said without much analysis. But that issue was nothing compared to the big one over taxes.

The idea that tax cuts paid for themselves was, virtually without exception, the expressed position of the Republicans on the House Budget Committee. In every debate we plowed the same ground. The Republicans celebrated the remarkable effect of tax cuts to stimulate economic growth so much that revenue for the government would increase, or, if they were pressed, decline by only an insignificant amount. Democrats argued that tax cuts considerably reduced federal revenues from what they would otherwise be and that we were borrowing from our children to give tax breaks to the rich. There was not a lot of evolutionary argument in the Budget Committee.

At the February 8, 2005, Budget Committee hearing, Chairman Nussle began by repeatedly invoking the beneficial impact of the president's tax cuts ("major tax relief that fueled recovery," "the strong economic growth unleashed by tax relief.") Then, during his debate with the ranking Democrat, John Spratt (D-SC), over the administration's goal of making the Bush tax cuts "permanent," Nussle enthusiastically pointed to a chart showing revenues rising even if the cuts were extended:

Now, wait a minute, how can this be? What kind of magic is going on in this world that you can cut taxes and the amount of money that comes into Treasury goes up? Isn't this a miracle? Well, let us go to chart No. 11, and I will show you how it works.[16]

In fact, the chart showed no miracle. It merely depicted the normal outcome of the American economy, which is almost always growing due to increasing population and productivity. The Republican fixation on tax policy leads them to vastly overstate its impact on economic growth. The economists who testified at our hearings testified that tax cuts, properly designed, could indeed stimulate the economy in the short run, but they would typically have only a small impact in the long run and could easily be a negative factor unless offset with reductions in spending or other increases in revenue. The economists agreed with each other, but the Republican members didn't accept their conclusions.

Even the way we talked about the economy often highlighted our differences. At the February 2005 hearing, Josh Bolten said, "In other words, by the end of the budget window [ten years], with the president's tax cuts made permanent, we will be at the historic levels of revenues that *income and other taxes take away from the economy*."[17] I responded by saying that I thought school teachers, police officers, firefighters, and the young men and women serving in our military were all part of the economy.[18]

One year later, on February 8, 2006, the Budget Committee went through the whole exercise again with committee Republicans and Bolten celebrating the economic power of tax cuts. Nussle confidently opined, "You cannot increase taxes and expect economic growth to continue," even though that is precisely what happened after the 1993 Clinton deficit reduction plan was passed without a single Republican vote. Josh Bolten again talked about the "economy" as if it consisted only of the private sector; he said the administration budget sustained only "essential spending" in order to leave other resources "back in the economy."

In response to one question, Bolten said the president's budget for future years had been adjusted on the assumption that the Bush tax cuts would be extended. When my turn came, I asked if that adjustment involved a reduction of estimated tax revenues. Bolten replied that economists didn't agree on the "dynamic" effect of tax cuts, but he admitted that "the revenues would be lower than they otherwise would have been without those tax cuts."[19]

That half-hearted admission from OMB director Bolten that tax cuts reduce revenues passed for a victory on that day, but it wasn't much of a victory. Bolten had said at the hearing, "I am not arguing that every dollar of tax cut produces more than a dollar of revenue. Some people believe that; I am not making that case here now."[20] In fact, he was adopting standard Republican fallback phrasing, which suggested that you might recover *most* of it. The believers in supply-side economics—most of the Republican House members—still insist that tax cuts are such a powerful economic stimulant that they increase revenues by most, if not all, of the reductions due to the tax cuts. In the real world it's not true. My notes of the February 8, 2006, Budget Committee meeting have a one word summary: "Wonderland."

After the change in control of Congress, Peter Orszag became the director of the CBO. Testifying before the House Budget Committee on January 30, 2007, Orszag said that reducing marginal tax rates could have a "slightly positive or slightly negative" effect on economic growth, although it would be "typically quite small."[21] His testimony was essentially the same as that of every economist who testified before the committee during my tenure.

The consensus of economic opinion had no perceptible impact on the Republican members. At one hearing in 2005 or 2006, after the usual back-and-forth on the effect of tax cuts, Ander Crenshaw in some frustration said, "I guarantee you that if taxes are increased, revenues will go down." Since at the time revenues had gone up for all but four of the previous fifty years, after multiple tax cuts and tax increases, that was preposterous. As of 2012, even in inflation-adjusted dollars, declines in federal revenue have occurred only ten times in the past thirty-five years, almost all during or just after a recession, including 2001, 2002, 2003, 2008, and 2009.

The gap in perspective arises from valuing different sources. Democratic members of Congress work with data from the CBO, CBPP, and the Department of the Treasury, and they listen to mainstream economists.

Republicans have argued for years that the prevailing economic models do not take account of the "macroeconomic feedback" effect of tax cuts in stimulating the economy; moreover, they listen to businessmen and women who regularly ask for lower taxes and less regulation. Consequently, Republican congressmen routinely dismissed Democratic arguments against tax cuts for the "wealthy" on the ground that tax cuts were necessary to restore or strengthen "confidence" among "job creators."

While business "confidence" is certainly a component of a growing economy, it is difficult to measure and even harder to quantify in relation to a specific action by Congress. It therefore becomes an argument that is always available but generally incapable of being proved or disproved. Combined with supply-side rhetoric that tax cuts pay for themselves, the Republican argument for reducing taxes became disconnected from any data-driven discussion we might otherwise have had. To Democrats, tax benefits for "job creators" was just the same old trickle-down economic theory that helping the rich would in the long run help the middle class and the poor. Given the thirty-year decline in the relative prosperity of the American middle class, the theory lacked evidentiary support.

PAUL RYAN—YOUNG GUN

The chair of the House Budget Committee, Rep. Paul Ryan of Wisconsin, is a mystery. He is warm, bright, eloquent, and energetic. Paul is a gentleman with real leadership potential—but his convictions about supply-side economics make it difficult for him to work across the aisle on those issues. Ryan requires all of his staff to read *Atlas Shrugged*, Ayn Rand's novel in praise of free markets and the pursuit of self-interest. At a celebration of what would have been Rand's one-hundredth birthday, Ryan said that if he had to credit one person with inspiring him to get into public service, it would be Ayn Rand.[22] Romney's selection of him as the Republican vice-presidential nominee confirms that Ryan's form of anti-government libertarianism is now in the party's mainstream.

I sat through four years of Budget Committee hearings with Paul Ryan. Like his Republican colleagues, he inveighed against "spending" (almost always in the abstract) and advocated for more and larger tax cuts. For example, after Democrats won control of the House in the 2006 elections, Paul opened our first hearing on January 23, 2007, by saying that deficits were due to excessive spending, not to the Bush "tax relief" (that brilliant focus-group phrase for tax cuts), which had led to increased economic growth and deficit reduction. The Republican Budget Committee mantra was always that "we don't have a revenue problem, we have a spending problem." That made sense to members whose working assumption was that taxes and spending were always too high—measured against some undiscoverable standard that Democrats could not comprehend. We believed the appropriate private sector analogy was that a company's success depends on getting a profitable balance between expenditures and revenues. To each side in the budget debate, its own position seemed obvious, but there was little comprehension across the aisle.

After President Bush's 2005 State of the Union speech I was standing next to Paul when he told a reporter that he liked the part of the speech on Iraq and foreign policy, but the second part reflected "too much of an industrial policy and I believe in free markets." President Bush had proposed an energy initiative with a 22 percent increase in clean energy research to deal with our "addiction to oil" and more funding for basic research to stimulate innovation in nanotechnology, supercomputing, and alternative energy sources. I am quite sure that not a single House Democrat would have seen those proposals as interfering in free markets, because we have a different view of the relationship between the public and private sectors.

To Paul Ryan and many Republicans, even a Republican president's proposals for funding clean energy research, innovation in cutting-edge technology, and math and science education conflicted with their faith in unfettered "free markets." But the federal tax code is riddled with provisions to help particular industries. State and local governments routinely offer tax breaks and other incentives for businesses to locate in their areas. Why should the federal government avoid funding research, technology, and education, all of which would make the country more competitive? We had been doing precisely that for our entire existence as a nation by funding canals, railroads, highways, and numerous other investments believed to have public value.

When relatively minor investments in research and education draw a negative reaction from an intelligent congressman like Paul Ryan, America is in trouble. European governments created and funded Airbus to compete with Boeing because they refused to be driven out of the airplane manufacturing industry. The Chinese government's direction of its market economy into profitable and socially beneficial directions like alternative energy technology is well known. More to the point, the clean energy technologies that were invented in America, such as solar receptors, are now flourishing overseas in Germany, Denmark, and China because of strategic decisions by those countries to invest public funds in these technologies.

Because I like Paul, I had trouble understanding how his ideological rigidity fit with his obvious intellect. For the better part of a year, I would think to myself, "Paul Ryan is too smart to believe the things he says." Then one day I wound up in a conversation with a Republican economist. Somehow the conversation turned to Paul and he said, "Paul Ryan is too smart to believe the things he says." Word for word. Today I suspect we were both wrong, but I will never be sure.

TAX CUTS DON'T PAY FOR THEMSELVES

Members of Congress have access to more information than we can ever digest. Articles, books, reports, studies, staff memos, and other material are always available and often thrust upon us. We are all subject in some degree to selecting material based on our preconceived opinions. But we learn from our daily contacts that there are usually several sides to an issue, and it is wise to listen to many voices. That doesn't mean that all voices are equally reasonable.

For economists the general effect of tax cuts on federal revenues is not a matter of serious dispute. Let's take a few examples. Greg Mankiw, the

Harvard economist who served as chairman of President George W. Bush's Council of Economic Advisors, wrote in his 1998 *Principles of Microeconomics* that there is "no credible evidence" that "tax revenues . . . rise in the face of lower tax rates." He likened an economist who says otherwise to a "snake-oil salesman."[23] Likewise, one of candidate John McCain's economic advisors, Mark Zandi of Economy.com, concluded in a lengthy 2004 report that Bush's tax cuts were not an efficient stimulus to the economy because so much of the benefits went to high-income households more likely to save than to spend what they received.[24]

During my early years in Congress, Republican supply-siders argued that the Treasury's economic models were faulty because they did not recognize "dynamic scoring," which they believed would prove that tax cuts stimulate economic growth enough to compensate for all or at least most of the revenue lost to the tax cuts. In 1981 the Reagan administration came to office with several supply-side advisors expecting to cut income taxes, increase defense spending, and balance the federal budget—an agenda with obvious internal conflicts.[25] Republican House members had been frustrated for years that CBO did not use "dynamic scoring" as a component of its predictive economic models.[26] But later, when Douglas Holtz-Eakin became CBO director, he incorporated nine different dynamic scoring models in evaluating President Bush's proposed 2004 budget. But there were "very little economic feedback effects."[27] Moreover, unless spending was reduced in line with the tax cuts, or alternative revenues raised by closing tax loopholes, annual deficits would increase and the long-term impact of the tax cuts on the economy would be wholly negative.[28]

The CBO conclusion in 2003 was reinforced in 2006 by President Bush's own Treasury Department, which forecast how people and institutions would react to the lower tax levels. That study didn't make the supply-siders' case. As the economist Jason Furman wrote, the Treasury report concluded that even under the rosiest of scenarios, at best only 10 percent of the cost of the 2001–2003 tax cuts could be recovered. In the absence of reductions in spending to offset the Bush tax cuts, those cuts would "end up *weakening* the economy over the long run."[29]

Jonathan Chait has described the Republican conviction that tax cuts pay for themselves as "crackpot economics." In an October 9, 2007, *New York Times* column, after pointing out that "every major Republican contender" for president had said that the Bush tax cuts had caused government revenues to rise, Chait concluded:

> Yet there is no more debate about this question among economists than there is debate about the existence of evolution among biologists. Most economists believe that it is theoretically possible for tax rates to be high enough that a reduction in rates could actually produce more revenues. But I do not know of any tenured economist in the United States who believes this is true of the Bush tax cuts.[30]

Mainstream economists agree that a recession recovery plan must include some combination of tax cuts and increased government spending to stimulate the economy. They necessarily result in short-term deficits; indeed, the goal is to compensate for lack of private sector demand. The more serious the recession, the stronger the medicine must be. That's why the stimulus package of the Bush administration, enacted in February 2008, and the Obama administration's stimulus, enacted a year later, made economic sense. Yet not one Republican in the House and only three in the Senate—Senators Snowe, Collins, and Specter—supported the Obama bill. Congressional Republicans appeared to be unconcerned about deficits created by tax cuts but alarmed by deficits they attribute to excessive spending, even when spending is designed according to standard Keynesian economic theory to boost aggregate demand to stimulate an economy in recession.

That is why the Budget Committee felt like Wonderland to me. We were arguing about an economic issue on which virtually all economists agreed, but the Republican committee members ignored the expert consensus. We felt that our job was to make concrete choices about taxes and spending; the Republicans wanted to reduce both as much as possible in pursuit of an elusive goal that made no sense to us. In those circumstances, it was hard not to question the integrity and motives of the other side. It is

no comfort now that the arguments we made then about the fiscal irre-
sponsibility of the Bush tax cuts proved to be accurate.

WHAT'S GOING ON HERE?

After listening for years to arguments not grounded in mainstream economics, I began to understand that the apparent issues are not the real
ones. The ideological debate over the role and size of government that has
been our national legacy, for better and worse, drives our differences on
specific matters. Our arguments about taxes and budgets did not involve
two competing views of the available evidence, because our values, fears,
and worldviews shape our specific positions on economic issues. That's
why in committee or on the House floor it felt as if we came from different
planets.

David Obey, who served in Congress for more than thirty years, was
known to get exasperated on a few occasions during his tenure. He was the
ranking Democrat on the powerful Appropriations Committee during the
Gingrich-Hastert years. I stood with Dave on the floor once when he was
expressing his frustration with the Republican majority. He said simply,
"These are not serious people." By this he meant they would not engage in
detailed debate over policy, they would not deliberate the long-term consequences of policy decisions, and they would not give up political rhetoric for the hard work of legislating. And they were in charge.

House Republicans now have a different core mission than when
Dave Obey came to Congress more than three decades ago. Today they
are trying to contain the growth of government to protect individual
liberty because they believe government necessarily infringes on the
freedom of the people. These are small government conservatives, not
fiscal conservatives. In 2005 I was walking from the House Chamber to
my office in the Longworth House Office Building with Jerry Moran, a
thoughtful Republican from Kansas (now a senator) and a morning
regular with me in the House gym. I said, "Jerry, your caucus must be
divided now between your tax cutters and deficit hawks." He replied,

"We don't have any deficit hawks left." I wondered where did they all go? If Republicans have essentially adopted a libertarian view of government, how can the two parties compromise on budget and tax issues when they cannot agree on the evidence that matters or the way it should be interpreted?

The faith of congressional Republicans in supply-side economics shows no sign of weakening. In July 2010, responding to a question about the budgetary cost of extending the Bush tax cuts, Sen. Jon Kyl said, "You do need to offset the cost of increased spending. And that's what Republicans object to. But you should never have to offset the cost of a deliberate decision to reduce tax rates on Americans."[31]

Mitch McConnell (R-KY) confirmed the next day that Kyl was speaking for his party. He said, "There's no evidence whatsoever that the Bush tax cuts actually diminished revenue. They increased revenue, because of the vibrancy of these tax cuts in the economy. So I think what Senator Kyl was expressing was the view of virtually every Republican on that subject."[32]

There are no kind words for what Republicans are saying about the effects of tax cuts. Their denial that tax cuts reduce revenues is the Big Lie at the center of their message, but yet they appear to believe it themselves. If you are looking for the sources of polarization, start here. The rudeness and bickering in Congress are symptoms, not the disease. And the disease is chronic and much more deeply rooted. One of the major American political parties simply refuses to acknowledge the most basic evidence about how tax cuts and spending affect the federal budget and the nation's economy.

The current Republican orthodoxy about taxes is a product largely of the last fifteen years. Bruce Bartlett, a senior policy advisor in the Reagan White House, points to eleven major tax increases passed by that administration from 1982 to 1988, which partially compensated for the 1981 supply-side-inspired tax cut in Reagan's first year.[33] The first President Bush signed a deficit reduction plan with tax increases and spending cuts in 1990; President Clinton did the same in 1993 and 1997. In short, although Republicans and Democrats have always had differences on budget and tax issues, compromise used to be possible.

The George W. Bush presidency represented a break with that past. According to the Treasury, his administration saw the passage of more major tax cuts and a greater aggregate revenue loss as a percentage of GDP than any prior administration. Moreover, despite rapidly growing deficits, President Bush never signed a single tax increase.[34]

Bartlett's book on the need for tax reform, *The Benefit and the Burden,* is a primer on tax policy and a plea for reforming the tax code. He has a long list of conservative credentials, including serving on the staff of Congressmen Ron Paul and Jack Kemp, working as staff director of the Joint Economic Committee of Congress, senior policy analyst in the Reagan White House, and deputy assistant secretary for economic policy at Treasury for President George H. W. Bush. Bartlett believes that federal revenues will need to rise as a share of GDP in order to reduce federal deficits and care for an aging society. But I believe he also sheds light on the trap into which so many members of his party have fallen.

After mentioning Michelle Bachmann's statement in a presidential debate that taxpayers should keep "every dollar you earn," Bartlett writes, "I have never once heard a conservative admit that there is a level of taxation below which it would be unwise to go."[35] In other words, the core Republican principle of "smaller government, lower taxes" has neither a stopping place nor a countervailing principle. In Congress, therefore, since members generally vote for measures that include some level of spending and taxes, Republicans can always be outflanked on the right, most recently by Tea Party–supported candidates, who promise even "smaller" and "lower." Apparently in some despair, Bartlett's last chapter is titled, "If Tax Reform Happens, It Will Be Because Grover Norquist Permits It." Since Norquist is opposed to any and all new taxes, and his organization, Americans for Tax Reform, has such power over Republicans in Congress, the prospects for reform are bleak.[36] Norquist is so widely feared for his capacity to take out Republican congressmen who stray from his anti-tax orthodoxy that until recently virtually all Republican candidates for Congress signed his pledge to *never* vote for a tax increase. In the 112th Congress only six Republicans in the House refused to take the pledge.

Although multiple factors have contributed to the growing anti-tax orthodoxy of the Republican Party, one is surely the intellectual slippery slope of its core principles. Without a concept of a legitimate role for government, Republicans have difficulty discussing how to make it work. The political power of "smaller government, lower taxes" keeps conservatives disengaged in the process of devising specific economic, education, health care, and environmental policies. That's why Democrats and Republicans in Congress and throughout the country speak past each other; general principles of "smaller and lower" provide little guidance on programmatic budget decisions, which largely determine whether the government is effectively serving the needs of the public.

The multiple Bush tax cuts and the war in Iraq, plus the associated added interest on the national debt, put the United States in a deep fiscal hole by adding more than $4 trillion dollars to the national debt between 2001 and 2011. One respected source found that "Just two policies dating from the Bush administration—tax cuts and the wars in Iraq and Afghanistan—accounted for over $500 billion of the deficit in 2009 and will account for almost $7 trillion in deficits in 2009 through 2019, including the associated debt-service costs."[37] The policies on taxes and Iraq were developed with only casual attention to the likely consequences. Administration officials believed that they knew all they needed to know about both subjects. Their convictions created barriers not only to new and contradictory information but to any form of disciplined inquiry. Vice President Cheney justified the 2003 tax cut to the Secretary of the Treasury by saying it was "their due," acquired by winning the 2002 midterm elections. That's not an argument that requires numerical calculations, only the faith that they are not needed.

The power of anti-tax orthodoxy on the right was apparent in the proposals for massive new tax cuts by all of the Republican 2012 presidential candidates. None of their plans for reducing taxes in the face of current annual deficits of roughly $1 trillion made economic sense. All continued to assume that economic growth always follows from cutting taxes regardless of time and circumstance—an assumption undermined by the actual experience of the Clinton and Bush administrations. All failed to explain that continuation of the Bush tax cuts, plus a few trillion in additional tax cuts, would necessarily lead to massive reductions in services and Social Security benefits to seniors and low-income Americans. Although both parties need to be engaged in data-driven budget negotiations, we cannot even agree on what counts as evidence.

The nonpartisan CBO has produced the data that explain the relative impact on current and projected deficits of the Bush tax cuts, the wars in Iraq and Afghanistan, the Bush and Obama stimulus programs, and the general economic downturn of the last five years. The CBPP developed the following chart with CBO data to highlight the factors contributing to our country's record deficits.

As of May 2011, the Bush-era tax cuts were estimated to be the largest contributor to the annual federal deficit from 2013 through the end of the decade, larger even than the economic downturn that began in 2007–8.

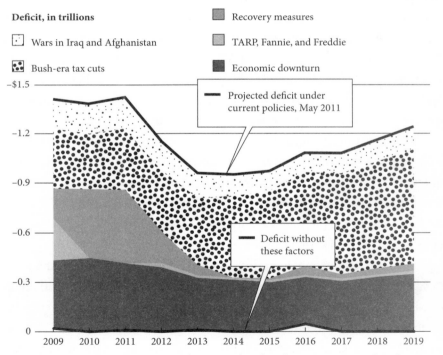

Figure 2.1 Economic Downturn and Legacy of Bush Policies Drive Record Deficits.
SOURCE: Center on Budget and Policies Priorities analysis based on Congressional Budget Office estimates.

The Bush and Obama stimulus packages were understood to provide a short-term fiscal injection to maintain aggregate demand for goods and services, and to have, consequently, a negative short-term effect on annual deficits. Indeed, without some increased deficit, there would be no stimulus.

Despite its explanatory value, the chart in figure 2.1 and the data it represents have had virtually no impact on Republican tax and budget policies. In January 2010, Paul Ryan issued a comprehensive proposal called the "Roadmap for America's Future" that combined huge tax and spending cuts, which, he argued, would restore fiscal discipline. The Tax Policy Center analysis found that his plan would cut in half the taxes paid by the wealthiest 1 percent of the public, and increase taxes on Americans making between $20,000 and $200,000. On the expenditure side, Ryan's roadmap would eliminate the tax exclusion for employer-based health insurance, end traditional Medicare, and abolish over time most of Medicaid and the Children's Health Insurance Program. These well-established programs would be replaced with tax credits or vouchers for people to buy private health insurance or block grants to states at shrunken funding levels, neither of which would keep pace with health-care costs. Consequently, rates for private insurance would rise and impose increasingly heavy burdens on individuals and states. Ryan also proposed to cut Social Security benefits and replace them with private accounts subject to the risks of market fluctuation.[38]

In 2011 and 2012 Congressman Ryan, as chair of the Budget Committee, secured House passage of substantially similar plans. Despite annual federal deficits of roughly $1 trillion, Ryan in 2012 again proposed big reductions in taxes, especially for upper-income Americans, and dramatic cuts in federal benefits for low- and middle-income people. These cuts were conveniently left unspecified. In explaining his 2012 proposal, Ryan said, "We don't want to turn the safety net into a hammock that lulls able-bodied people . . . into complacency and dependence."[39] The big expense items were, of course, Medicare and Social Security, which primarily cover retired people, not those still in the workforce. In February 2012, a CBPP analysis of census and budget data revealed that "more than 90 percent of the benefit dollars that entitlement and other mandatory programs spend go to assist people who are elderly, seriously disabled, or members of working households (who benefit from, among other things, the earned income tax credit, the Children's Health Insurance Program and the school lunch program)."[40] To critics, the Ryan budget proposals laid out a path to an on-your-own society, which would reduce taxes for the wealthy, cut benefits for the most vulnerable, and even increase taxes for many low- and middle-income Americans by scaling back some of their deductions and tax credits. For people who do not share the conservative worldview that government services impinge on personal liberty and create dependency, those budget proposals make little sense.

Paul Ryan has been unable to reconcile, and perhaps has not tried to reconcile, his own religious beliefs with the inspiration he draws from Ayn Rand's celebration of selfishness and rejection of altruism. When he claimed that his 2012 budget was inspired by his faith, the U.S. Conference of Catholic Bishops sent letters to Congress criticizing the Republican budget for failing to meet the moral criteria of the Roman Catholic Church, specifically for not helping the "least of these," the poor, hungry, homeless, and jobless. A group of Jesuit scholars and the Georgetown University faculty wrote that Ryan's budget "appeared to reflect the values of your favorite philosopher, Ayn Rand, rather than the Gospel of Jesus Christ."[41] Ryan is not alone. My Republican colleagues who were most vocal about their religion seemed to me the least interested in using their office to serve what I and many others understood as the social gospel of Christianity. That conflict of conservative political and religious values was as puzzling as their rejection of evidence relevant to our political disputes. In the first few weeks after being selected by Mitt Romney to be his running mate, Ryan tried to disavow Ayn Rand's influence on him and to reject her atheism. But Rand understood that her philosophical and political beliefs were incompatible with the social gospel of Christianity. As hard as he may try, Paul Ryan cannot make the relentless pursuit of self-interest into a Christian virtue.

In the real world tax cuts don't pay for themselves; they have to be offset or "paid for." Supply-side proponents deny that conclusion. All of us—Right or Left—are potentially subject to adopting convictions that are not true. A large body of research has confirmed that for many of us our emotions, cognitive styles, or worldviews lead us to reject evidence that conflicts with our preexisting convictions. We attempt to reason with each other about politics and religion, but our views are not easily changed. Our representative form of government requires that elected officials reason together, not just emote in the same space. The more difficult reasoned deliberation becomes, the less effective the government. In our checked-and-balanced system the advocates of "no" have an advantage over the proponents of "yes." In a crisis, that's a big problem.

In 2008, with some large American financial institutions in free fall, we were lucky to have Henry Paulson as Secretary of the Treasury and Ben Bernanke as chairman of the Federal Reserve, two of President Bush's best appointments. Moreover, the 2006 elections gave Democrats control of Congress and elevated Rep. Barney Frank and Sen. Chris Dodd to be chairs of the critical House and Senate finance committees. These four major players do not have the ideological blinders that keep others from finding common ground. Without their leadership, we would probably be trying to dig our way out of an epic global depression. President Bush let Bernanke and Paulson develop unprecedented forms of relief for financial institutions, and Senator Dodd and Congressman Frank helped to build legislative support. In the current climate of opinion we have no reason to believe that we will be so fortunate the next time.

Our ability to debate and decide public issues is crippled when government is always seen as the problem, not as part of the solution. To deny to the federal government some role in strategic planning for the country is to weaken America in a world that Bill Clinton rightly describes as "increasingly inter-connected but insufficiently integrated." Nothing matters more to our future prosperity than being able to engage in pragmatic, constructive debates and decision making about federal taxes and expenditures. It didn't happen while I was in Congress, and it is now close to impossible.

After she stepped down as head of President Obama's Council of Economic Advisors, Christina Romer observed, "The polarization of fiscal policy is one of the worst legacies to come out of the recession. Before the crisis, there was agreement that what you do when you run out of monetary tools is fiscal stimulus. Suddenly, it's like we're back in the 1930s."[42]

But there had been no such "agreement" in Congress for more than a decade. My Republican colleagues, long before they were joined by the Tea Party candidates after the 2010 elections, had locked in on an economic theory that transcended time and place and was immune to the most widely used economic models: projections from the CBO could be safely ignored; the less the government spends, the healthier our economy will be. The conviction that tax cuts pay for themselves has no support in mainstream economic analysis; it was and remains faith-based.

In the twenty-first century an American government tangled in ideological rigidity will lose economic influence and power to the rest of the world. Other developed countries are not burdened with such a strong anti-government, anti-tax movement as is our country. They may dismiss their governments as corrupt or ineffective, but our sustained, widespread, well-funded hostility to government is uncommon in the rest of the developed world. The irony is that the United States is still the longest surviving democracy in the history of the world—and, we once believed, the model for others.

Americans, most of them, fail to understand the lifeline between the public and private sectors, the necessity of spending public dollars to invest in fairness today and opportunity tomorrow. For all but five or six weekends in twelve years, I returned to Maine to meet and talk with my constituents. I saw, as few Americans do, the intricate web of support and dependency that tie us together. Half of Maine's revenues come from the federal government. The public, acting through federal, state, and local governments, sets rules of the road for private sector activity and provides an enormous variety of incentives and funds for infrastructure upon which our private enterprise system is built. Our children are educated, our streets protected, our elderly housed and kept from poverty, our sick and disabled cared for, our businessmen and women supported, among many others, by the public through public decisions.

Our discouraged constituents may assume that those they elect to Congress choose partisan combat for personal political reasons and are comfortable with that choice. It's not generally true. Now that I am out of office, I continue to find that for both Republicans and Democrats in Congress, the inability to work across the aisle is the major frustration of the job, and neither side knows how to overcome it. The struggle of widest consequence occurs on the ground defined by budget and tax policy.

I believe that conservatives cling to the old conviction that tax cuts pay for themselves, or come close to doing so, because it works politically and allows them to set aside otherwise difficult choices of reducing spending or increasing other revenues to offset their tax cuts. A black-and-white portrait of big government versus innovative job creators is more politically arresting than a painting in shades of gray. If even popularly elected governments restrict personal freedom, then in America it is best to stand for freedom. That worldview is in stark contrast to the Democratic belief that government is a vehicle for creating individual opportunity and taking collective action for the common good. If American politics continues to be a battle of worldviews, a struggle—not a balance—between our archetypical individualism and our engagement with others, our national politics is likely to remain dysfunctional. In Congress today a gulf of incomprehension that no bridge can cross has left us stranded in our separate provinces.

Iraq

Evidence Doesn't Matter

Bush wanted to remove Saddam, through military action, justified by the conjunction of terrorism and WMD. *But the intelligence and facts were being fixed around the policy.* The NSC had no patience with the UN route, and no enthusiasm for publishing material on the Iraqi regime's record. *There was little discussion in Washington of the aftermath after military action.* (emphasis added)

—*Downing Street Memo, July 23, 2002*

On the morning of September 11, 2001, I was in the Cannon House Office Building at a meeting with the chair of the Pew Oceans Commission, Leon Panetta, a former congressman and chief of staff to President Clinton. Shortly after 9 a.m., Leon was handed a note and told us that a plane (we envisioned a small plane) had crashed into the World Trade Center. I returned to my office and saw the television images of smoke billowing from one tower. My staff and I watched in horror as another jetliner struck the second tower.

A short time later, Todd Stein, my legislative director, shouted, "The Pentagon's been hit!" We could see the smoke from our Longworth House

Office windows and could only imagine the loss of life in New York and Washington. Within seconds we and other offices decided to evacuate the building. We descended six flights of stairs and went outside past Capitol Police who had not yet been informed of the attack on the Pentagon.

Standing in the sunshine in the park behind Cannon, we were cut off from information and desperately wanted to know what was going on. I took all of my staff to my small apartment a block away. There we turned on the television to follow the tragic developments. We knew our family and friends would be worried, so with landline and cell phone service suddenly inoperative, we shared my newest technological gadget, a Blackberry, to send them emails saying we were safe.

In the weeks and months that followed, Americans were uncharacteristically subdued; we turned inward, reaching out to each other rather than erupting in anger. American flags hung from bridges and porches everywhere. Strangers on the streets of New York and Washington treated one another with unusual politeness, even benevolence. After al-Qaeda, the terrorist network in Afghanistan, was identified as the culprit, support for retaliatory action by our government was widespread.

I was struck by the vehemence with which the administration and its media allies attacked any questions or comments about the "root causes" of terrorism. They viewed the attacks as a clear manifestation of evil in the world. They had a point, obviously, but their determination to suppress discussion of causes suggested that they feared that discussion about the sources of Islamic fundamentalism would somehow suggest that American policy was at fault and thus weaken America's willingness to act. Many people raised a question that required serious thinking, "Why do they hate us?" The administration avoided a direct answer by repeating: "This is the face of evil," making the statement more a matter of theology than of politics.

The single most stunning fact about the war in Iraq is that President Bush never called a meeting of his defense and foreign policy advisors to debate the potential ramifications of and alternatives to an invasion. Bob Woodward, who interviewed the key people who formulated the policy, including the president, told a group of Democratic members that "no one could remember a meeting" held to discuss the pros and cons of an invasion. On the most fateful decision of his life, President George W. Bush, the only president with an MBA, failed a first rule of decision making. As Secretary of State Colin Powell later observed, the president made his choice for war "even though the NSC [National Security Council] had never met—and never would meet—to discuss the decision."[1]

The failure was not his alone. Given the array of top-level cabinet members and advisors around any president, one can only conclude that others on President Bush's team didn't believe that a meeting was necessary. They took America to war without the fundamental analysis of options that any American corporation would make before introducing a new product. Why? Dick Cheney's obsession with Saddam played a critical role. Beyond that, the president's convictions and those of his advisors appeared to be set in stone; more detailed information about Iraq, its history and circumstances, was apparently irrelevant. They planned how to mobilize American forces to invade Iraq, but they avoided debating the question "why."

The legacy of the Bush administration was cemented by its response to 9/11 and by the invasion of Iraq. That response and the invasion were shaped by the attitudes and worldviews of the decision makers in the administration and Congress. The price of their decisions was measured in a staggering loss of life and direct costs of close to a trillion dollars. The result was an America weaker abroad and more divided at home. What went wrong?

Some recent research explains the polarization of American voters based on where they fit on a spectrum of authoritarian to nonauthoritarian attitudes or worldviews. People with an authoritarian worldview increasingly gravitate to the Republican Party, while nonauthoritarians move toward the Democrats. There is evidence that authoritarian personalities see the world in black and white rather than shades of gray, are more predisposed to the use of force over diplomacy in foreign affairs, and are impatient with details and evidence. Those with authoritarian worldviews were, therefore, more likely to adopt the Bush administration's policy of preemptive war against Iraq than a roomful of people with the opposite outlook. And this may explain why President Bush never called a meeting to debate whether to invade Iraq. Perhaps he did not want to referee a meeting in which Secretary of State Colin Powell would clash, as he undoubtedly would have, with Secretary of Defense Rumsfeld and the rest of the war council. But that meeting should have been held.

Resistance to government engagement in issues connected to the federal budget, health care, and climate change are connected to concerns about threats to personal freedom, but a predisposition to use military force is more directly linked to an authoritarian worldview. People who are hostile to government action on domestic issues and those with an authoritarian worldview tend to be impatient with evidence and extended deliberation. Inattention to or disdain for evidence helps explain the administration's conviction that we would be welcomed "as liberators" and that Iraq had weapons of mass destruction, both of which proved to be untrue. For the first four years of the war the president and his supporters neglected the tangled complexity of Iraqi politics and culture, the nature of the resistance to the American occupation, and the impact of our policy on the rest of the world. The result was catastrophic. But the recovery of the American effort in 2007 was in large part the result of a dramatically different approach—the development of a counterinsurgency strategy specific to conditions on the ground in Iraq—for which a handful of creative military leaders should get credit. In the end, however, the surge succeeded only in extricating the United States militarily, leaving Iraq with a government significantly influenced by Iran and the country at risk of continuing internal civil conflict.

The politicization of the Iraq war led to another casualty: the institutional integrity of the Congress. The Senate's historic responsibility to oversee administration action was neglected with respect to the massive waste, fraud, and abuse by independent contractors working in Iraq. Billions of American dollars and Iraqi assets were squandered without a single contractor ever being called before the Senate to testify. Senators Byron Dorgan (D-ND) and Frank Lautenberg (D-NJ) tried for years to rally press and public support for aggressive oversight hearings, but they were defeated by Republican resistance and a cowed, complicit media.

THE RHETORIC OF ANTI-TERRORISM

To understand the difference that worldviews can make in describing the choices created by the attacks of 9/11, consider two speeches on terrorism with contrasting values and visions: George Bush's State of the Union address on January 29, 2002, and Tony Blair's speech to his Labor Party Conference in October 2, 2001.

Bush and Blair were united in their response to al Qaeda. Both were forceful in arguing there could be no compromise with terrorists and that they must be attacked and destroyed. However, the values and the language of the two speeches were miles apart. Blair used the word "community" seventeen times; Bush not once. Blair invoked the concept of our mutual interdependence repeatedly; Bush only occasionally. No Republican and few Democrats could have given Blair's speech when Americans were hungry for revenge, but a different American president could have taken Blair's values and set the attacks in a broader context. Bush played to the public's fear and desire for revenge when we needed something more.

Here is Tony Blair:

> I believe their memorial [those who lost their lives on 9/11] can and should be greater than simply the punishment of the guilty. It is that out of the shadow of this evil, should emerge lasting good: destruction of the machinery of terrorism wherever it is found; hope amongst all nations of a new beginning where we seek to resolve differences in a calm and ordered way; greater understanding between nations and between faiths; and above all justice and prosperity for the poor and dispossessed, so that people everywhere can see the chance of a better future through the hard work and creative power of the free citizen, not the violence and savagery of the fanatic.[2]

Here is George Bush:

Thousands of dangerous killers, schooled in the methods of murder, often supported by outlaw regimes, are now spread throughout the world like ticking time bombs, set to go off without warning.

North Korea is a regime arming with missiles and weapons of mass destruction, while starving its citizens. . . . Iran aggressively pursues these weapons and exports terror . . . Iraq continues to flaunt its hostility toward America and to support terror. The Iraqi regime has plotted to develop anthrax and nerve gas and nuclear weapons for over a decade. . . . States like these, and their terrorist allies, constitute an axis of evil, arming to threaten the peace of the world. By seeking weapons of mass destruction, these regimes pose a grave and growing danger. . . . In any of these cases, the price of indifference would be catastrophic . . .

I will not wait on events while dangers gather.[3]

Tony Blair and George Bush understood that al Qaeda could not have free rein in Afghanistan. Britain had experienced decades of terrorist attacks related to Northern Ireland, and dozens of British citizens died in America on 9/11. But Blair and Bush came to this moment of crisis with very difference perspectives. Blair held out hope for greater collaboration, while Bush made the case for an impossibly long war on "terrorism."

Tony Blair called for the strengthening of the bonds of community. George Bush urged Americans to revive the economy by traveling to Disney World. Blair understood that the forces driving Islamic terrorism must be confronted on many fronts. Bush was stuck with the limitations of his individualistic perspective: individual Americans should spend money to boost the economy; individual terrorists would be killed until jihad was stopped.

In the end, as the world knows, Blair meekly followed Bush down the warpath to Iraq, much to the fury of his own countrymen. I believe, however, that if Bush had shared Blair's perspective, the United States, together with its principal ally, would have formulated a very different policy, one that would have left the world less divided and dangerous.

MUNICH IN FEBRUARY 2002

Ten days after President Bush gave his 2002 State of the Union speech linking Iraq, Iran, and North Korea in an "axis of evil," I flew to Munich, Germany, with a congressional delegation. The CODEL (congressional delegation) had been organized by Senators John McCain (R-AZ) and Joe Lieberman (D-CT), perhaps the most hawkish senators on an invasion of Iraq. The occasion was the thirty-eighth annual Wehrkunde Conference, a gathering of defense ministers from the United States and Europe that had been expanded in the aftermath of the 9/11 attacks. Our American delegation included McCain, Lieberman, Jon Kyl (R-AZ), and Chuck Hagel (R-NB), and ten members of Congress.

The president's State of the Union message had sent shock waves through European military and diplomatic circles. By linking together three countries that rarely cooperated with each other in an imaginary "axis of evil," the president lost credibility abroad, and his thinly veiled threats to invade Iraq seemed reckless to European observers.

I remember standing with a group that included Senator Lieberman and Lord George Robertson, the secretary general of NATO and previously Tony Blair's minister of defense, shortly before the meetings commenced. Robertson looked at Lieberman and said, in a voice mixed with concern and incredulity, "Is the president serious about action against Iraq?" Lieberman replied, "Absolutely. We need to take action against Saddam; sanctions haven't worked." Robertson was not persuaded.

Traditionally, the U.S. secretary of defense had led the American delegation to the Wehrkunde Conference, but Donald Rumsfeld sent his deputy secretary, Paul Wolfowitz, in his place. Wolfowitz read a speech to the conference filled with promises of consultation and engagement with European governments. By the time he finished, I was pleasantly surprised by the respectful tone of his remarks, which I believed was what was needed at that moment.

Then Wolfowitz took questions. His tone and content changed. He made it clear that the United States was going to act on its own and that our allies could decide whether they would join us. I could feel the mood in the room change and tension rise. Careful staff-written remarks could not contain Wolfowitz from voicing his real views about our European allies. They had only one choice: they could be with us or against us.

On the plane back to the States, I was sitting across a table from Senators Kyl and Hagel. On the subject of weapons of mass destruction, Kyl said, "We've shown what we can do in Afghanistan. Now we'll show the Iraqis. Pretty soon, these countries will learn they just can't have these kinds of weapons." Hagel responded, "I disagree, Jon. It's more complicated than that. There are always unintended consequences."

Kyl's comments reflected the attitude toward the use of force that took us headlong into Iraq. Hagel's views embodied the caution that logically called for continuing sanctions and inspections, although in the end he was, like every Republican senator, a supporter of the invasion. Given Kyl's Manichean mind-set on terrorism, I was not surprised in November 2011 that the collapse of the so-called Super Committee charged with reducing the national debt by $1.2 trillion was attributed, by Democrats and Republicans alike, to Kyl's refusal to compromise.

A few weeks after the conference in Munich, I went to Afghanistan on one of the first congressional delegations after our invasion. Our CODEL flew from Kuwait into Bagram Air Base on a C-130 military transport plane with a small group of army soldiers. Spectacular mountains rose from dry valleys turned to dust by four years of drought. Our troops had gone into Tora Bora the night before and were taking casualties, although the spirits of those at Bagram were high because they knew the difficulty and significance of the assignment.

For the next day and a half, we had military briefings and talked with Harmid Karzai, then the chair of the Afghan Interim Authority. I won't forget the Afghan children at an orphanage who sang to welcome our delegation and asked only for "pens and pencils." Or the mothers at the "best" hospital in Kabul crowded beside their children because nursing care was nonexistent.

Afghanistan had no experience of an effective central government. One of every four children died before the age of five; the adult life expectancy was forty-six. Only 4 percent of the women were literate and only

27 percent of the men. One of the poorest countries in the world, Afghanistan in 2006 had an annual average income of $250. Although hope was in the air because of our military success, the task of stabilizing Afghanistan was sure to be daunting. I returned from Afghanistan convinced that the poverty and the terrain I had seen meant that we would be there for many years.

But the administration had already turned its attention to Iraq. From the "Axis of Evil" State of the Union speech in January through the summer of 2002, the administration ramped up its alarmist rhetoric about Saddam Hussein's regime. The president and his aides continued to deny that any decision to use force had been made.

Years went by before the administration's internal thinking became public. On May 1, 2005, the *Times* of London published the previously secret "Downing Street Memo" of July 23, 2002. An unnamed British official reporting on his recent trip to Washington was recorded as saying:

C reported on his recent talks in Washington. There was a perceptible shift in attitude. Military action was now seen as inevitable. Bush wanted to remove Saddam, through military action, justified by the conjunction of terrorism and WMD. *But the intelligence and facts were being fixed around the policy.* The NSC had no patience with the UN route, and no enthusiasm for publishing material on the Iraqi regime's record. *There was little discussion in Washington of the aftermath after military action.* (emphasis added)

The government of America's principal ally recognized that the Bush administration had somehow come to a decision to invade Iraq and thus was both manufacturing evidence to support the decision and ignoring its potential consequences. That's what it seemed at the time to me and many others, but we had no prior experience of America rushing to war with so little apparent thought of alternatives and risks. In my time on the House Armed Services Committee I had learned that the American military was fiercely committed to detailed planning in advance of combat. The same was not true of the Bush White House.

By late summer 2002, Democratic House members were wondering if the president would stoop to make an invasion of Iraq into a fall campaign issue. President George H. W. Bush had waited to seek authority to wage the first Gulf War until January 1991—after the fall elections. But Karl Rove and others in the second Bush administration saw the benefits of campaigning as a "war president." Scott McClellan, the president's press secretary, later admitted that the administration chose to use the war resolution as a political issue for the fall congressional campaigns and sold the war to the public as the administration had done with far less consequential and risky policies.[4]

On September 20, just a few days after the first anniversary of 9/11, the White House released "The National Security Strategy of the United States of America," which laid out the "Bush Doctrine" of preemptive war: the United States would take anticipatory action to prevent hostile acts by its adversaries. The White House appeared unconcerned that this bellicose doctrine clashed with American historical practice and established international law. The Bush Doctrine was broad and vague enough to provide an excuse for waging a first strike against almost any country whose leadership we opposed.

In the fall of 2002 I was completing my sixth year on the House Armed Services Committee. I had participated in briefings, both classified and open, on a wide range of military topics, and had developed great respect for the men and women who rose to the top ranks of the U.S. military. They demonstrated, with few exceptions, considerable breadth of understanding about the threats and opportunities the United States faced around the world and the limits of military action. From all I could see, the invasion of Iraq was not a priority of the American military—it was driven by the civilian leadership in the White House.

As a practical matter, invading Iraq to depose Saddam never made sense to me. I was no expert on the Middle East, but Iraq was not Afghanistan. There was no credible connection between Saddam and the attacks of 9/11. Nor could I comprehend how a force of 150,000 American soldiers could control 25 million people in a country the size of California in the middle of the Arab Islamic world.

Like most members of Congress, I had no reason at that time to question the possibility that Saddam possessed chemical and biological weapons. He had never denied that he did, and he had used them in the past. But I did not think that justified an invasion, since that would put U.S. soldiers within range of such weapons. That turned out to be the CIA's position as well. The administration's terror-inducing speculation about a "mushroom-shaped cloud" appeared to be a fear tactic designed to cut off further discussion. I had heard no evidence to support the claim that Iraq possessed nuclear weapons. Moreover, I believed that the administration would have given any hard information about an Iraqi nuclear program to the UN inspection team led by Mohammed el Baradei, and he had indeed reported that there was no evidence of such a program.

I talked every few weeks about Afghanistan and Iraq with Larry Pope, my Middle East advisor, personal friend, and Bowdoin College classmate. Pope had served in State Department posts in the Middle East and Africa, including the post of ambassador to Chad under President Clinton. Larry had capped an extraordinary diplomatic career by serving as political advisor to then-commander of the U.S. Central Command, General Anthony Zinni. President Clinton nominated Larry, after he retired from the Foreign Service in 2002, to be ambassador to Kuwait. He was denied a hearing by the staff of Sen. Trent Lott and Sen. Jesse Helms in retribution for Zinni's publically expressed objections to the Iraq Liberation Act of 1998 along with his objection to relying on Ahmad Chalabi as a source of intelligence and as a potential leader for a democratic Iraq. In fact, it was later revealed that Chalabi was a master of disinformation that played a crucial role in leading the United States into the war. He is now considered aligned with Iran.

Larry and I periodically discussed the prospect of military action against Iraq. My instincts lined up with his experience. He thought an invasion would be a "disaster." But the rhetorical buildup to war increased during the summer of 2002.

Soon after we returned to Washington following the Labor Day recess in 2002, President Bush met with congressional leaders. He announced that before we left town again for the midterm elections, Congress would take up a "strong" resolution authorizing military action in Iraq. The eventual resolution was shockingly open-ended: it authorized the president to use U.S. Armed Forces "as he determined to be necessary and appropriate in order to defend the national interest of the United States against the continuing threat posed by Iraq."

Andrew Card, the president's chief of staff, was blunt about the administration's political motivation: "If you are rolling out a new product, you don't introduce it in August." The vote in the House was held on October 10, just weeks before the midterm elections; the Senate vote followed a few days later. The timing ensured that the vote would be a lose-lose proposition for Democratic incumbents: a vote *for* the resolution would alienate our liberal base; a vote *against*, portrayed by opponents as unpatriotic or weak on security, would undermine our support in the political center.

Nevertheless, I didn't hesitate to encourage my colleagues, including Maine's Second District congressman John Baldacci, to vote against the resolution giving President Bush authority to invade Iraq. Even if there might be negative political consequences, we had to try to stop the momentum for a second war. There are no do-overs with military invasions. The odds were against us, but we had to take a stand.

General Wesley Clark testified at one of our Armed Services Committee hearings on September 26, 2002. He argued that our diplomatic efforts in the UN would be strengthened if Congress adopted a resolution expressing U.S. determination to act if the United Nations could not. He said:

> The use of force must remain a U.S. option under active consideration. . . . Such congressional resolution need not, at this point, authorize the use of force. . . . In the near term, time is on our side and we should endeavor to use the United Nations if at all possible. This may require a period of time for inspections or the development of a more intrusive inspection regime . . . if necessary backed by force. It may involve cracking down on the eroding sanctions regime and countries like Syria who are helping Iraq illegally export oil enabling Saddam Hussein to divert resources to his own purposes.[5]

After the hearing, Rep. John Spratt (D-SC), a high-ranking Democrat on the committee, spoke with me, Vic Snyder (D-AR), and David Price (D-NC). He suggested we work together on an alternative to the president's proposed resolution that had been drafted to give him complete discretion to use any military force "necessary and appropriate" to remove Saddam.

We agreed to develop a resolution to allow the president to use armed force to protect and support arms inspectors and to undertake enforcement actions under UN auspices. It would not, however, give the president open-ended authorization to use force unilaterally or preemptively. He would need a second vote from Congress after other prescribed means had been exhausted. After all, the administration's justification for military force, or the threat of it, was that Saddam had flagrantly violated repeated UN resolutions demanding full cooperation and access for UN inspectors; all avenues to achieve this access had not yet been exhausted.

We started lobbying our colleagues. We sent out Dear Colleague letters describing our resolution to every member of Congress, brought the alternative up in Democratic caucus meetings and at informal gatherings on the House floor, enlisted the support of advocacy groups, wrote op-ed articles for newspapers, sat for radio and TV interviews, and otherwise used every means at hand.

At home I held a number of town meetings, which were flooded with constituents opposed to the president's proposal. Opponents to a controversial policy generally tend to outnumber proponents, but in this case I was struck by the number of parents who brought their children to the meetings to teach them something about democracy and to demonstrate their fear for their children's future.

Vice President Cheney predicted that the conflict would last "weeks rather than months" and that American soldiers would be "welcomed as liberators." John Tierney of Massachusetts and I talked on the House floor one day and were incredulous at the claim. We even tried to recall analogous historical examples without success. At one meeting, Rumsfeld was asked why he believed we would be received as "liberators." His response was simplistic: "Because they have been oppressed for so long." He said nothing about Iraqi attitudes and history that might dampen their joy at having U.S. military in their midst.

The Democratic leaders felt the political pressure and caved: minority leader Dick Gephardt (D-MO) in the House and Tom Daschle (D-ND) in the Senate sponsored the resolutions, and many Democratic House members felt betrayed by our leadership. Virtually all Republicans, even thoughtful senators like Chuck Hagel, whose clear thinking had impressed me on the trip to Munich, supported the war resolution. I believe the Democratic leadership was trying to compensate for the long-standing public perception that Democrats are "soft" because they are slower to resort to the use of force. In general, most Democrats prefer negotiation to force when foreign crises arise, though that aspect of our world view carries risks of its own. Military intervention in Rwanda, for example, might well have stopped the genocide during President Clinton's term.

On the morning of the House vote, October 10, 2002, I heard Martin Frost, the chair of the House Democratic caucus, tell National Public Radio that he was confident that a majority of Democrats would "support the president" on the Iraq war resolution. I knew he was wrong, because we had created our own vote-counting operation. In the end, a majority of Democrats in the House refused to follow our party leadership. We had 126 of the 208 House Democrats on our side.

But the resolution passed (296 to 133) and we set off down the road to an invasion. Like the Clinton impeachment and the disputed 2000 election, the debate over Iraq generated an avalanche of phone calls to my offices and huge turnouts at some of the town meetings I held. It's hard to convey the sense of foreboding and alarm that I felt about the administration's manipulation of public opinion. The New York Times's Iraq reporter, Judith Miller, seemed to have been taken in by the neocons promoting the war. In the end, Congress and the country followed a president and administration willfully blind to information that would contradict their convictions about the threat from Iraq and their assumptions about how easy it would be to withdraw from that country. They lifted the lid to Pandora's box.

None of this had to happen. Looking back, the underlying factors seem somewhat clearer, although the precise relationship between the president and his vice president may always be murky.

From the start, President Bush heeded the counsel of the neocons who dominated his inner circle. They embraced an alternative mind-set, dismissive of contrary facts and unconcerned with detailed evidence about Iraq, but convinced that removing Saddam would be a relatively easy way to transform the Middle East. Many were driven by a desire to make the Middle East a safe place for a Greater Israel. At the same time, others in the government, not among the president's closest advisors, held a more complicated understanding of Iraq and the region, which suggested a more cautious policy. To some extent, the split reflected the traditional difference of outlook between the Defense and State Departments. But in my opinion it had more to do with the ideological makeup of the president's chief civilian advisors.

From the beginning of the internal debate in the fall of 2001, as Stuart Bowen, the special inspector general for Iraq Reconstruction (SIGIR) and his staff wrote in "Hard Lessons," "Secretary of Defense Donald Rumsfeld believed that, after Saddam's fall, power should rapidly transfer to an interim Iraqi authority. . . . In this scenario, the United States would not need to administer the functions of Iraq's government after major combat operations ceased."[6]

By contrast, the State Department "concluded that invading Iraq and replacing its totalitarian regime would require a U.S. commitment of enormous scope, carried out over a period of years, engaging everything from Iraq's judiciary to its electrical grid." Colin Powell told the president that "when you hit [Iraq], it's like crystal glass. It's going to shatter. There will be no government. . . . There will be civil disorder."[7]

Rumsfeld and Doug Feith, the undersecretary of Defense for Policy believed that "minimizing the military's presence would force local populations to rely more rapidly on their own leaders to resolve problems." The inspector general's report noted that Feith and Rumsfeld were "convinced that by limiting the military's postwar role in Iraq, the United States could avoid the 'culture of dependency' that had taken root in other post-conflict interventions."[8]

That phrase, "culture of dependency," says it all. That concept is part of a larger worldview about individualism and collective action. It is a perspective that plays a central role in battles over domestic issues, including welfare, that involve debates over the role of government. But it is surprising to see its influence on decisions affecting the people of a country with no history of democracy about to have its leadership forcefully deposed by an outside power.

Rumsfeld won the internal battle. He forced General Tommy Franks, commander of the allied forces in the region, to accept a much smaller invasion force than had ever been conceived as sufficient. He made sure that the Pentagon, not State, would control U.S. policy in Iraq after Saddam was deposed, even though he paid little attention to planning for the aftermath of his overthrow. General Franks and the Defense Department's job was to depose Saddam and the aftermath was someone else's problem. Yet Rumsfeld wanted to keep the authority, without understanding the nature of the responsibility. No one in the inner circle was strong enough to stand up to Rumsfeld or to make sure that the president heard other views. The person who could have played this role, National Security Advisor Condoleezza Rice, was no match for Rumsfeld, and she failed in her primary duty to coordinate the presentation of different views within the administration for a decision by the president.

Rumsfeld's view, frozen in time by his prior experiences, was laid out in his speech on February 14, 2003, in New York, shortly before the invasion of Iraq. Titled "Beyond Nation Building," he made clear the administration's distaste for the Clinton administration's approach to dealing with troubled states. In Afghanistan, he proclaimed, "The objective is not to engage in what some call nation building. Rather it's to try to help the Afghans so that they can build their own nation. This is an important distinction. In some nation-building exercises well-intentioned foreigners arrive on the scene, look at the problems and say let's fix it. This is well motivated to be sure, but . . . when foreigners come in with international solutions to local problems, if not very careful they can create a dependency."[9]

Rumsfeld found evidence of "dependency" in both East Timor and Kosovo in the alleged facts that, "Educated young people can make more

money as drivers for foreign workers than as doctors and civil servants."
Moreover, he said, "A recent *Wall Street Journal* story described how three
years after the war, the United Nations still runs Kosovo really by executive orders."

For those who see the world through lenses of radical individualism,
"dependency" at home and abroad is the greatest danger. How different
our experience in Iraq might have been if the Administration had been
run by people who took off their ideological glasses long enough to see
and care about the specific history, condition, needs, and beliefs of those
who lived there.

Finally, in the ultimate irony of his limited knowledge of the country,
Rumsfeld described the twin "advantages" of time and resources that we
would have in dealing with post-invasion Iraq as compared to Afghanistan. First, he said, "With Iraq, . . . there has been time to prepare," and
second, "Iraq has a solid infrastructure with working networks of roads
and [resources] and it has oil to help give free Iraq the means to get on its
feet."[10]

The truth proved to be that the planning was pathetic and the Iraqi
infrastructure was a mess; electrical and basic services were destroyed, the
oil production that was supposed to pay for the reconstruction remained
a trickle for years. The State Department and outside observers were
largely correct, but their arguments and evidence could not penetrate
Rumsfeld's convictions or those of his allies. Estimates vary, but so far the
Iraq invasion and occupation have cost American taxpayers close to a trillion dollars.

Strongly held—but mistaken—preconceived convictions litter the history of our engagement in Iraq. The insistent personal pressure that Cheney
put on CIA operatives to prove that Saddam was connected to 9/11 is well
documented. Rumsfeld took a similar approach with Lt. Gen. Jay Garner,
the first head of the post-invasion mission. Garner had hired Tom Warrick, the State Department leader of its Future of Iraq reconstruction planning project. But Rumsfeld soon instructed Garner, "You've got two people
working for you—Warrick and [Meghan] O'Sullivan—that you need to get
rid of." When Garner protested because they were smart, knowledgeable

people, Rumsfeld said it was out of his hands. Garner was deeply puzzled by the order to get rid of his experts and eventually concluded that Cheney's office was vetting people based on perception of their politics.[11]

The American military was undermined by civilian ideologues who thought they had all the answers—and therefore ignored the ambiguity and complexity of the mission and the country they were trying to change. Paul Wolfowitz urged the president to attack Iraq before Afghanistan but was overruled. Frank Luntz, the notorious Republican wordsmith, urged his clients when talking about Iraq to always begin with a reference to 9/11. They followed that advice consistently for years. No wonder that years later a substantial percentage of Republican voters still believe that Saddam Hussein had been involved in the 9/11 attacks.

The "decision" and the marketing of the invasion of Iraq were not the product of thoughtful consideration of risks and benefits. The pattern of administration statements and actions indicates that the principal source was out of sight, in the convictions, attitudes, and worldviews of the neo-cons who dominated the administration's civilian war council.

For those of us opposed to the policy, there was a craziness to the administration's arguments and actions. What they were doing was outside the bounds of our political experience. They were stirring up arguments they knew to be false, politicizing matters of war and peace, and above all, paying little attention to what would happen after Saddam's removal. Deception and recklessness at the highest level of the federal government, together with the quiescence of the mainstream media, led me to feel for only the second time in my life (the other being 1968) that even American democracy—the oldest and most stable democracy in history—was not guaranteed to survive indefinitely.

STRATEGIC FAILURE TO TACTICAL PROGRESS

By 2006, America and the "coalition of the willing" were losing in Iraq. The violence and the casualties in Iraq were growing month by month in the third year of the war. That country was barely functioning: electrical and other services in the cities were erratic at best; oil production was a trickle; corruption was rampant. Americans were being maimed and killed at an alarming rate. The antiwar movement in the United States was growing stronger, and the Bush's approval numbers were below 40 percent. In November 2006, Democrats won control of the House.

In December President Bush gave his approval for a dramatic change in American policy that turned the tide in the war, a change driven by the ugly facts on the ground instead of wishful thinking.

Although not known at the time by Congress or the public, an extraordinary debate within the administration culminated in a new strategic approach. The "surge" was implemented over the objections of nearly all relevant leaders of the U.S. military establishment. A few insiders, led by retired General Jack Keane, managed to persuade President Bush to adopt a more effective strategy built around protecting the Iraqi people.[12]

After dismissing the need for detailed planning before the invasion, the administration had protected American troops by keeping them on large bases away from the Iraqis until they went out on patrol. The theory was that Iraqi troops would "stand up" as the Americans "stood down." It hadn't worked. In *The Gamble*, Thomas Ricks' second book on Iraq, he argues, "By making the protection of their own troops a top priority, and by having them live mainly on big bases and only patrol neighborhoods once or twice a day or night, [U.S. commanders] had wasted precious time and ceded vital terrain to the enemy." They had not made the protection of Iraqi civilians part of their mission.[13]

General Keane stepped into the breach created by the ineffectiveness of the chairman of the Joint Chiefs of Staff, Gen. Peter Pace, and the dysfunctional relationship between Rumsfeld and other military and civilian officials, including Condoleezza Rice. Rumsfeld was adept at accumulating bureaucratic power but lacked the flexibility to change a failed strategy. Without consulting the U.S. commander in Iraq, Gen. George W. Casey Jr., Keane worked with the second in command, Gen. Ray Odierno, to plan how they could use additional troops to protect Iraqis, not just our military.[14]

The change in strategy that was eventually sold to the president in December 2006, just after Democrats won control of the House, was the result of a small, determined group of military and civilian realists who understood that the United States was losing the war and who understood Iraqi culture and the Iraqi people as they found them. This acceptance was built on experience about what worked on the ground in Iraq and what didn't. The new approach was evidence-based, not grounded on wishful thinking about Iraqis falling by default into some form of democracy after Saddam was overthrown.

Different values accompanied the change in strategy. Advocates for the new strategy emphasized that Americans dealing with Iraqis needed to acknowledge Iraq's communitarian values, often expressed by showing and receiving respect. Wolfowitz thought otherwise. When told that the fundamental characteristic of Iraqi society was its tribal nature, he said that it is a "cosmopolitan society."

David Petraeus was the third critical player in the change of strategy. He had conducted his troops along counterinsurgency lines during his first tour, had led the rewriting of the army manual for this type of warfare, and later replaced Casey in 2007 as the top commander in Iraq. Both Petraeus and Odierno were able to adjust rapidly to new circumstances and evolving situations by changing tactics when the existing approach was not working.[15] That type of flexibility was in short supply at the top levels of the Bush administration.

Most members of Congress, including me, did not understand the change in policy. I understood the "surge" for what the word implied—an increase in troops with no change in approach—simply to compensate for a failed policy. Most Democrats, like most Republicans, reacted to Bush's proposal for more troops with the somewhat murky lenses through which we had come to understand our Iraq policy. I spoke out emphatically against the "surge" because it felt too much like the increase in troops that Lyndon Johnson had sent to Viet Nam.

Even when I visited Iraq, Afghanistan, and Pakistan in August 2007, the status of the Iraqi conflict was much in doubt. Our congressional delegation met with Ambassador Ryan Crocker and General Petraeus; Petraeus stated only that we had "tactical momentum" against al-Qaeda in Iraq because the Sunni sheiks had turned against them. Months would pass before confidence grew that the path in Iraq was becoming somewhat smoother, though still not easy.

It may always be impossible to determine how much of the reduction in violence in Iraq was due to the American military's adoption of a counter-insurgency strategy, how much to the Sunni Awakening, how much to the standing down of Shia militias, and how much to luck. The change in our military strategy clearly helped. The important point is that the Bush administration's initial strategy was based on assumptions and convictions, not grounded in evidence. That strategy failed and the second strategy—counterinsurgency—was given birth by a handful of military leaders taking Iraq as it was, not as the administration wanted it to be. In the end, the counterinsurgency strategy may be viewed as a tactical success, reducing the level of violence and laying a foundation for U.S. withdrawal several years later. The vision of a democratic, peaceful, prosperous Iraq stabilizing the Middle East may long remain a mirage. Iraq has rejected any cooperative relationship involving a residual U.S. troop presence, the State Department's massive police training plans have been abandoned, and our fortress embassy is certain to be a flash point for conflict for years to come.

Flexibility beats rigidity not just in military strategy but in public policy as well. The denial of evidence contradicting the administration's wishful thinking about the invasion and reconstruction of Iraq, and the failure to learn from experience, led to catastrophic personal, economic, and geopolitical losses.

AN UNEXAMINED CASUALTY OF THE WAR: CONGRESSIONAL OVERSIGHT MIA

Americans paid a terrible price for the convictions of those who led us into Iraq convinced it had weapons of mass destruction, that the Iraqis would welcome our troops as liberators, and that democratic institutions would arise after Saddam's overthrow. The cost of the war in Iraq has been crushing, in lives lost or shattered, and close to a trillion dollars in direct costs. Other countries in North Africa and the Near East, led by despots have now, eight years later, spontaneously arisen in revolt on their own, inspired by their people's own hunger for democracy and dignity. I still remember Secretary Rumsfeld at an Armed Services Committee hearing telling me that Iraq's leadership would never change without our intervention. We'll never know.

Before the invasion, Bush administration neocons dismissed inconvenient evidence, and Cheney did all he could to manufacture supportive evidence by putting pressure on the CIA. Unfortunately, during the conflict the administration's allies in the Congress circled their wagons to prevent hearings on waste, fraud, and abuse by American contractors, suppressing important evidence about the conduct of the conflicts in both Iraq and Afghanistan. In short, congressional leaders sacrificed the institution's integrity to protect the administration. The result was a massive waste of taxpayer funds and enormous profiteering by American companies, which reinforced Iraq's existing culture of corruption.

The military drive to Baghdad went so smoothly that the administration assumed that all was well. Yet not long after the president stood on a U.S. carrier in front of a massive sign announcing "Mission Accomplished," sectarian and insurgent violence began to take a heavy toll on Americans and civilian Iraqis. The Iraqi people were without the most basic services. The Pentagon's failure to plan for rebuilding Iraq's government and infrastructure was proving to be costly and dangerous, and its rejection of the State Department's planning foolish.

Although it was not clear from administration pronouncements, it became obvious that one of the world's largest oilfield services contractors, Halliburton, was profiting enormously from having its former CEO Dick Cheney as vice president of the United States. Halliburton and its subsidiary, Kellogg Brown and Root (KBR), received multibillion dollar no-bid contracts to serve and supply American troops and manage the Iraqi oil fields. Clues to the corruption, self-dealing, and wasteful practices were leaking out, but there were no systematic efforts to unearth the problem and deal with it. A number of House Democrats pushed legislation to open up the contracting process and create an independent commission to investigate wartime contracting. Our inspiration was the 1941 Truman Committee, led by then-Senator Harry Truman during the thick of World War II, which unearthed war profiteering by army contractors and took steps to prevent further abuses.

On my second trip to Afghanistan in August 2007, the optimism I had seen five years earlier had dissipated. The discouragement was partly the result of witnessing unchallenged greed and incompetence by U.S. contractors. Outside Kabul, I listened to a command sergeant major describe his utter frustration at how KBR, a former subsidiary of Halliburton, was routinely ripping off the federal government. As one example, he said KBR was paid for drilling water wells that always came up dry because, as he discovered, they never drilled to the depth required by the contract.

At that meeting, George Close, the chief official in Afghanistan of Dyn-Corp, a private military contractor, admitted that "as an American tax-payer," he believed what had happened was inexcusable. He said that for years after the invasion of Afghanistan, the State Department had only two "contract oversight representatives" to oversee thousands of contracts in that country. Years later the final report of the Commission on Wartime Contracting (CWC) in Iraq and Afghanistan (the "Contracting Commission"), issued in August 2011, confirmed that there were too few federal contract specialists to prevent billions of dollars in waste, fraud, and abuse. Despite the enormous increase in contracting activity between 1992 and 2009, the number of contract specialists had risen by only 3 percent.[16]

The more extensive waste was ongoing in Iraq. An Air Force Reserve mechanic from Maine told me in 2005 about a giant electric generator dump north of Baghdad. He and his fellow mechanics begged to be allowed to service the huge KBR generators that provided electricity to the U.S. compound. The KBR contract, however, prevented anyone but their employees from even changing the oil or checking the coolant; the company didn't do any maintenance, so when the generators broke down they just hauled them off to the dump and bought replacements at great cost to taxpayers and huge profits to KBR.

It was not just American funds that went missing. In the closing days of the Coalition Provisional Authority in 2004, more than 363 tons of American currency, about $12 billion in cash, was flown in Air Force C-130 cargo planes from New Jersey to Iraq for distribution to Iraqi agencies. Much of it was shipped in Saran-wrapped "bricks" of $10,000 each. The money represented Iraqi assets seized by the United States and was part of the Iraqi contribution to the reconstruction effort. In January 2005, Stuart Bowen reported that $8.8 billion of this cash could not be accounted for.[17] The American press covered Bowen's report, but no congressional hearings were held to investigate the disappearance of almost half of the planned Iraqi contribution to the reconstruction budget.

Paul Bremer, the head of the Coalition Provisional Authority (CPA), later said about the missing funds: "These are not appropriated American funds. They are Iraqi funds. I believe the CPA discharged its responsibilities to manage these Iraqi funds on behalf of the Iraqi people." Bremer's financial advisor, retired Admiral David Oliver, was blunt; he told the BBC World Service, "I can't tell you whether or not the money went to the right things or didn't—nor do I actually think it's important." When the interviewer noted, "But the fact is billions of dollars have disappeared without trace," Oliver continued: "Of their money. Billions of dollars of their money, yeah I understand. I'm saying what difference does it make?"[18]

Of course, it did matter, not only to the millions of Iraqi civil service families who had not been paid salaries or pensions for months but also to the safety of American armed forces, since the delay in restoring the Iraqi banking system and economy exacerbated the nascent insurgency. A congressional inquiry could have revealed the enormous waste, fraud, and abuse and created the public pressure to stop it.

Senators Frank Lautenberg (D-NJ) and Byron Dorgan (D-ND) pressed the Senate to exercise its traditional oversight authority. Dorgan used the Senate Democratic Policy Committee to conduct informal hearings on contractor fraud and abuse, but since the group was not a standing committee, it had no subpoena power and attracted little attention. In the House, Rep. Henry Waxman (D-CA) tried to use his position as ranking minority member of the oversight committee to shed light on the debacle. Their efforts failed, and American financial and human losses continued to swell.

The story of how Senate and House Republicans blocked oversight hearings on the waste, fraud, and abuse of American contractors in Iraq and Afghanistan is central to understanding that congressional dysfunction is not just about legislation. In this case it was a stew of tragic reinforcing components: weak committee leadership, media neglect, the triumph of partisan loyalty over institutional responsibility, the deference of Congress to the White House, and the tendency of both press and public to view even legitimate debate as "partisan bickering."

The Senate Committee on Governmental Affairs and Homeland Security describes itself on its website as "the chief oversight committee for the United States Senate." But Sen. Susan Collins (R-ME), the committee chair, consistently resisted appeals for investigations into questionable conduct by American contractors working in Iraq. On May 9, 2003, Senator Lautenberg wrote Collins a letter urging her to conduct hearings on the Army Corps of Engineers' sole-source contract in Iraq with KBR. He asked for an investigation of the no-bid process by which Halliburton received the contract—worth up to $7 billion. Senator Collins responded to Lautenberg on May 19, 2003. She avoided answering his request for a hearing, mentioned legislation on the topic, and added, "What is currently needed, in my view, is the public disclosure of the terms of these contracts and the reasons that they were not subject to full and open competition." But she scheduled no hearings on what was "currently needed."[19]

On September 23 and December 11 Lautenberg asked for oversight hearings on the Defense Department's internal audit agency's finding of contractor overcharges. Collins refused, on the ground, as she wrote, that "I do not wish to overlap or duplicate work already being conducted by the appropriate authorities." On February 20, 2004, Lautenberg reminded Collins that "the Committee on Governmental Affairs often conducts investigations and hearings that 'overlap or duplicate' work done by other governmental bodies," citing the multiple Enron investigations.

Lautenberg gave compelling reasons to hold hearings. In December 2003, Defense Department auditors had determined that KBR had overcharged the federal government by $61 million for fuel shipments from Kuwait to Iraq. In January 2004, Halliburton had been forced to repay

$6 million in overcharges because a Kuwaiti subcontractor had bribed two KBR employees. In February, Halliburton and KBR had to credit the federal government $20–$34 million for overcharges for meals they never served to our troops in Iraq.

Lautenberg raised the committee's inactivity on contractors at hearings on other matters and sent additional letters on June 1, 2004, August 6, 2004, April 26, 2005, June 20, 2006, and October 30, 2006, but Collins never called contractors to testify at a public hearing during her four years as chair of the committee. She had the support of the ranking Democrat on the committee, Sen. Joe Lieberman, who tried to discourage Lautenberg's requests for hearings. Lieberman's support for suppressing hearings was critical. Tim Yehl, Lautenberg's chief of staff at the time, says that Lieberman's staffer Joyce Raufcausen would call and "scream" at him whenever Lautenberg fired off another letter to Collins, or suggested at a hearing on another topic that waste, fraud, and abuse by private contractors in Iraq was more important. According to Yehl, Raufcausen accused him of "going around the ranking member [Lieberman] and interfering with his special relationship with Collins."[20]

Nothing changed when Lieberman became chair of the Committee on Governmental Affairs and Homeland Security. Defeated in the Democratic Party primary in 2006 largely because of his support for President Bush's Iraq policies, Lieberman was reelected as an Independent but secured his chairmanship of the committee by caucusing with the Democrats. In this role, he followed Collins's practice of using the gavel of the chief Senate oversight committee for issues other than contracting in Iraq.

After the Abu Ghraib scandal broke in April 2004, there were developments in the Armed Services Committee, which although not public at the time, effectively assured that Republican senators would not allow hearings on contractor waste, fraud, and abuse in Iraq. Senator John Warner (R-VA), chair of that committee, initiated oversight hearings to discover what had happened at the Abu Ghraib prison in Iraq and who was responsible for the apparent torture of U.S.-held detainees. The resistance from other Republican senators was swift and strong.

In 2008, more than four years after the fact, Jonathan Mahler reported that Warner came under intense pressure from Republican colleagues to stop the hearings. Senator Ted Stevens (R-AK), a longtime friend and Senate colleague, angrily confronted Warner one afternoon in the Senate cloakroom. "'No more hearings,' he said." Mahler quotes a former Armed Services staff member who told him: "Their attitude was that these hearings were just going to provide propaganda for the insurgents and be politically embarrassing for the Republican president during an election year."[21]

In May 2004, several Republican senators on the Armed Services Committee gave Warner an ultimatum: if he continued the hearings, they would withdraw support for his continuing to chair the committee. They presented him with a letter signed by all the committee's Republicans except Senators McCain, Graham, and Collins. For junior senators to confront their chair was unprecedented, and Warner was convinced that Rumsfeld had pushed them to do it.

Warner refused to stop the hearings, but he became less confrontational and less engaged in assigning blame. The message could hardly have been lost on Collins: stick with your team if you want to keep your position as committee chair.

At the time the press had no inkling of the private letter to Warner from his Republican colleagues. But one article in *CQ Weekly* got the drift of what was going on. The author reported that the third hearing of Warner's on Abu Ghraib on May 19, 2004, was a "potential blockbuster" and that the "Iraq prison investigation could give Warner the opportunity to leave a legacy as a chairman who transcended partisan politics during a time of national scandal, in the spirit of Senators Sam Nunn, D-GA. (1972–97), Sam Ervin, D-NC (1954–74) and Frank Church, D-ID (1957–81)."[22]

Warner, however, was "polite and deferential" to Generals John Abizaid, Ricardo Sanchez, and Geoffrey Miller, and "in the end, there were no major revelations." Other Republicans had openly opposed investigations into Abu Ghraib; Rep. Duncan Hunter, chair of the House Armed Services Committee, even refused General Sanchez's offer to testify on the matter and urged the general to "return to your troops."

CQ Weekly summarized Warner's position concisely: "In the coming months, Warner might have to choose between the institutional responsibility of Senate oversight and loyalty to his party." He chose party loyalty. At the time Warner said that Republican pressure to back off the Abu Ghraib hearings would have no effect. "They are entitled to their views," he told *CQ*, "Nobody is pressuring me."[23] Quite the contrary.

The Washington press rarely highlights the institutional responsibilities of members of Congress. Yet the best newspapers in the country should have been much more aggressive investigating the obvious potential conflict with Halliburton getting no-bid, cost-plus contracts from an administration with its former CEO as vice president.

Elections focus the attention of members of Congress. As the 2006 election loomed, both the Senate and House oversight committee chairs decided to hold a hearing. Senator Collins held a hearing on August 2, 2006, with only one witness: Stuart Bowen. Three years after Senator Lautenberg had urged hearings on single-source contract abuses in the U.S.–Iraq reconstruction effort, Bowen told the committee: "The use of sole-source and limited competition contracting in Iraq should have virtually ceased after hostilities ended [the fall of Baghdad] and previously sole-sourced limited competition contracts should have been promptly re-bid." One hearing, one witness, three years late.[24]

Since both Collins and Warner had prevented effective hearings in the Senate committees of jurisdiction, Sen. Byron Dorgan, chair of the Democratic Policy Committee, worked to expose contractor abuse. This "committee" constituted an informal group of senators rather than a legislative committee of Congress, so it lacked subpoena power to compel testimony and documents. Dorgan therefore had to rely on whistleblowers, watchdog groups, and outside experts.

In 2005, at one of his multiple DPC inquiries, Bunnatine Greenhouse, then the top civilian contracting official with the Army Corps of Engineers (ACE), testified that the awarding and implementation of enormous contracts for repair of Iraqi oil fields and support of U.S. troops by KBR was the "the most blatant and improper contract abuse" she had seen in her long career. For blowing the whistle on those abusive procedures, she was demoted.[25] That obvious suppression of a whistleblower wasn't enough to trigger a formal Senate hearing. Eight years later, in 2011, Greenhouse recovered nearly a million dollars from the Army Corps of Engineers for her wrongful demotion.

Senator Dorgan has concluded that "the contracting to supply the war and the contracting for the reconstruction of Iraq represent the greatest waste, fraud, and abuse in the long history of our country. It is a sordid story of graft, corruption, incompetence, and neglect."[26] That conclusion is confirmed by the two post-mortem reports of the American reconstruction experience in Iraq.

In Special Inspector General Bowen's five-hundred-page report, "Hard Lessons: The Iraq Reconstruction Experience," he concluded that "the United States was unprepared to manage the increasing chaos it faced . . ." and lacked the ability to manage large-scale contingency relief and reconstruction operations.[27]

What he didn't say is that the Republican-controlled Congress was as ineffective and unprepared as the executive branch. The "Hard Lessons" report highlights a long list of problems that could have been managed earlier if an aggressive press and aroused public had demanded that the key congressional committees do their job. But for Senate Republicans it was more important to protect the president and the illusion of progress in Iraq than to assert their institutional and constitutional responsibilities.

The equivalent of the "Truman Committee" was the bipartisan Commission on Wartime Contracting (CWC), which was created by Congress only after Democrats won control of the Senate and House in 2006. As mentioned earlier, its final report was issued in August 2011. After three years of investigations, hearings, and interim reports, the CWC concluded that American funds lost to waste, fraud, and abuse in Iraq and Afghanistan were between $31 and $60 billion. Dov Zakheim, the comptroller and CFO of the Defense Department from 2001 to 2004, told a reporter, "I personally believe that the number is much, much closer to $60 billion."[28] That $60 billion represents 29 percent of the $206 billion estimated by the CWC to be the total spending on grants and contracts in the two countries through 2011. It doesn't count the billions wasted in Iraqi funds.

The CWC also concluded that "Money lost as a result of the inability to sustain projects could easily exceed the contract waste and fraud already incurred."[29] Commissioner Zakheim cited a water plant in Iraq, a large prison, schools without teachers, 130 health clinics in Iraq, none of which was being used and all of which were unlikely to be sustained by the host country.[30] In other words, many investments made with U.S. financial aid will not be maintained for lack of interest, funds, or appropriate skills. Poor planning, corruption, and inadequate oversight all contributed to the unprecedented waste and fraud in both countries.

The CWC's final report identifies and analyzes multiple factors that undermined the reconstruction process—with one exception. The report is silent on the failure of Congress to conduct aggressive oversight hearings into allegations of waste, fraud, and abuse by Halliburton, DynCorp, and other contractors during the years from 2003 through 2009. It is not surprising that the commission, authorized and funded by Congress, would not see criticism of Congress as within its jurisdiction. But congressional neglect, *intentional* neglect, is the rest of the story and in many ways the most important part.

Whatever happened to investigative reporting? Why was the story of congressional collaboration limited to a few partisan outlets? At a meeting in 2007, I asked one national media executive why his organization ignored this problem for so long. He said that they typically rely on congressional hearings for stories of this kind and that those hearings were not being held. Perhaps the media can no longer sustain difficult investigative undertakings. Perhaps reporters were reluctant to take on senators they respected.

In his classic 1861 work, *Considerations on Representative Government*, John Stuart Mill wrote, "the proper office of a representative assembly is to watch and control the government." Yet we saw in the years after the 2000 election—with homeland security, Abu Ghraib, Hurricane Katrina, and the reconstruction and war efforts in Iraq and Afghanistan—how costly it can be when Congress fails to do its job. The Bush administration was neither closely watched nor controlled. Party politics was clearly a major factor.

The risk of embarrassing the Bush administration might have had less influence if discovering the truth had been more important. The devaluation of data and the lack of concern with evidence seem to have broadly infected the Republican Party and its federal officials. The decision to invade Iraq was apparently made in private conversations between President Bush and Vice President Cheney without vetting by other top administration officials. The post-conflict planning of the Defense Department reflected disdain for detail and complexity. It is perhaps not surprising that Republican senators had no interest in hearing evidence about who was responsible for Abu Ghraib and what Halliburton was doing in Iraq. Political considerations crept into the space that should have been occupied by a hunger for information.

CONCLUSION

Convictions can be dangerous when they create barriers to doubt and evidence. The invasion and occupation of Iraq were based on convictions that Saddam was the root of evil in the Middle East, that democracy would emerge in that "cosmopolitan" society if he were deposed, and that an early American exit was necessary to avoid creating a "dependency" of Iraqis on outsiders. The signature domestic policy of the Bush administration and the Republican Congress came down to the tax cuts of 2001 and 2003, which were based on unshakable convictions about the power of free markets, the stimulating effect of tax cuts, and the vital role of the very wealthy in driving investment in new businesses.

The advocates for the Bush tax cuts and the invasion of Iraq were fiercely resistant to contrary information concerning the administration's policies. Yet they were wrong. We were *not* welcomed as liberators. Iraq could not pay for its own reconstruction. Democracy is not a default form of government but an incredibly difficult culture to create and maintain. The 2001 and 2003 tax cuts reduced federal revenues and restored large deficits, and the consequences were enormous. By the end of 2011, the direct costs of our invasion and occupation of Iraq were approximately $1 trillion, and not a penny in new taxes was authorized to pay for it. The Bush tax cuts, depending on how long they continue, will have increased the national debt by several trillion more.

The convictions that inspire the Republican passion for tax cuts are not the same as those that drove America into Iraq without adequate deliberation and planning. For conservatives, taxes should be lower and government smaller because of perceived risks to personal freedom. Conservatives also tend to be more inclined to resolve international disputes by the use of force. That's why the worldview of conservatives has a libertarian cast on issues like taxes, health care, and climate change, and what appears to be an America-against-the-world component on some foreign policy matters. Perhaps these two aspects of a conservative worldview are generally, but not always, found in the same people. In both cases, the consequence can be a tendency to block contrary evidence from undermining the internal coherence of the conservative worldview.

The August 2011 final report of the CWC in Iraq and Afghanistan emphasizes the deficiencies in agency planning and coordination that contributed to the American failures in Iraq. It does not cover the deeper source of those failures—the worldview of the policy's architects that was impatient with complexity and disdainful of evidence and expertise.

The most painful part of all this for me was attending so many funerals across Maine for the young men and women who lost their lives in our war of choice in Iraq. I remember the school gymnasium jammed with more people than live in the town of the deceased soldier and the many smaller rural churches in communities where everyone knows everyone else. Our governor and the congressional delegation occupied a front row in every case. But the men and women who gave their lives for our country deserved both a deliberate high-level evaluation of the risks and benefits before the administration decided to invade Iraq in addition to aggressive congressional oversight during the conflict. They got neither.

The world as it is exacts a price from those who deny its complexity—and sometimes from many others as well.

Health Care

Principle before People

Before you know kindness as the deepest thing inside,
you must know sorrow as the other deepest thing.
You must wake up with sorrow.
You must speak to it till your voice
catches the thread of all sorrows
and you see the size of the cloth.

—NAOMI SHIHAB NYE, *"Another Voice"*

Leon Currier, the retired firefighter who told me he could not afford the prescriptions ordered by his doctor, had set me on a path of concentrating on health-care legislation. Throughout my twelve years in office, there were tens of millions of Americans without adequate health care and millions of small businesses that could not afford to cover their employees.

The cost and availability of health care was a growing concern for people in Maine. Over the years, my staff heard many heartbreaking stories of families who could not get the care or coverage they needed and, in some cases, had been driven into bankruptcy by medical bills. I recall one two-income couple with two children but no insurance who had their lives transformed when the wife developed multiple sclerosis and could no longer work. I talked with uninsured self-employed people in their late fifties and early sixties hoping to stay healthy until they qualified for Medicare at age sixty-five. At first, the stories seemed exceptional; over time, though, they described an epidemic of anxiety.

The cost of health insurance for individuals and businesses rose year after year at double-digit rates. Wherever I went in Maine, men and women with small businesses vented their frustration with rapidly rising premiums. On a walk down Main Street in the midsize former mill city of Biddeford, nine of ten shop owners raised the issue without being prompted. A woman in Gorham told me she was about to close her business and lay off her twelve workers because she had to provide health care to attract quality employees, but the business lost money when she did.

Many small business owners obtained health-care coverage through a spouse who worked for a large corporation or in the public sector. Other people complained of the businesses they couldn't start or employment opportunities missed because they were locked into jobs that provided health insurance. During my last six years in Congress, most Mainers who bought individual coverage could afford only catastrophic coverage with enormous $5,000 or $10,000 deductibles. That's not health insurance; that's home insurance.

Providers also were deeply concerned. Visitors to my office in Washington included hospital administrators, long-term care providers, consumer advocates, nurses, nurse anesthetists, nurse practitioners, home-health suppliers, medical device manufacturers, medical school faculty and students, surgeons, primary care doctors, anesthesiologists, and representatives of every other specialty in the medical field. Moreover, the major diseases have advocacy groups of afflicted families who urged greater investment in targeted research. About 25 percent of my office meetings involved health-care issues.

No member of Congress could fail to see the human cost and the financial burden imposed randomly on their constituents. Yet with the prominent exception of prescription drugs for seniors, health-care coverage and cost were essentially Democratic issues. The past fifteen years have been marked by a movement from piecemeal bipartisan engagement by Republicans in Congress to consistent rejection of federal proposals to expand coverage and contain systemic costs, culminating in their vociferous opposition to President Obama's Affordable Care Act (ACA). The Republicans' own limited reform plans included voucher or premium support proposals not adjusted to keep up with medical inflation; consequently, those proposals would effectively increase costs to individuals over time without reducing overall health care costs.

The Tea Party–inspired takeovers of congressional town meetings in the summer of 2009 appear to have driven Republican senators like Olympia Snowe and Chuck Grassley from continuing their bipartisan conversations on President Obama's health-reform proposals. That uncompromising attitude had not been evident when the State Children's Health Insurance Program (SCHIP) was enacted in 1997, my first year in Congress. SCHIP was widely considered a major bipartisan accomplishment and led to coverage for millions of children.

Cost, access, and quality: that's the health-care trifecta. The best policy would provide the fairest, most efficient, and most effective balance among those factors. The U.S. health-care system has by far the highest per person cost in the world; it has left up to fifty million Americans without the security of health insurance; it provides high-quality care for many but often leaves the uninsured to seek care in emergency rooms. No other developed country neglects such a large proportion of its people. Polling in developed nations puts approval of our health care system twenty or thirty points below public support for the health-care systems in Canada and Europe. For decades we have had a problem too big to ignore— but ignore it we did. When the Obama administration made health-care reform a major priority in 2009 and 2010, why was there no equally comprehensive Republican proposal?

The primary answer, I believe, is that only one party had a worldview that could accommodate government action on the scale needed to address the lack of coverage and high cost of health care in America. We argued over innumerable details, but the real conflict was, first, about the role of government, and second, about whether individuals should share the risk of illness and accident—or leave the sick and injured to bear the financial consequences on their own—a classic "me" versus "we" choice. Comprehensive health insurance means sharing the risk of illness and injury among a large group, whether the insurer is a private company or a government agency. For Republicans in Congress the principle of "smaller government, lower taxes" was an intellectual roadblock to health-care reform on the scale needed to compensate for the failure of the private insurance market to provide affordable coverage for millions of Americans. For those who believe government regulation inevitably infringes on personal liberty, health-care reform was worse than the status quo, and expanding coverage never became an important part of a Republican political agenda. Instead, they promoted allowing insurance companies to sell plans across state lines (and thus avoid stricter state regulation) and tax credits for health savings accounts; neither policy would have made a significant dent in the ranks of the uninsured.

Of course, the cost and complexity of the American health-care system made comprehensive reform a daunting task for any Congress and administration. During my first congressional campaign in 1996, I visited Don McDowell, the respected head of Maine Medical Center. He suggested that I think of the health-care system as a huge tub of money, at that time 14 percent of our GDP (now about 17 percent). Imagine, he said, that the tub is surrounded by all the providers in the health-care system, each of whom takes a certain amount of money from the tub each year. "Now," Don said, "try to change it."

Complexity is only part of the story. The other components include money, ideology, and neglect. Let's start with neglect. Republican congressmen had to know about the financial stress and bankruptcies caused by the cost of health insurance for small businesses. But comprehensive universal health care was not on their agenda during the Republican ascendancy; they had no apparent free-market solution for a market failure that makes health insurance too costly for tens of millions of Americans. Democrats had already staked out this territory; why help them take credit for health-care reform? Moreover, for many Americans with quality health insurance, it is easy to look past their fellow citizens who cannot afford the same. I have spoken on health-care issues hundreds if not thousands of times, and the gap in worldviews was most apparent when someone from the audience would ask, "Why should I have to pay for health insurance for someone who can't afford. . . ."

With so little common ground between the parties, President Obama's signing of the Patient Protection and Affordable Care Act on March 23, 2010, was remarkable. The administration had to cut a deal with the pharmaceutical industry at the beginning, because the Pharmaceutical Research and Manufacturers of America (PhRMA) and the health insurers are too powerful to take on together. PhRMA agreed to pay millions of dollars over ten years to close the "donut hole" that had left many seniors without adequate coverage for their drugs—and not to oppose the administration bill. During the legislative struggle the final bill was stripped of a public option, which would have established a government-run insurance entity to compete with other private insurers. As enacted, the ACA established state-regulated insurance exchanges where competing private insurance plans could be offered to consumers with subsidies to make them affordable for all. Moreover, the ACA's most controversial provision, the individual mandate requiring everyone to purchase health insurance, had been a central part of a Heritage Foundation plan as early as 1989. The ACA is much more of a free market system than Medicare or the VA today.

Yet the bill, or more accurately, its ideological opponents, aroused a firestorm of protest. Ultimately, Republicans could not support new restraints on the insurance industry, a mandate that everyone carry health insurance, or spending billions of dollars to subsidize its cost for lower-income Americans. But there was no other plan with a comparable increase in coverage or containment of costs. Like congressional minorities in the past, the Republicans, on the advice of Frank Luntz, a Republican pollster and strategist, complained about "process" and pleaded for "more time" or to "start over" as a cover for their substantive objections.

The evolution of health-care policy in the dozen years I served in Congress is a case study in the different realities inhabited by Republicans and Democrats. Republicans start with the fixed belief that government involvement is inherently bad because it creates personal dependency and is always inefficient compared to the private market. If government is bad for the soul and economic well-being, big government is anathema. With this mind-set, Republicans instinctively and shrewdly turned health-care reform into a metaphor for intrusive government. Democrats, on the other hand, argued that high costs and nearly fifty million uninsured Americans constituted compelling evidence that the private market was not working. The mainstream media and members of the public focused on the chances for compromise between the two parties without understanding their incompatible worldviews about health-care reform.

Republicans argued as if government-supported health-care programs were untested or had proved unsuccessful. Yet, more than half of all Americans get health care through public programs. Our veterans, for example, have a largely "socialist" health-care system with government facilities staffed by government health-care providers, and this system had been established in 1930. Although not without problems, the VA system has become efficient and effective. For every veteran who complained to me (with some justification) about long delays in being assigned a primary care physician, many others told me that the attention they had received at Maine's veteran hospitals and clinics was compassionate and first class. The VA was an early adopter of electronic medical records and coordination of care among providers. Without a profit incentive, their providers embraced treatment protocols that had been tracked and found to produce the best outcomes. Likewise, Medicare, which is essentially our national single-payer system for seniors and the disabled, and Medicaid, which serves that function for low-income Americans, although less well coordinated and funded, are popular among beneficiaries and have largely achieved their medical purposes.

On the other side of the aisle, Democrats had their own myopia. The Medicare payment formulas were inefficient, favoring specialists over primary care, procedures and numbers of office visits rather than outcomes. Medicaid, which served a largely nonvoting population with little political clout, was dangerously underfunded. For the Democratic Party, responding to our base and special interests—more delicately referred to as "stakeholders"—too often trumped the need for honest talk about the problems of these publicly funded health programs. In particular, long-range cost projections suggested the programs were unsustainable without a combination of additional revenue, some reduction in benefits, and fundamental reform of financial incentives for providers. The hard political truth is that those issues are so contentious they require engagement and sacrifice by both parties, which appears impossible without a broadly shared objective, for example, either to preserve the basic structure of the programs or to convert them to vouchers or block grants.

From 1994 to 2008 neither congressional party aggressively promoted comprehensive health-care reform. Republicans objected to existing federal regulation of the insurance and health-care industries, so an expansion of the public role was off their table. They had some success in partially privatizing aspects of Medicare, including the addition of prescription drug coverage and a private insurance option to Medicare Part B called Medicare Advantage. The latter program was the result of an agreement with the Clinton administration to reimburse private insurers in the Medicare market at 95 percent of the cost of care for the average beneficiary; over time for technical and political reasons the reimbursement grew to an average of more than 110 percent, a substantial overpayment to private industry.

Democrats in Congress had their own reasons for resisting calls from the Left for wide-ranging reform. In 1993, with Democrats in control of the House, the Clinton health-care plan failed even to get out of the House Energy and Commerce Committee. It had been developed by First Lady Hillary Clinton and aides with insufficient outside and congressional input. Even before it was announced, the proposal was subjected to withering public attack by the health-insurance industry. The failure of the Clinton plan led many Democratic officeholders to back off any proposals for comprehensive change for several years.

Incremental steps, however, seemed possible. In 1997, the Clinton administration reached a compromise with congressional Republicans to create a State Children's Health Insurance Plan (SCHIP) to cover millions of children from families with personal financial resources too high to qualify for Medicaid and too low to purchase health insurance on their own. For Republicans the compromise made some headway in privatizing the federal-state government program; in most states SCHIP would be run by private insurers, rather than Medicaid.

The passage of SCHIP seemed to suggest a capacity for compromise on major issues. In hindsight, it looks more like an aberration. The plight of children without health insurance and affordable quality care was especially compelling, and expanding health care for children was a bargain; as a category they are the cheapest to keep well, and health care for the young is a particularly good investment. In addition, the SCHIP expansion was enacted as part of a larger package. As a stand-alone bill, it might not have passed. Indeed, when Democrats, in control of Congress in 2008, tried to expand SCHIP as part of a larger bill, President Bush vetoed the bill because, he said, it "would lead to more Americans getting their health care through a government program." The expansion was reintroduced in 2009 and was the second bill signed into law by President Obama.

During the Bush administration, beneath the surface, the movement toward a larger public role was gaining cohesion and strength, driven by trends that were making the health-care system unsustainable. In 1996, according to the Census Bureau, there were about forty-two million Americans without health insurance. Over the next few years the number of uninsured fluctuated narrowly because strong economic growth and the expanded coverage of children under SCHIP compensated for a decline in employer-based coverage. After the 2000 election, however, the number of uninsured accelerated. By 2008 about forty-seven million Americans lacked coverage and millions more were underinsured or insured only for part of the year. The 2009 census figures showed that the uninsured population had increased by 4.3 million people to a total of 50.7 million. A major contributing factor was the continuing decline in employer-based coverage.[1]

Now, this was not just a problem for the uninsured. Those who had coverage found their premiums, deductibles, and co-pays going up; for insured Americans, health care was rapidly growing more expensive, in part because the providers, like doctors and hospitals, had to recover from paying patients the cost of the charity care they gave to the uninsured. In addition, health care costs for all working Americans are reflected in higher taxes to recover the costs of uncompensated care for the uninsured and higher system-wide costs because the uninsured do not receive adequate preventive care.

The major challenge for health-care reformers was that most Americans had decent health insurance and liked what they had. Many insured people had little familiarity with the plight of those without insurance. The frightening lack of care, looming bankruptcies, or fear that a divorce or lost job would leave an entire family without health insurance: these situations were largely invisible except to those directly affected.

I concluded that for any member of Congress who wanted change, the challenge was to find a legislative opening for new ideas on discrete health-care issues. I concentrated on making prescription drugs affordable for the elderly and disabled, and supporting research that would compare the effectiveness of different treatment options for particular conditions. The latter was inspired by a promising approach to improving quality and reducing costs that was already underway in Oregon, Australia, and New Zealand.

With both initiatives, I appealed for Republican support by developing an approach that would be cost effective for the federal government. My prescription drug legislation was designed to negotiate a significant discount for Medicare beneficiaries at minimal public cost, and my comparative effectiveness bill would reduce system costs and improve quality. But even these modest proposals for change drew considerable opposition.

In chapter 1, I described the origins of the prescription drug discount legislation I introduced for Medicare beneficiaries late in 1998, at the conclusion of the 105th Congress. The bill provided that Medicare beneficiaries would be able to purchase prescription drugs at the "best price" given to the federal government either through the Veterans Administration or Medicaid. At very little cost to the government, millions of Americans would receive significant price discounts negotiated by Medicare on their behalf.

In February 1999, I dropped my revised proposal in "the hopper," the simple wood box in front of the Speaker's podium that has long been used for filing bills in the House. The clerk assigned a number (H.R. 664) to the

Prescription Drug Fairness for Seniors Act. The bill attracted broad support; eventually we signed on more than 150 Democratic House members as co-sponsors.

The timing was ripe. Since the enactment of Medicare in 1965, prescription drugs had become a far larger component of medical treatment, and the cash prices that seniors were paying for medicine were skyrocketing. Most Americans not yet on Medicare seemed to assume that the program covered prescription drugs. In fact, only drugs provided in hospitals or for a few specific conditions were covered.

Throughout 1999 my staff and I helped other House Democrats replicate our studies of the problems that high prescription drug prices created for seniors. Activists began organizing bus trips to Canada and Mexico to buy less expensive medicines. Each rider saved hundreds of dollars. It was a compelling human story that attracted much press attention. And at this point we had momentum.

Given the power of the pharmaceutical companies in Washington, change was possible only with inspired grassroots activity to mobilize the public. In Maine, John Marvin and Viola Quirion, ordinary citizens blessed with extraordinary courage and passion, took up the cause. John was a retired teacher and labor organizer who put together the first chartered bus trip to Canada so that Maine seniors could get their prescriptions filled there for far less than they cost in Maine. John milked the issue for all the press he could get in order to highlight the dilemma of Medicare beneficiaries who were forced to choose between medicine and food or heating oil.

Vi Quirion became a public face of the Medicare population in need of help. She had gone to work at the Hathaway shirt factory in Waterville, Maine, at the age of fifteen and, apart from a few years in a Massachusetts convent, stayed for forty-four years. Her wages as an inspector at the factory were just above minimum wage, but she was never on welfare and never collected an unemployment check. Vi walked with the help of two brace crutches but went on every one of the approximately eight bus trips to Quebec and New Brunswick that she helped organize. She admitted that the trips were tough: "We're a bunch of senior citizens with canes and crutches and oxygen."[2] She knew many others who could not afford to buy the medicines their doctors prescribed and she was determined to help them.

On October 17, 1999, the CBS program *60 Minutes* did a profile on the price of prescription drugs and my legislation. Vi Quirion told Mike Wallace that she lived on Social Security and a very small pension, which together came to about $900 a month; she spent a quarter of that income on prescription drugs for her arthritis and severe stomach problems. For her the choice between food and medicine was often painful. Another bus rider said, "We are all refugees from the American health care system . . . thank goodness, Canada is here."[3]

I argued that the most profitable industry in the country was charging the highest prices in the world to people who could least afford them. The pharmaceutical industry was then spending tens of millions of dollars to build opposition to Democratic bills to establish a discount or a Medicare prescription drug benefit for our seniors. The principal industry ad concluded with an elderly woman facing the camera exclaiming, "I don't want big government in my medicine cabinet."

I had believed a bill that provided seniors with significant financial breaks at relatively little cost to the federal government would attract Republican support. I was wrong. The industry and congressional opponents charged that a discount negotiated by the federal government constituted "price-fixing," which would dry up drug industry research. Lobbyists for PhRMA worked the halls of Congress, and the industry was successful—not one Republican signed on to the bill.

The issue, however, gained traction among Democratic leaders, and the minority party leaders on the Energy and Commerce Committee—John Dingell (D-MI) and Henry Waxman (D-CA)—pressed for the more comprehensive and more expensive approach of a Medicare prescription drug benefit based on a proposal from the Clinton administration. Both the discount and Medicare benefit had more than a 70 percent approval in the Democratic leadership's polls.

As the public learned that Medicare beneficiaries were paying the highest drug prices in the country, the Republican leadership concluded that they needed to act. In June 2000, Bill Thomas, chair of the House Ways and Means Committee, introduced a bill that provided assistance for prescription drugs by relying on the insurance and pharmaceutical companies. It passed the House by a narrow margin of three votes but never became law. But in the 2000 presidential campaign, both Vice President Al Gore and Governor George W. Bush promised to help seniors get access to the medicines they needed. After Bush was elected, the competing proposals were refined.

The Republican prescription drug bill covered Medicare beneficiaries, but instead of adding a drug benefit to the existing program, the bill relied on private insurance companies competing against each other to offer prescription drug coverage. Each insurer would be free, within some limits, to set premiums and co-payments, and to designate or exclude specific medications.

The Republican bill was embraced by the pharmaceutical industry because it vastly increased their market share without government pressure to reduce their prices. In fact, the Secretary of Health and Human Services was specifically precluded from using the purchasing power of Medicare's forty million recipients to negotiate lower prices. While the government routinely negotiated lower prices on goods and services to protect taxpayers, the Republican majority concluded that PhRMA should be treated differently. They argued that allowing the government to negotiate prices was akin to price-fixing and would drive prices so low that drug research and development would be compromised. At the same time, Republicans contended that competition among providers would produce the lowest possible prices for beneficiaries. Both could not be true.

November 23, 2003, when the Republican prescription drug bill came up for a vote, was the strangest night on the floor during my twelve years in Congress. (The impeachment debate was the strangest day.) Custom and precedent were set aside in order to ram the bill through a reluctant House. The majority leader, Tom DeLay, and Speaker Dennis Hastert, had become accustomed to holding controversial votes very late at night, apparently to reduce press coverage of the debate.[4] But the votes on the prescription drug bill broke all the records.

After extended debate, the vote began at 3 a.m. Typically, a vote is held open for fifteen minutes and then, on important or highly contested matters, the presiding officer often stands by for ten or fifteen more minutes, gavel ready to drop, to accommodate members who are on the way to the floor from their offices. On this night, given the significance of the bill and the time, most members were already in the chamber. The voting dragged on. By 3:48 a.m., the opponents appeared to have prevailed. The electronic voting board on the wall showed 215 yeas and 218 nays—an absolute majority in opposition. At least two dozen or so Republicans had voted against the bill because they opposed the creation of another government benefit, estimated to cost $400 billion over ten years. Some had even left the House floor to avoid being pressured by their leadership.

As the voting remained opened, we had nowhere to go and nothing else to do, so we watched the leaders scramble. DeLay and Speaker Hastert surrounded Nick Smith (R-MI), and then other Republicans opposed to the bill, trying to get them to change their votes. Smith later said he had been told that the leadership's financial campaign support for his son, Brad, to replace him in Congress was dependent on Smith's voting yes. Smith decided to vote no; Brad Smith was defeated in the Michigan primary in November 2004. In the chamber, as the early morning hours passed, we talked and waited for Tom DeLay to signal the Speaker to close the vote.

Contrary to past practice, Speaker Hastert allowed Health and Human Services Secretary Tommy Thompson onto the floor of the House to lobby reluctant Republicans. In the wee hours, President Bush personally called some who had voted no to urge them to change their position. Finally, DeLay succeeded in getting Butch Otter (R-ID) and Trent Franks (R-AZ) to change their votes from nay to yea to pass the bill. A few others switched their votes in both directions, and the gavel came down just before 6 a.m.

As I walked out of the East Side of the Capitol, the sky was light and the sun would soon rise. The previous night seemed unreal. We had been part of the longest roll call vote in the history of the House of Representatives. We had witnessed one of its ugliest moments as Republican leaders threatened their own members to get them to vote against their beliefs on an issue vital to the well-being of tens of millions of Americans.

I voted against the bill because the pharmaceutical companies and health insurers could list whatever drugs and charge whatever prices they wanted. As Rep. (now Sen.) Sherrod Brown (D-OH) said to me, the pharmaceutical industry had won again, as they always did in Congress.

When the plan went into effect, my office was besieged with calls from seniors who were totally baffled by the confusing choices the law had created, as well as by the many gaps in statutory coverage, such as the infamous "donut hole," a period of zero coverage for some people who were dependent on multiple prescriptions. Seniors would have to sort through a labyrinth of plans and options to decide which plan would best meet their needs. Depending on where one lived and what prescriptions were needed (along with predictions about what might be needed in the future), the choices varied enormously and were rarely clear. But the plan once in place would be hard to change, and benefits once created are difficult to alter.

Two years later, I was not surprised when I read a *Wall Street Journal* article confirming that the Bush prescription drug plan had been a "financial bonanza" for pharmaceutical companies. Moreover, since Republicans made no effort to raise taxes or reduce other spending to cover its cost of several hundred billion dollars over ten years, Medicare Part D was a significant factor—along with the Bush tax cuts and the wars in Iraq and Afghanistan—in weakening the financial condition of the federal government. It was no "financial bonanza" for the American people, but the Republicans had dealt with the pressure from the public for action and still protected the private sector companies with the most at stake.

Although I did not approve the final product, it brought a measure of relief to a population in need of help. After the initial confusion of its early implementation, Medicare beneficiaries learned to cope with its complexity, and the complaints to congressional offices abated. In my view the bill inappropriately enhanced the power of the pharmaceutical industry in Congress and expanded annual federal deficits. However, its prominent gap in coverage, the so-called donut hole, was closed by President Obama's Affordable Care Act by an agreement struck with PhRMA to win their support of ACA. There are sometimes more possible solutions to public challenges than people on either side will admit.

COMPARATIVE EFFECTIVENESS RESEARCH

Another health-care issue—independent research into effectiveness of prescription drugs—demonstrates how conservative policy and political support can erode over time in the face of ideological opposition. Approval of the Food and Drug Administration means less than most people think. The FDA approves drugs after extensive testing designed to answer only two questions: (1) Is it safe? and (2) Is it more effective than a placebo? That's all. In the United States no evidence is required of a new drug's effectiveness compared to existing medicines or other therapies. The drug companies are free to make assertions in their ads supported only by their own privately funded studies.

Pharmaceutical companies often compete more by advertising than reliance on product effectiveness or price. For several years the huge ad budgets for Vioxx and Celebrex, anti-inflammatory medicines widely used for the treatment of arthritis, were symptomatic of an industry that had found it could maintain much higher prices for marginally more effective drugs with a huge onslaught of advertising for a "new and improved" drug. In 2004 both Vioxx and Celebrex were pulled from the market; they never should have been widely prescribed.

Before the end of his second term in 2002, Oregon's governor John Kitzhaber had approved legislation that instituted a preferred drug list (PDL) for the Oregon Medicaid program, which required that effectiveness be the primary consideration, and if two drugs were equally effective, cost would be a secondary consideration. Since the vast bulk of research on the safety and efficacy of prescription drugs was funded by pharmaceutical companies, the public and providers could not be confident of its validity. In fact, media accounts of adverse research results being buried and "independent" researchers being funded by the drug manufacturers had undermined public confidence in claims by manufacturers about their products.

Governor Kitzhaber, Mark Gibson, his former chief of staff and health policy advisor, my health-care legislative assistant Susan Lexer, and I met for lunch in the Members' Dining Room in the Capitol. The governor gave me an overview of Oregon's legislation, which involved publically funded research to compare the relative effectiveness of drugs approved to treat the same illness or condition, based on a review of existing scientific studies and evidence. His program later became a multistate collaborative effort—the Drug Effectiveness Review Project (DERP).

I also studied the systems used by Australia and New Zealand, which had relatively sophisticated ways of evaluating whether a "new" prescription drug was significantly more effective than existing drugs in treating a particular illness or condition. In those countries, the information was used to determine the price at which the cost of the drug would be reimbursed by the government and whether it would be included on its formulary. That was not my approach. I simply wanted accurate, independent, comparative information to be readily available to patients and providers, and I hoped that would lead patients and providers to see the value in the less expensive of equally beneficial alternatives.

For many health policy experts, investing in comparative effectiveness research was a cutting-edge idea with significant potential to improve the knowledge base of health-care providers. It fit in well with the movement toward "evidence-based medicine." The idea was to create an independent source of information about the relative effectiveness of drugs, not tainted by pharmaceutical company investments. It carried great promise for improving health-care quality and reducing cost.

In 2002 I introduced the first House bill to fund comparative effectiveness research. It authorized $25 million for the Agency for Healthcare Research and Quality (AHRQ), a body within the Department of Health and Human Services that was funding and overseeing health-care research. The following year, in the 107th Congress, I was able to build bipartisan support for a revised version, H.R. 2356, the *Prescription Drug Comparative Effectiveness Act*, which authorized $100 million for AHRQ to conduct systematic reviews of existing evidence on prescription drug effectiveness. Representative Joanne Emerson (R-MO), was the lead cosponsor; she and Rep. Zach Wamp (R-TN) were able to attract further support from their Republican colleagues. The bill was introduced with the public support of twelve members, equally divided between Republicans and Democrats.

In Maine and across the country, there was no significant constituency for funding comparative effectiveness research; few even knew what it was. On the other hand, there was in the beginning no significant constituency against it. Insurers, individuals, and businesses could reduce costs and improve quality with good information; patients and providers had a common interest in optimizing care. Even the opposition from the pharmaceutical industry was diffused, for while the information would likely diminish sales of some expensive blockbuster drugs, the large companies were also poised to come out on top in other comparative effectiveness studies. Thus, the bill cut across the typical ideological divisions on health-care reform.

Chris Jennings, the former White House point person on health care for President Clinton, recognized this confluence of interests. He had put together a "Purchasers' Coalition" to support health care proposals on which they agreed. The coalition was an unlikely group: General Motors, Caterpillar, labor unions, consumer groups, and even some insurance companies. GM, for example, had come to realize that one pricey purple pill, Nexium, which treated heartburn, was consuming a huge portion of its health-care costs. Were other medications just as effective for most people? Getting a better understanding of unnecessary expenditures would make a serious difference to the bottom line. The coalition was the first and most impressive example of what I had been hoping for: a diverse organization of health-care purchasers to protect their own financial interests.

Marion Berry (D-AR), a former pharmacist and my co-chair of the Prescription Drug Task Force in the House, Joanne Emerson, Zach Wamp, and I met with the coalition in 2003 to discuss our proposal. The coalition became an important advocate for the concept of comparative effectiveness research, but it worked mostly behind the scenes.

H.R. 2356 became the basis of a provision (Sec. 1013) included in the Medicare Modernization Act of 2003 (MMA), the legislation that added prescription drug coverage to Medicare benefits. The language had not been included in either the House or Senate versions of the bill. But Reps. Nancy Johnson and Doug Bereuter, both Republicans, had made favorable comments about comparative effectiveness research during an earlier

House floor debate. The Purchasers Coalition quietly supported adding Sec. 1013 comparative effectiveness funding of $15 million to the MMA, and Senate majority leader Bill Frist (R-TN) and Sen. Tim Johnson (D-SD) were able to get it done. To this point the effort was clearly bipartisan.

By itself, Sec. 1013 was just a foot in the door; it authorized the AHRQ to conduct "systematic reviews of existing evidence" on the clinical comparative effectiveness of drugs and other treatments, and authorized $50 million over several years for that effort. No money was provided for AHRQ to do its own research. Moreover, the first $15 million appropriation was not available until fiscal year 2007. And PhRMA clearly had exerted some influence. Sec. 1013 included a provision that the information gathered could not be used by Medicare or Medicaid to make coverage decisions regarding prescription drugs.

In the health-policy world, comparative effectiveness research continued to gain ground. In November 2006 Gail Wilensky, director of the Centers for Medicare and Medicaid (CMS) under the first President Bush, published an article in the journal *Health Affairs* supporting a major investment in this approach.[5] After Democrats won control of the House and Senate in 2006, I could argue for an investment that would be more than just a foot in the door. In May 2007, with Joanne Emerson as the lead Republican, I introduced H.R. 2184, the *Enhanced Health Care Value for All Act*, which built on the steps that AHRQ had already taken. The bill created an "all-payer" financing mechanism to fund $3 billion of comparative effectiveness research over five years, with contributions from Medicare (a maximum of $1 billion), self-insured health plans, and insurance companies. Since comparative effectiveness research would benefit public programs like Medicare and private health insurance plans, the goal was to get a financial investment from both public and private sources.

The bill did not become law in the 110th Congress, but after the 2008 elections, a major investment in comparative effectiveness research was included in the Obama administration's stimulus package in February 2009. The stimulus bill included $1.1 billion over two years for research for drugs, medical devices, and certain treatments. In that form it was broad enough over time to improve the quality of many medical decisions and eventually reduce the nation's reliance on overly expensive drugs, devices, and treatments.

What happened? The issue itself—better information more widely distributed—did not engage the ideological passions generated by some other health-care issues. The pharmaceutical industry was isolated by past allies who acted in their own interests as consumers or purchasers of prescription drugs. This allowed us to attract enough Republican support to reduce the intensity of the conflict over the legislation. Still, the most important factor in funding was the change in party control after the 2006 elections, which led to a more comprehensive commitment to independent research.

The bipartisan consensus on the value of independent research into the comparative effectiveness of drugs, devices, and eventually medical practices did not survive the political and ideological battles after the 2008 election. Vociferous Republican opposition to the 2009 Obama stimulus package and the 2010 Affordable Care Act included attacks on the comparative effectiveness provisions in both bills. The health reform law established the Patient-Centered Outcomes Research Institute (PCORI) as an independent advisory board with a $3 billion budget to support comparative effectiveness research. The mission of PCORI was broadened from research on medical prescriptions and treatments to include how health systems can best organize to deliver care and how to reduce health-care disparities. Its nineteen-member board includes patients, physicians, nurses, hospitals, drug makers, device manufacturers, insurers, payers, government officials, and health experts. PCORI does not have the power to mandate or endorse coverage rules or reimbursement for any particular treatment.

The conservative critique of comparative effectiveness research focused on the specter that individual patients might be denied coverage for expensive drugs deemed not effective by independent panels. In fact, the Democratic stimulus legislation was written to prevent that outcome. For Republicans attacking the Obama stimulus and health-care plans, the overall cost of the health-care system paled in comparison to the prospect of an individual without access to an expensive medicine. The value of accurate information about the effectiveness of drugs and devices was minimized. In response, Democratic advocates learned not to mention the cost-savings potential of the legislation, because it would trigger the response that some patients might be denied expensive drugs they needed. In today's media environment, explaining the text of the bills is a sure loser compared to invoking threats to individual choice.

No matter how careful proponents were to protect the professional judgment of physicians from government interference, Republicans who believed government spending was out of control oddly insisted that no individual should be denied the right to have the government pay for a more expensive but no more effective drug.

Members of the two parties were looking at comparative effectiveness research in dramatically different ways. Democrats believed we were trying to reform the system to improve quality and reduce costs: if some people needed additional approval for a more expensive medication, that was an insignificant price to pay for a more efficient health-care system. For Republicans, acutely sensitive to any incremental addition of government power or regulation, the efficiency of the overall system paled into insignificance. We were not engaged in debating the same topic.

COMMON THEMES OF HEALTH-CARE DEBATE

Health-care issues occupied a significant portion of my time in Congress. Patterns of argument soon became apparent. I had hoped to attract Republican support for a negotiated prescription drug discount for Medicare beneficiaries because it would produce substantial relief at very low cost to the federal government. However, conservatives turned out to be wary of increasing governmental influence over drug prices and rejected that approach. Investment in comparative effectiveness research, which promised both higher quality care and long-range cost savings, attracted Republican support for early modest initiatives, but less when the proposals increased in scale under the Obama stimulus plan and the ACA.

In those contexts, conservatives argued against comparative effectiveness research because it might deprive an individual of a needed drug, even though both bills had been written to avoid that outcome. For all the alarms raised about the growing costs of Medicare and private health plans, systemic cost issues were trumped by fears of individuals being short-changed. In other cases, the claims were even more bizarre. Take the fabricated charge in the summer of 2009 that the ACA established "death panels" that would decide whether Grandma would live or die. That section of the bill authorized compensation to health-care providers for counseling family members concerning profoundly personal end-of-life decisions about their own or loved ones' medical care.

Fox News played a major role in promoting the "death panel" story. The claim was first made by Betsy McCaughey, who had been New York governor George Pataki's lieutenant governor. Fox immediately picked up the claim and repeated it as "news" long enough to force the story into the mainstream media and for Sarah Palin to give it credibility among many Republicans.[6] The pattern had become common; a provision to improve patient choice was again characterized as government heavy-handedness.

If we turn to the ACA itself, for which not a single Republican voted, the conservative assault was primarily directed to the "individual mandate." The concept of requiring individuals to purchase private health insurance found its earliest expression in a 1989 proposal by Stuart Butler, the leading health-care specialist at the conservative Heritage Foundation. In a nine-page summary of the Heritage Plan, Butler described the three serious underlying problems with the American health-care system: (1) inviting runaway costs, (2) failing to channel government assistance to those who need it most, and (3) failing to require households to protect themselves against health-care needs.[7] He proposed an individual mandate to obtain insurance, with government assistance to lower-income families, as an alternative to an employer mandate to provide health insurance for full-time employees. Three years before Bill Clinton was elected president, Butler wrote that, "I believe that eventually the U.S. will have a 'national health system,' in the sense of a system that assures each citizen of access to affordable health care."[8]

The Heritage Plan was designed as a conservative response to the deficiencies of a health-care system that in 1989 represented more than 11 percent of GDP and still left thirty-seven million Americans without adequate insurance. In 2010 the comparable numbers were 17 percent and nearly fifty million people. Butler argued that families should bear primary responsibility for obtaining health insurance, not businesses. He explained that health insurance is different from other insurance because "If a man is struck down by a heart attack in the street, Americans will care for him whether or not he has insurance."[9] The individual mandate would deal with "free-riders" who avoided paying for insurance in the knowledge that the system would care for them if they became ill or were injured.

Although every year their health insurance premiums rose significantly, most small business owners leaned toward Republican because they wanted lower taxes and less government regulation. In my view, their interests were not well represented in Washington by the National Federation of Independent Businesses (NFIB), the largest lobbying group for the small business community, because it gave Maine businesses so little help on health care. The NFIB was an intensely partisan organization, an active player in the right-wing "Wednesday morning" planning sessions organized by Grover Norquist of Americans for Tax Reform. The NFIB consistently supported Republican health-care policies, which advanced the interests of their big business allies like the insurance companies, but left behind many of their own members—who in Maine and elsewhere were desperate for help. The legal assault on the ACA was led by the NFIB, which had no credible alternative plan for comprehensive reform.

Back home, people trying to keep a small business afloat had little time for health-care policy. But it was still frustrating to have small businessmen and women come to my office, carefully prepped by a national association, to argue for legislation that would work just fine for the health insurers but not for them. As the crisis grew worse and Congress failed to act, some business owners began to change their minds. Over time, I heard from more than a few who were ready to embrace a single-payer system, equivalent to our Medicare. Still, it was only in my last few years in office that I sensed that some small business groups began to understand that tighter regulation of the insurance industry was essential.

The congressional debates over health-care reform during the Bush and Obama administrations exposed the underlying clash of ideas and values that breeds the polarization about which the press and public complain. I spoke to countless rooms of people about the crisis in the American health-care system. Often, the room was divided between those who believed health care should be available to everyone, regardless of wealth, and a smaller number who believed they should not be required to share the costs of illnesses or accidents suffered by others. It's not that the latter group was cruel-hearted; many undoubtedly gave generously to churches, temples, and charitable efforts. But many also harbored the view that the poor brought on their own misfortune. The factions had fundamentally different moral views.

This dichotomy mirrored the various perspectives on the role of government: one believed that only the federal government could expand coverage and contain the excesses of the health insurers, and the other believed in "free markets," even in health care. Advocates for comprehensive reform typically found it intolerable that millions of Americans lacked both adequate insurance and health care. Opponents typically preferred to do nothing rather than to expand the role of the federal government.

It is harder to understand that attitude among members of Congress, who meet thousands of their constituents every year. I visited subsidized housing facilities whose residents, mostly women, lived on $700 a month and were unable to pay for their prescriptions. I talked with students forced to leave college because of health issues, who then lost their health insurance when they left. My staff dealt with hundreds of constituents struggling with inadequate care and no insurance. The thought often ran through my mind, "How do Republican congressmen respond to these personal stories of neglect and lack of care?" I don't know.

In short, each side finds the position of the other incomprehensible. That's why my Democratic colleagues concluded that Republicans must be completely beholden to the health insurance and pharmaceutical industries, and Republicans concluded that Democrats wanted to expand the power of government for their own political purposes. The bottom line is that compromise on major reform, even the Affordable Care Act in 2009–10, was never realistic.

Before that bill passed the House I ran into a Republican colleague in Washington. He complained that the minority had been denied the opportunity to offer amendments. But when I suggested that even if given that chance and the amendments passed, he still couldn't vote for the bill, he agreed. When the congressional minority party, Republican or Democratic, complains about being denied the opportunity to amend a bill, extend the debate, or a similar process issue, the real objection is almost always about the substance. The mainstream media typically gives too much credibility to the red herring of abuse of process claims and not enough to the decisive conflict of values and ideas.

A sign at a Tea Party rally in 2010 read: "Big Government Means Less Individual Freedom." President Obama told a town hall audience: "I got a letter the other day from a woman. She said, 'I don't want government-run health care. I don't want socialized medicine. And don't touch my Medicare.'" That's the level at which major political issues are fought today. The concept that better (or even some) health care, or more education, or improved services for children can create opportunity for Americans rather than limit them, or that government services need not make beneficiaries "dependent" is rarely debated in specifics—where evidence might matter.

When one side will only debate vital public issues in terms of "big government" and "individual freedom" instead of the nuts and bolts of policy, no amount of evidence can stop our slide to intensifying polarization. Meanwhile, the people without adequate care and the businessmen and women struggling to provide coverage for their employees could only wait—and wonder when relief might come. That question for millions is now tied to whether the systemic changes signed into law by President Obama can survive the continued relentless attack from the Right during the next few years.

The full-throated Republican opposition to the ACA, including the appeal to the Supreme Court, masked the underlying reality that they had no alternative proposal to expand coverage to the more than thirty million (of the fifty million now uninsured) projected to gain coverage under the ACA. I believe that if the Republican leadership had somehow been *forced* to produce a plan for comparable coverage, they would have relied on a somewhat less regulatory, competitive private insurance market with either an individual mandate or tax penalties or inducements to achieve the same result. In other words, they would have adopted legislation much like the bill they condemned. They had no free-market option that could expand coverage to millions of Americans for whom the current free market was impossibly expensive.

In the last two decades, despite the increasing saliency of health care concerns, no national Republican leader offered a plausible plan to expand coverage. There were, I believe, two reasons: (1) politically it wasn't necessary to respond to their base, and (2) conceptually they could not escape the confinement of "smaller government, lower taxes." Those core principles and the absence of any countervailing conservative principles took Republicans out of the health-care coverage debate—except to say no to Democratic proposals. In that effort, they isolated the part of the ACA that by its very name would in America arouse intense opposition: the "individual mandate." For a party sliding down a road of ever-increasing hostility to government, there could hardly have been a more inviting rhetorical target.

The equally troubling conclusion is that the combination of forty million to fifty million uninsured Americans and the financial consequences for American businesses large and small was not enough to make health-care reform a pressing issue for both parties. In every congressional district there were thousands of people struggling with the costs and consequences of an inadequate health-care system, and hundreds of businesses burdened by rapidly increasing insurance premiums. But that was not enough for Republican congressional leaders to develop an updated version of the 1989 Heritage Plan. The party's fierce opposition to government action in health care ensured that their only viable political choices were small-bore proposals allowing insurance companies to sell policies across state lines, medical malpractice limitations, and health savings accounts. In the end the ACA, although it included significant conservative ideas, attracted only Democratic support.

The legal challenges to the ACA reached the Supreme Court in March 2012. After listening to conservatives on the Supreme Court repeatedly describe the issue as "freedom," one commentator wrote, "It's about freedom from our obligations to one another, . . . the freedom to ignore the injured, walk away from those in peril, . . . the freedom to be left alone, . . . the freedom to live like it's 1804."[10] The clash of worldviews that played out in the political, legislative, and courtroom debates over Obamacare was intense and irreconcilable primarily because it was so abstract.

In the two years after its enactment Republicans had frequently claimed that they would "repeal and replace Obamacare." After the Court upheld the law, Sen. Mitch McConnell was pressed three times by Chris Wallace on Fox News to explain how Republicans proposed to cover the thirty million Americans who would be covered under the ACA. McConnell's response was, "That's not the issue."

> WALLACE: You don't think the thirty million people who are uninsured is an issue?
> MCCONNELL: Let me tell you what we're not going to do. We're not going to turn the American health-care system into a western European system.[11]

It would be hard to find a clearer contemporary example of how ideological principles devalue people. Tens of millions of uninsured are "not the issue" because a libertarian ideology has no room for their problems and no respect for "western European" systems that provide near-universal coverage at lower cost and with better health outcomes than our own system. At some point, there is a moral equivalence between leaving millions of Americans stranded with the health and financial risks of being uninsured, and walking by a stranger lying bleeding in the street. And at nearly fifty million insured, we have long passed that point.

In *NFIB v. Sebelius* the Supreme Court upheld the central components of the ACA, including the individual mandate, although under the taxing power of Congress, not the Commerce Clause. Justice Roberts's opinion protected the Court from being perceived as an institution driven entirely by conservative politics and yet confined the reach of the Commerce Clause for potential future cases. The Court's resolution of the constitutionality of the ACA, passed by Congress without a single Republican vote—despite its conservative roots—will leave health-care reform as another example of how deep-seated convictions about dependency, liberty, and the role of government can render nearly impossible the bipartisan congressional engagement that our largest, most complicated and pressing challenges require.

Climate Change

Denial as Public Policy

When despair for the world grows in me
and I wake in the night at the least sound
in fear of what my life and my children's lives may be,
I go and lie down where the wood drake
rests in his beauty on the water, and the great heron feeds.
I come into the peace of wild things
who do not tax their lives with forethought
of grief. I come into the presence of still water.
And I feel above me the day-blind stars
waiting with their light. For a time
I rest in the grace of the world, and am free.

— WENDELL BERRY, *"The Peace of Wild Things"*

We may stop to rest in the grace of the natural world, but humans now have the capacity to enhance or destroy it. When I was growing up, the paper mill to the west of Portland spread its rotten-egg, sulfur dioxide smell over the city. Houses along the nearby Presumpscot River were stained brown by the pollutants discharged by the mill. When we went on family vacations in the 1950s and 1960s to fish the pristine trout ponds near Mount Katahdin, we passed through Millinocket, which like all Maine towns with paper mills, had the same familiar odor that residents tolerated as "the smell of money." The foaming polluted rivers of Maine in the 1950s and 1960s steeled Sen. Ed Muskie's determination to pass the

Clean Water Act. That was a simpler world—in which we could see and smell the effluent and emissions of industrial plants.

Today the danger we pose to the planet's air, water, and oceans is greater but less visible. Carbon dioxide, the major greenhouse gas, is natural, undetectable through our senses, but accumulating steadily in the atmosphere. Its concentration is the highest in millions of years; its absorption by the oceans has made them about 30 percent more acidic since the Industrial Revolution.[1] The Arctic ice sheets are shrinking and parts of that region have warmed by four or five degrees Fahrenheit since the 1950s—three times faster than the increase in global average temperature of 1.4 degrees Fahrenheit during the same period.[2] The 1980s were the hottest decade on record until the 1990s; the 1990s took that record only until the 2000s. Global warming turbocharges more violent and costly weather events. Ocean acidification kills coral formations and threatens tiny shell-forming organisms at the bottom of the food chain.

The 1960s were defined by three popular movements—for civil rights, for women, and for a cleaner environment—marked by significant increases in citizen activism. All sought to change patterns of the past to create better policies for the future. All had significant bipartisan support. Environmental concerns about air and water pollution grew as evidence of harm to human health became clearer. Rachel Carson published *The Edge of the Sea* in 1951 and *Silent Spring* in 1962, both of which helped galvanize public concern about the ocean and the dangers of DDT. The Clean Water Act provisions of 1972, the Clean Air Act of 1970, the National Environmental Policy Act, the Endangered Species Act, and the creation of the Environmental Protection Agency were all accomplished during the Nixon administration. Beyond the sight of the Cuyahoga River in flames and the first Earth Day in 1970, Americans of both parties understood that pollution respected no state boundaries and had to be in large part a responsibility of the federal government.

The environmental legislation of the 1960s and 1970s was largely successful. The Clean Water Act produced a dramatic improvement in America's rivers; over three decades in Maine, the foam disappeared, the fish returned, and the "no swimming" signs vanished. The Clean Air Act has saved hundreds of thousands of lives and reduced illnesses related to air pollution.

In the 1980s international collaboration successfully addressed the danger presented by higher levels of ultraviolet-B radiation from the opening in the ozone layer over the Antarctic. As scientific evidence proved that the "ozone hole" in the stratosphere was caused by chlorofluorocarbons (CFCs), emitted by aerosol spray cans, refrigerators, and air conditioning equipment, the affected countries and stakeholders negotiated the 1987 Montreal Protocol on Substances that Deplete the Ozone Layer. The protocol was signed by every member of the United Nations and ratified by the U.S. Congress at the request of President Reagan.[3] It was a signal achievement in response to an unprecedented risk, yet more easily managed than climate change because CFCs were produced by only a handful of multinational corporations—and substitute products were soon available.

Bipartisan compromise was still possible when Sen. George Mitchell (D-ME) and Rep. Henry Waxman (D-CA) led the charge for the Clean Air Act Amendments of 1990, a bill signed into law by President George H. W. Bush. That legislation included provisions to implement the Montreal Protocol and, more significantly, adopted a cap-and-trade program to reduce sulfur dioxide emissions from coal-fired power plants, which were killing fish and plant life in northeastern lakes and streams. New York had bodies of water in the Adirondacks where increased acidity had killed off all fish. Because the wind blows west to east, the same fate awaited us in Maine even though we have no coal-fired power plants.

In hindsight, environmental issues became increasingly partisan after 1994, when the Republicans won control of the House for the first time in forty years. Industries opposed to regulation of pollutants reacted negatively to Kyoto and other Clinton-Gore initiatives and began to invest heavily in Republican candidates; environmental groups countered by increasing their financial support of Democrats. As the two parties coalesced into pro- and anti-regulatory camps, money and messaging intensified the differences. Senators with strong environmental records, like John Chafee of Rhode Island, became outliers in the Republican Party, and Democrats from coal-producing states found themselves a minority in their party.

The first part of this chapter examines the forces contributing to the polarization of environmental issues in the last twenty years, including the attitudes toward science and economics that have made the United States slow to acknowledge and react to the growing threat of climate change. Then I turn to the "other CO2 problem," the chemically related, emerging concern about the risk that ocean acidification poses to coral reefs and the planetary food chain. Finally, given the intriguing conflict between science and public attitudes about climate change, recent surveys have produced remarkable data that paint a fuller picture of how our underlying worldviews move us to select information that reinforces our own opinions and blinds us to those of others.

CLIMATE SCIENCE AND ITS ADVERSARIES

I won election to Congress in 1996 partly because Jim Longley Jr., a first-term Republican incumbent caught up in the heady days of the Gingrich revolution, had voted with his Speaker of the House to weaken several environmental laws, which signaled he was no Republican moderate. After taking my seat, I knew that the House was unlikely to pass legislation to reduce emissions from power plants and other industrial facilities, including carbon dioxide and mercury, both then unregulated. But like others in Congress I hoped for a more favorable political alignment in the future. Moreover, President Clinton and Vice President Gore were committed environmentalists, and the House Republicans were limited in what they could do to reverse existing laws or regulations.

The election of George W. Bush and Dick Cheney, both with backgrounds in the oil industry, removed almost all hope of further bipartisan collaboration on environmental issues. Republicans controlled both the House and Senate for five of the next six years. President Bush abandoned his campaign promise to regulate carbon dioxide, formally rejected the Kyoto Protocol on global warming, made no effort to renegotiate its provisions, and promoted rules and legislation to weaken existing clean air and water regulations.

Opponents of the administration attacked its policies on the ground that they were simply designed to serve allied business interests, like the fossil fuel industries, utilities, heavy manufacturers, and steel mills. Although Republicans in the 1970s understood that only the federal government could effectively cope with air and water pollution, neither of which respected state boundaries, the Bush administration and its allies were opposed to environmental regulation in part because they were opposed to regulation generally.

Pollution can be understood as a kind of market failure. Fossil fuel utilities and heavy industry produce pollutants that damage the environment and human health, but the polluters typically do not pay for those costs unless required to do so. Historically, the auto industry and its labor unions vehemently resisted regulations to improve automobile mileage; fossil fuel and manufacturing companies fought regulations to reduce air and water pollution. They argued that environmental regulations would have an adverse effect on the economy. These industries, however, avoided the cost of cleaning up part of the waste stream from their own business activity, and so regulation was one way that the broader public could make them bear those costs.

The science of climate change has faced political resistance from the beginning, most notably in the United States. In 1992 the United Nations Framework Convention on Climate Change established voluntary emissions reduction objectives to deal with the threat posed by global warming. Five years later, industrialized countries agreed to binding emissions reductions pursuant to the Kyoto Protocol. Concerns about the economic consequences of ratifying Kyoto and tensions between developed and developing countries eventually undermined the prospect of a comprehensive global treaty.

In May 2001 I attended an Aspen Institute program for senators and members of the House on the "Convergence of U.S. National Security and the Global Environment." We reviewed the latest report of the Intergovernmental Panel on Climate Change (IPCC) on the accumulation of unprecedented levels of carbon dioxide and other greenhouse gases in the atmosphere. The report concluded that about three-quarters of the anthropogenic emissions of CO_2 to the atmosphere in the previous twenty years were due to the burning of fossil fuels, and the rest to deforestation and other land-use changes. Like prior reports, it predicted that greenhouse gas emissions would raise global surface temperatures, increase precipitation, induce more severe weather events, and increase the risk of drought over mid-latitude continental interiors.[4]

For more than fifty years the concentration of atmospheric carbon dioxide has been measured daily by weather balloons at the research station at Mauna Loa in Hawaii. The data show—with standard seasonal variations—a steady climb in atmospheric CO_2. The change in ocean chemistry is a more recent discovery. Ocean acidification is caused when the ocean absorbs carbon dioxide from the atmosphere and converts it to carbonic acid. Surface ocean data generated since the early 1990s at Ocean Station Aloha northwest of Mauna Loa show that the acidity of the seawater at Aloha is increasing with a parallel regularity to atmospheric carbon dioxide (see figure 5.1).

To get a brief view of the rapid warming in the Arctic, go to NOAA Climate Services on the agency's website and watch satellite images of year-to-year physical changes in the Arctic sea ice formation (http://www .arctic.noaa.gov/detect/ice-seaice.shtml). As of December 1, 2011, the highlights of NOAA's 2011 Arctic Report Card included scientific evidence from around the world of "extreme melting on the surface of the Greenland ice sheet, declining summer sea ice cover, rapidly receding glaciers, and changing ocean pH—all of which have wide-ranging consequences for people, plants, and animals in the Arctic and beyond."[5]

The Arctic is changing much faster than the rest of the planet because of the feedback between its ice covers and air temperature, or "Arctic amplification." The NOAA text explains, "As air temperature increases, ice melts; as the bright, reflective ice melts, it reveals darker ocean and land surfaces. These dark surfaces absorb more solar energy during the Arctic's summer season, when the Sun never sets. This causes more heating, which causes more melting . . . and so on." This cycle carries substantial risks that

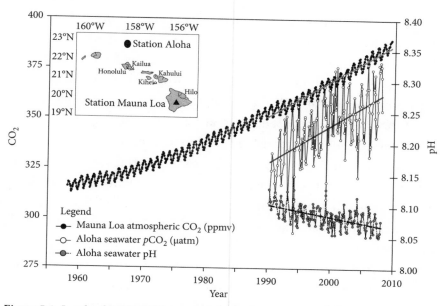

Figure 5.1 Levels of Acidity of Seawater at Ocean Station Aloha Compared with Levels of Atmospheric Carbon Dioxide.

SOURCE: S. C. Doney, W. M. Balch, V. J. Fabry, and R. A. Feely, "Ocean Acidification: A Critical Emerging Problem for the Ocean Sciences." *Oceanography* 22(4): 16–25, 2009, http://dx.doi.org/10.5670/oceanog.2009.93.

warming of the Arctic region will release vast amounts of methane, long safely frozen in the tundra, and accelerate the projected rate of change.

The contrast between the physical world and American politics is stark. Take Texas for example. In 2011 Texas suffered through the driest twelve months in its history, and the hottest three months (June–August) of any state in American history since records have been kept. Between one hundred million and five hundred million trees were killed by drought, not counting those burned by the wildfires that scorched four million acres. Governor Rick Perry, a Republican candidate for president, urged Texans to pray for rain and dismissed global warming as a theory that "still has not been proven" and is driven by a "substantial number of scientists who have manipulated data" to secure research grants.[6] We might have hoped that in states where the impact of climate change is most apparent, like Texas and Alaska, elected officials would provide political leadership to cope with climate change—but that has not happened.

During my last six years in Congress, from 2003 to the end of 2008, I served on the House Energy and Commerce Committee, which has jurisdiction over energy and environmental legislation. By then the attitude of the Bush administration to those issues was clear: the president's campaign promise to deal with the threat of greenhouse gases like carbon dioxide had been scrapped, and overt and covert campaigns against environmental regulations were well underway. From my side of the aisle it did not appear that our Republican colleagues were looking for more effective ways to accommodate both environmental and economic concerns. They appeared to be fixed on helping favored industries reduce their costs.

I believe now that many conservatives in Congress and the Bush administration viewed environmental issues as they did others—seeing America's coal resources as helpful in making us more self-reliant on domestic sources, and America's energy companies as major contributors to the health of our economy. It was another example of valuing the principle of "stand on your own two feet" and the prosperous "job creators" so important to the economy. Moreover, energy and environmental regulations have both costs *and* benefits, and legitimate differences need to be debated and resolved. Finally, all members of Congress have constituents, so it should not be surprising that Democrats from coal-mining and coal-burning states tend to reflect local interests. Yet it is one thing to argue about the details of energy and environmental policies, and another to deny the overwhelming evidence of the human contribution to climate change and the consequences of ignoring it. That political attitude, now characteristic of Republicans in Congress, is potentially catastrophic.

Debates over more conventional struggles over energy and environmental policies can more easily be attributed to interest group politics. Here is one example. I worked extensively on legislation to reduce emissions of sulfur dioxide, nitrogen oxide, carbon dioxide, and mercury from aging power plants. Mercury is a potent neurotoxin especially dangerous for expectant mothers and young children. It is emitted by coal-fired utility plants, converted in water to methylmercury, absorbed by fish and then by the people, loons, eagles, and others that eat the contaminated fish. Coal-fired power plants in the U.S. emit about forty-eight tons of mercury annually. The Clinton administration had adopted Maximum Achievable Control Technology regulations to reduce such emissions up to 90 percent by 2008. Yet the Bush administration proposed revisions of the mercury rule that would reduce emissions by only 30 percent over the next fifteen years. Given the influence of energy industries with the Bush administration, I was not surprised when the news broke that the proposed mercury rule contained twelve paragraphs lifted, sometimes verbatim, from documents filed by industry lawyers.[7]

In March 2005, the EPA's proposed rules were released; later they were adopted, challenged in court, and eventually thrown out by the court. More stringent science-based regulations were adopted by the Obama administration in December 2011. Because efforts to reduce mercury emissions also produce lower levels of sulfur dioxide, the health and economic benefits of the Obama administration's rules will be substantial. Nonetheless, industry had bought years of delay before being required to install available technology to protect the health of Americans.

At Energy and Commerce Committee hearings I let no opportunity pass to grill Jeff Holmstead, the Bush administration's point person on air quality, about the dangers of mercury to public health. Yet despite one effort to suppress data on mercury's effect on children, the administration was not engaged in full-blown denial of the science of mercury pollution. That's what makes the politics of climate change so dangerous. By *denying* evidence that climate scientists agree is overwhelming, conservatives in Congress need not participate in any discussions about how to cope with it. Trust and respect across the aisle cannot survive circumstances when one worldview is incomprehensible to the other side and is defended by making up so-called evidence.

The conscious denial of climate science has been going on for two decades. Frank Luntz, the Republican communications advisor, is credited with popularizing "death tax" to describe the federal tax imposed on the estates of the wealthiest Americans, urging Bush administration officials to begin every argument for invading Iraq by saying "9/11 changed everything" and suggesting "Clear Skies" as the right name for the administration's proposal to weaken the Clean Air Act. In early 2003, in a memo on climate change, Luntz advised Republican congressmen to express their commitment to "sound science" and refer to "climate change" instead of "global warming" because the former is "less threatening." He went on to say:

The scientific debate is closing [against us] but not yet closed. There is still a window of opportunity to challenge the science. (bold and brackets in original)[8]

The memo contains no suggestion that its author cared whether his words were true. Years later Luntz said to a *New York Times* reporter, "I'm not a policy person. I'm a language person."[9] In other words, he's for whatever words work, whatever their connection, if any, to policy. The substance of the issue was buried by political rhetoric.

It still is. Five years after the Luntz memo, the Republican presidential nomination went to Sen. John McCain, even though he was a party outlier as the sponsor of the leading cap and trade bill to deal with power plant emissions. By the 2012 cycle, however, all the leading Republican candidates were in full denial of the human contribution to climate change, in some cases (e.g., Romney and Gingrich) rejecting their own past views to the contrary. In short, more Republican candidates are in denial about the science of climate change even as climate scientists have become more confident of their conclusions.

During the George W. Bush administration the denial and suppression of scientific conclusions bearing on public policy became commonplace— about global warming and other fields. Seth Shulman's book, *Undermining Science: Suppression and Distortion in the Bush Administration,* exposed the widespread practice of mid-level administration political appointees revising scientific reports for political purposes. In January 2007 the Union of Concerned Scientists surveyed sixteen hundred climate scientists at seven federal agencies. The scientists reported personal knowledge of 435 incidents of political interference in their conclusions, and 46 percent indicated they or others had been pressured to remove the words "climate change" or "global warming" from their official documents.[10]

From his position as chief of staff from 2001 to 2005 to the White House Council on Environmental Quality (CEQ), Phil Cooney, previously a lawyer for the American Petroleum Institute, altered numerous scientific reports to weaken or remove language concerning the existence and consequences of global warming, including the 2002 and 2003 annual reports of the Climate Change Science Program. He had support from the top. In May 2003 when the EPA and State Department issued the "U.S. Climate Action Report," President Bush dismissed it as a "report put out by the bureaucracy."[11] In April 2003 Cooney and his colleagues applied such pressure on the EPA to make "a host of major amendments" to its *Report on the Environment* that the administrator, Christie Todd Whitman, and agency scientists decided to eliminate that entire section of the report rather than mislead the public.[12] The next month Whitman resigned. As Ron Suskind reported, on the day in May 2003 when Christie Todd Whitman resigned as EPA administrator, she told him: "In meetings, I'd ask if there were any facts to support our case. And for that, I was accused of disloyalty!"[13] Suskind indicated in 2004 that Whitman "denies making these remarks and is now a leader of [Bush's] re-election effort in New Jersey."[14] But Paul O'Neill, after he was fired from his position as Secretary of the Treasury, recalled Whitman asking White House advisor Larry Lindsey, "Do you have any facts" to back up your assertions that "thousands of power plants . . . have not been constructed" because of EPA regulations. Whitman believed the number not constructed for that reason was zero.[15]

The gap between most Republicans and most Democrats on climate change and other environmental issues continues to widen. In the fall of 2011 *National Journal* reporters contacted every Republican senator and congressman to ask if they thought climate change was causing the earth to become warmer, how much of any warming was due to human activity, and what should be the appropriate governmental response. Only sixty-five of the roughly three hundred Republicans in Congress agreed to respond, and only twenty replied that they believed climate change was causing the earth to warm. Refusals to comment were the norm. For Republican federal officeholders today, the issue is so politically toxic that it's better that they not speak at all. However, the refusals to respond suggest that express denial is no longer an easy option.

Nevertheless, the House Republican leadership decided after the November 2010 elections to "attack the Obama administration relentlessly on fossil-fuel and climate-change regulations, but to keep silent on the issue of climate science" because, in the words of one Republican operative, "the science argument's a loser."[16]

The science argument is a political loser because the scientific consensus *accurately* explains the factors driving global warming. So what is the Republican plan to deal with it? Apparently, just attacking the Obama administration "relentlessly on fossil-fuel and climate-change regulations." Why? Because there are no Republican "principles" that could shape a conservative climate-change policy. "Smaller government, lower taxes" provides no guidance. It seems likely that some Republicans are alarmed by estimated costs of dealing with the consequences of climate change. In addition, Rick Santorum and others argue that God gave human beings dominion over the earth and believe it is to be exploited for our benefit. How did this happen? If the national party is in thrall to the Republican "base," how did the "base" become so hostile to the science? Why is there such an overwhelming consensus among scientists and such division and uncertainty among conservatives?

Money is part of the reason. For years the oil, coal, and gas companies funded the Global Climate Coalition to challenge the growing scientific consensus on the facts and causes of global warming; Exxon Mobil was a major funder. Through the 1990s, the coalition argued first that "the role of greenhouse gases in climate change is not well understood" and that "scientists differ," and later, that the scientific evidence did not justify sharp cuts in emissions. The coalition dissolved in 2002 as its position became untenable, but individual members continued to lobby against any law or treaty that would reduce emissions.[17]

More recently the principal funders of the anti–climate change crowd have been Charles and David Koch, owners of Koch Industries, an oil, gas, and pipeline company thought to be the second largest privately held company in America. The Koch brothers are libertarian billionaires who have spent tens of millions of dollars to attack climate science and the politicians who urge action to deal with its consequences. Jane Mayer reports that as their fortunes grew with the company founded by their father, "Charles and David Koch became the primary underwriters of hard-line libertarian politics in America." In 1980 they arranged for David to become the Libertarian vice presidential candidate running against Ronald Reagan from the Right, because he could legally contribute millions of his own money to the campaign. The party's platform included abolition of the FBI, CIA, SEC, and the Department of Energy, and urged abolition of Social Security, minimum wage laws, and all personal and corporate income taxes.[18]

Disillusioned with conventional politics after 1980, the brothers and their family foundations poured millions into policy organizations, universities, lobbyists, and advocacy groups to spread their anti-government messages. From 2006 through 2010 Koch Industries, one of the top ten air polluters in the country, led all other energy companies in political contributions. In 1977 the Koch brothers funded the creation of the Cato Institute, the first libertarian think tank, which now has more than one hundred employees. Ed Crane, Cato's founder and president, once explained the institute's opposition to climate change, "global-warming theories give the government more control of the economy."[19] Recently, the Koch brothers sued Cato in an attempt to make it more engaged in supporting Republican Party positions. The Koch brothers may now believe that their libertarian philosophy can best be advanced through a Republican Party that is increasingly libertarian in its positions.

Crane's comments reflect the explicit connection between radical individualism and the denial of the scientific consensus about climate change. Apart from the self-interest of companies producing or using fossil fuels, the passionate resistance to government action on climate change is rooted in the quintessential American fear that collective action undermines rugged individualism in what is seen as its last bastion on earth. That worldview shapes the conclusions of the climate change deniers before they consider the science—if they ever get that far.

The Koch brothers also funded and promoted the Tea Party activists who turned August 2009 into a storm of congressional "town meetings" that led many members of Congress to give up on that means of communicating with their constituents. The Koch vehicle for inspiring and training Tea Party activists is Americans for Prosperity (AFP). Tom Phillips, its president, has tried to assume a position on climate change similar to that of Grover Norquist on tax policy. In response to a *National Journal* reporter's questions about declining Republican recognition of the threat of climate change, Phillips bragged about his group's pressure and influence: "Most of these [Republican] candidates have figured out that the science has become political, . . . if you . . . buy into green energy or you play footsie on this issue, you do so at your political peril."[20] To understand why Republicans are opposed or silent on this issue, one has to recognize the power of the Koch brothers.

In short, Tom Phillips, Frank Luntz, Charles and David Koch, and the conservative media have been able to undermine a clear scientific consensus on the greatest threat to the planet in the twenty-first century and to prevent one of the two major political parties from participating in a meaningful discussion of what to do about it. In 2009 when Sen. Lindsey Graham (R-SC) engaged in discussions about a bipartisan climate-change bill with Senators John Kerry and Joe Lieberman, Graham warned his colleagues, according to reports, that they had to move quickly "before Fox News got wind of the fact that this was a serious process" because then their coverage would "be all cap-and-tax all the time, and it's gonna become just a disaster for me on the airwaves. We have to move this along as quickly as possible."[21]

Those who deny climate change use conservative media outlets like Fox News and take advantage of the mainstream media's tendency to cover both "sides" of "political" issues, even if the basic scientific conclusions are clear. Environmental groups also raise and spend huge amounts of money to persuade the public to take action. But climate deniers, like the tobacco companies and the creationists, only need a stalemate—enough coverage and confusion to obstruct action.

The prospects for a more rational debate are not promising. The latest development is the emerging attacks on teaching climate science in the classroom, following the pattern of Christian fundamentalist attacks on evolution. Texas and Louisiana now require that denial of climate change be taught in science classrooms and two other states (Tennessee and Oklahoma) have similar bills pending; Utah and South Dakota legislatures passed resolutions denying climate change.[22] In all likelihood the debate over climate change will intensify whenever concrete proposals to contain its effects are brought to the floors of the House and Senate, which may be a year or many years away.

A Democrat urging action to combat the growing threat of climate change and a Republican who denies the existence of the threat are not speaking the same language about the same subject. When members of the press and public urge them to "compromise their differences," they have no common language or understanding to do that. Their incompatible worldviews, of which their opinions on these subjects are only a part, make compromise impossible.

For Democrats who take climate science seriously it is hard to conclude that Republican skepticism is honest. Denial of the scientific consensus does not appear to be another case of genuine disagreement; it looks and feels to be a product of intentional distortion or willful ignorance. That's why, when added to our divergent positions taken on taxes, health care, and Iraq, it contributes to the breakdown of trust between the two parties and the capacity of Congress to address current challenges.

Republicans who care about environmental issues are muzzled by their leadership and outside conservative media and financial enforcers. Mitt Romney, former governor of Massachusetts (one of the nine states in the northeastern cap-and-trade market for carbon dioxide), is intelligent enough to understand the science but cannot discuss it as the Republican nominee for president. Conservative groups concerned about the environment are seeking ways to engage more Republicans as active supporters of action. Even some evangelical leaders have argued that responsible stewardship of the earth is closer to what God expects of human beings than our dominion and exploitation of the earth. Yet the conservative campaign to undermine climate science because it conflicts with orthodox hostility to government has been largely successful. As shown by the polling data discussed later, conservative Americans are more skeptical of the science and more opposed to government action than they were a decade or two ago.

Most members of the public have heard little about the effect of carbon emissions on the chemistry of the ocean and the risks it poses to the sustenance and livelihoods of hundreds of millions of people around the globe. Yet the impacts on some coastal fisheries, especially in the Northwest, provide some reason to believe that this aspect of our rapidly changing planet can be thoughtfully addressed by Americans and our governments.

ACCELERATING ACIDIFICATION OF THE OCEAN

The ocean that covers 70 percent of the globe is the earth's life-support system. It is the primary driver of our weather and climate, and through evaporation and rainfall the source of most of our clean water. The plankton (microscopic plants) that live in the ocean are responsible for almost one-half of the oxygen we breathe. Despite the vast size of the ocean, human activity is rapidly changing the ocean's chemistry. Since the Industrial Revolution the ocean has absorbed about one-third of carbon emissions from burning fossil fuels and from deforestation. Because the ocean converts carbon dioxide to carbonic acid, seawater acidity has increased by about 30 percent in the last two hundred years. Samples from glacial ice and ocean sediment indicate this rapid rate of change is virtually unprecedented in the last three hundred million years; the only comparable period (fifty-six million years ago) involved a massive extinction of microorganisms at the bottom of the food chain—and undoubtedly higher forms of life as well.[23] Studies in the Pacific have shown that the steady increase in ocean acidity tracks the similar increase in carbon concentrations in the atmosphere, as shown in figure 5.1.

Without conscious design, the burning of fossil fuels by human beings and the absorption of carbon dioxide emissions by the ocean constitutes the world's largest chemistry experiment—conducted in the ocean for the past two centuries. In a few decades ocean acidification could disrupt the planet's food chain at the bottom by destroying coral reefs, phytoplankton, and other tiny organisms, which have evolved over millions of years in an ocean with stable chemistry. Today 90 percent of the world's coral reefs are at risk, and the consequences for ocean health are alarming.

Ocean acidification is already having a measurable impact on oyster farmers in Oregon and Washington. In 2007 at the Whiskey Creek Shellfish Hatchery in Oregon, batch after batch of oyster larvae were dying in the tanks where they began their lives. The same was happening at Taylor's Shellfish, the largest oyster grower in the United States, at their facilities near Seattle. West Coast growers of oysters, clams, and mussels have come to rely on hatcheries to provide larvae because natural reproduction is declining. Testing at Whiskey Creek revealed that ocean acidification was causing the larval die-offs. Upwellings of deep, more acidic ocean water drawn into the hatchery's larval tanks was threatening an important part of the Oregon/Washington economy. Hatchery owners now know they must monitor the acidity of ocean water near their facilities—and treat the water when it becomes dangerous. But that's only a temporary response to the rapidly changing chemistry of the ocean. With support from NOAA, Washington and Oregon are beginning to address local "exacerbators" of ocean acidification, such as storm water and runoff, but global carbon emissions have primed the ocean for rapid acidification for decades to come.[24] In the Northeast, upwellings are one cause of near-shore acidification, but the growth and decomposition of plankton and seaweed are bigger factors there than in Oregon and Washington.

The House Oceans Caucus that Curt Weldon, Jim Greenwood, Sam Farr, and I had created in 1999 drew ideas for legislation from the recommendations of two prominent national commissions. The Pew Oceans Commission issued its final report in June 2003; it concluded that "more than 60 percent of America's coastal rivers and bays are degraded by nutrient runoff. Crucial species like groundfish and salmon are under assault from overfishing. Invasive species are establishing themselves in the nation's coastal waters."[25] The U.S. Commission on Ocean Policy, funded by Congress, issued its report and recommendations in September 2004.[26]

Both reports dealt comprehensively with oceans issues. Acidification was one. I wrote a bill, often cited as FOARAM (Federal Ocean Acidification Research and Monitoring), that established the nation's first program to improve our understanding of what ocean acidification means to our fisheries and coastal communities.

Although members of the caucus built some bipartisan support for several bills, the Republican House leadership was resistant to new money and new programs. At the end of the session in 2006, we secured productive changes in the principal federal statutes regulating the fishing industry in the Magnuson-Stevens Act. However, progress was limited until after the 2008 election.

President Obama incorporated the ocean observing bill and the acidification research bill into larger legislation passed in March 2009. On July 19, 2010, the president issued an executive order creating a National Policy for Stewardship of the Ocean, Coasts, and Great Lakes, and a National Ocean Council to coordinate the policy across agencies. The executive order adopts a flexible framework for effective coastal and marine spatial planning to address conservation, economic activity, user conflict, and sustainable use of the ocean, our coasts, and the Great Lakes. I believe that these ocean policies could have been bipartisan but for the Republican resistance to any "new spending" or "new programs." It is another measure of congressional dysfunction that the National Oceans Policy had to be implemented by an executive order; who knows how long it would have taken Congress to act.

Ocean acidification can be dismissed by conservatives for the same reason as global warming—their distaste for proposed remedies—or for any remedy. For example, consider the House floor debate held on June 9, 2010, on H.R. 989, a resolution sponsored by Jay Inslee (D-WA):

> Expressing the sense of the House of Representatives that the United States should adopt national policies and pursue international agreements to prevent ocean acidification, to study the impacts of ocean acidification, and to address the effects of ocean acidification on marine ecosystems and coastal economies.

A House resolution does not have the effect of law and, in any event, H.R. 989 did not specify any "national policies" that Congress might later adopt to address ocean acidification. The Republicans opposed acknowledging the problem because they opposed a cap-and-trade system to reduce carbon dioxide emissions. Here is Jason Chaffetz (R-UT) for the majority Republicans:

> I do find that this House resolution is ambiguous when it talks about adopting national policies, which I think is a thinly veiled attempt to say that we should be adopting the cap-and-trade bill.

And later:

> But, Mr. Speaker, when it says in the very first sentence that the United States should adopt national policies, in my mind, Mr. Speaker, this is clearly an attempt to try to say that we should be passing the cap-and-trade bill, which I am totally opposed to.

Inslee argued that the resolution only acknowledged the problem and did not propose any specific remedy. But the two-thirds majority of the House required for such a resolution could not be secured because of Republican opposition. In its effect this debate on the House floor was inconsequential, but the language of the opponents speaks volumes about our dysfunctional Congress. Most House Republicans cannot and do not acknowledge the existence of a looming environmental crisis for fear they might then have to do something about it.

The scientific consensus is that climate change will disrupt our way of life, increase the number of weather-related disasters, make fresh water a scarcer commodity, and lead in time to relocation of populations worldwide. Ocean acidification, caused by higher levels of atmospheric carbon dioxide, threatens the food chain that sustains much of life on earth. Those threats require collective action on a scale to which we have been unaccustomed since World War II. We need strong political leadership because climate transcends jurisdictional boundaries, and private enterprise is part of the problem—although it could be part of the solution.

Believers in "smaller government, lower taxes" have no corollary principle to provide guidance on coping with climate change. If efficiency were a complementary conservative value, then Republicans could follow the many economists who argue that taxation of carbon emissions is the most efficient way to reduce them. Higher fuel taxes would make vehicles with higher gas mileage more attractive, and an assessment on power plant emissions would stimulate development and use of new control technology. But Republicans are so opposed to *any* tax increase that "cap and tax" rhetoric is their favored message to undermine cap-and-trade legislation.

As the science has become more established and more alarming, the Kochs and others have stepped up their disinformation campaign. Climate change can only be addressed on a bipartisan basis in Congress, and that cannot happen without Republicans who acknowledge the science. At the moment, the most prosperous nation on earth is crippled in addressing its greatest long-term challenge by our widespread hostility to government. We have in effect decided that we should let our children and grandchildren bear the cost and disruption of climate change rather than make inconvenient policy decisions to abate its effects.

PUBLIC OPINION: TRENDS AND INFLUENCES

As better information about the nature and risks of global warming has become available, public opinion has changed, but not as people might expect. Despite the greater scientific consensus, politicians and the American public are more polarized today on the subject than they were twenty years ago. Multiple surveys have been designed to determine the reasons for that polarization. The evidence suggests that the widening gap has been largely driven by members of Congress and other political elites, from which the public takes its cues. In addition, the division between those most alarmed by climate change and those most dismissive of its existence is strongly correlated with religious divisions between evangelical and fundamentalist Christians and mainline traditions. The worldviews that shape our religious differences have a similar effect on the intensifying struggle over the major energy/environmental challenge of the century.

Democratic and Republican congressional leaders work hard to coordinate their respective messages to maximize coverage on topics of particular importance to the party and the country. Speeches on the floor of the House during and after legislative sessions are organized so that several members address the same topic. Votes will be called on bills to make a political or substantive point on an issue, even if everyone knows they will never become law. Events back home will be arranged so that most House Democrats discuss health care or energy at the same time, while Republicans may try to attract attention on taxes. On the House floor I sometimes felt we were speaking into a void without being sure that anyone was listening. It turns out, though, that people were.

One recent survey confirmed that public opinion on climate change was much more polarized in 2008 than in 1997, the year the United States signed the Kyoto Protocol. For example, asked in 1997 whether global warming was occurring, 52 percent of Democrats and 48 percent of Republicans agreed that it was; eleven years later, 76 percent of Democrats agreed but only 42 percent of Republicans—an enormous thirty-four-point gap. Likewise, in response to a question of whether global warming was due mostly to human activity or natural changes, the partisan difference of seventeen points in 1997 (70 percent of Democrats and 53 percent of Republicans responding yes) grew to a difference of thirty-two points in 2008 (72 percent and 40 percent saying yes, respectively).[27]

Another study reviewed seventy-four surveys completed between 2002 and 2010 to identify the reasons for the movement in public opinion. Concern about climate change increased significantly in 2006 and 2007, and then declined. The release of Al Gore's film *An Inconvenient Truth* in May 2006, the advocacy of Sen. John McCain for legislation, and former Speaker Newt Gingrich's video with Speaker Pelosi all contributed to a lessening of partisanship. Then, at the beginning of 2008, with Democrats in control of Congress trying to move climate-change legislation,

Republican no votes increased and the partisan gap widened. In addition, unemployment increased and the economy declined, both of which drove down attention and concern about environmental issues.[28]

The authors concluded that "the most important factor in influencing public opinion on climate change . . . is the elite partisan battle over the issue."[29] Democratic statements in support of action and Republican votes against proposed bills moved their followers in the public in opposite directions. Polarized political elites sending conflicting cues to voters are likely to trump any science-based information campaign to persuade individuals of the need for action.[30] In short, politicians and their allies are successfully influencing the attitudes of the public on this issue and undoubtedly others. For better or worse, the increasing sophistication of political communication enables politicians and allied groups to shape the attitudes of their constituents and increase the polarization of the public.

That is one reason that the millions invested in Americans for Prosperity by the Koch brothers have such impact. Tom Phillips, AFP's president, corralled much of the most influential Republican political elite on climate change by his bizarre statement about buying into green energy and the "political peril" of such actions. Together, the right-wing organizations that openly fund primary challengers to Republican incumbents, especially Americans for Prosperity, Americans for Tax Reform, and the Club for Growth, are successfully enforcing ideological conformity on Republican members of Congress. Money matters in myriad ways.

A deeper analysis of the contrasting worldviews of voters with respect to climate change can be found in the ongoing work of Edward Maibach and colleagues at Yale and George Mason University. In 2009 they conducted an "audience segmentation analysis" that identified—and then studied—six groups of Americans who differ in their beliefs about climate change, their level of engagement with the issue, their actions, and the governmental policies they support. The authors describe the six groups as follows:

These six audience segments describe a spectrum of concern and action about global warming, ranging from the Alarmed (18 percent of the population), to the Concerned (33 percent), Cautious (19 percent), Disengaged (12 percent), Doubtful (11 percent) and Dismissive (7 percent).

The Alarmed have the highest belief in global warming and are the most concerned and most motivated. On the other end of the scale, the Dismissive have the lowest belief and are least motivated and least concerned about [climate change], but almost as engaged in opposition as the Alarmed are in support of action to deal with it.[31]

There is certainty at both ends of the spectrum. Asked "how much do you think global warming will harm future generations of people," 91 percent of the Alarmed say "a great deal" and 90 percent of the Dismissive say "not at all." Even 68 percent of the Concerned chose "a great deal" in answer to the question.[32]

The six groups differed markedly in party affiliation. The Alarmed are 58 percent Democrats, 24 percent Independents, and 9 percent Republicans. The party identification of the Concerned is 47 percent, 23 percent, and 19 percent, respectively. At the other end of the spectrum, the Doubtful are 9 percent Democrats, 24 percent Independents, and 56 percent Republicans; the Dismissive are 3 percent, 19 percent, and 64 percent, respectively.

It is not surprising that the Dismissive score highest of the six groups in individualistic values (accepting wealth inequality and opposing government regulation/interference) and lowest in egalitarian values (wealth should be divided more equally and discrimination against minorities is a serious problem). For example, 70 percent of the Dismissive oppose government programs to get rid of poverty. The Doubtful and Dismissive are the least likely to trust scientists and the mainstream media, and the most distrustful of government. In short, on this issue the abiding tension between individualism and community has split the most engaged and active Americans into adversarial groups with little understanding of each other.

There is a striking correlation between views on climate change and fundamentalist religious beliefs. Less than one-quarter (23 percent) of the Dismissive believe in human evolution compared to 47 percent nationally.

Almost two-thirds believe the world was created in six days (62 percent), compared to 54 percent nationally. Skepticism and lack of concern about climate change are much more prevalent among people who say that they are "born again" or evangelical. About 50 percent of the Dismissive describe themselves as born again or evangelical, in contrast to about 15 percent of the Alarmed (see figure 5.2). Many of those who take their religious doctrine most literally are also likely to deny the scientific consensus on climate change, presumably because it does not fit their worldview.

Despite the differences in beliefs between the Alarmed and the Dismissive, they are the two groups with the greatest civic engagement. Moreover, they are most likely to say they are well informed about climate change and the least likely to say they could change their views.[33]

Figure 5.3 is a picture of polarization in America. More than conventional polls, Maibach's audience segmentation analysis on climate change explains why Americans feel we are divided into warring political camps. The Alarmed were 18 percent of the population at the time of this survey;

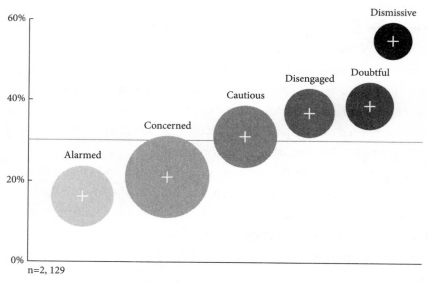

Figure 5.2 Views on Climate Change of Fundamentalist Christians.
SOURCE: E. Maibach, C. Roser-Renouf, and A. Leiserowitz, "Global Warming's Six Americas 2009: An Audience Segmentation Analysis" (Fairfax, VA: George Mason University Center for Climate Change Communication, 2009).

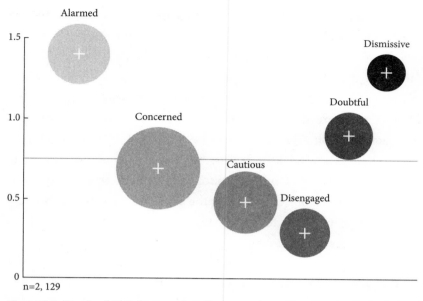

Figure 5.3 Levels of Civic Engagement. Participants were asked, "Which of the following have you done in the past 12 months?": Written or called any politician at the state, local, or national level; attended a political rally or speech or organized protest of any kind; attended a public meeting on town or school affairs; held or run for political office; served on a committee of a local organization; served as an office of a local club or organization; written a letter to the editor of a newspaper or magazine or called a live radio or TV show to express an opinion; written an article for a magazine or newspaper; worked for a political party; made a speech; been an active member of any group that tries to influence public policy or government.

SOURCE: E. Maibach, C. Roser-Renouf, and A. Leiserowitz, "Global Warming's Six Americas 2009: An Audience Segmentation Analysis" (Fairfax, VA: George Mason University Center for Climate Change Communication, 2009).

the Doubtful and Dismissive at the other end of the spectrum were another 18 percent. One pole is mostly Democrats; the other mostly Republicans. The Democrats are more communitarian in their outlook; the Republicans more individualistic. Both are more active in civic affairs than people in the middle. Both are also more certain of their opinions. Few of the Alarmed are fundamentalist or evangelical; most of the Dismissive are. The Alarmed on one side and the Doubtful/Dismissive on the other are not debating the science of climate change but are struggling with emotionally laden worldviews that shape our respective rights and responsibilities for each other.[34]

Recent research confirms that Americans, despite our general respect for science, are divided on climate change not by our level of scientific literacy. Instead, people with "hierarchical, individualistic" worldviews tend to be skeptical of environmental risks, while people with "egalitarian, communitarian" perspectives take them more seriously. These cultural worldviews are more significant than our understanding of climate science. In fact, hierarchical individualists become more skeptical of climate change as their knowledge increases, because they are more facile in explaining away empirical evidence about the climate. Improving scientific communication alone cannot close the gap in understanding, because "to avoid dissonance and to secure their group standing, individuals unconsciously seek out and credit information" that supports the worldviews that they share with those around them.[35] Climate science has acquired all the emotional and ideological baggage of "social issues."

Yet there is a big difference between the Alarmed and the Dismissive of the Six Americas, between individualists and communitarians. The views of the Alarmed/communitarians are supported, and the views of the Dismissive/individualists are contradicted, by an overwhelming number of peer-reviewed climate studies and by eleven national academies of science. If scientific truth means anything, the people worried about climate change are right and those who dismiss the scientific consensus are wrong. The scientific evidence, leaving aside our competing worldviews, calls for action on our part to address it. But that appears to be precisely why so many Republicans and their congressional representatives deny the science; for them admission would mean accepting an intolerable level of governmental regulation to contain the damage from a warming planet.

Members of Congress do not often dwell publicly on the frustrations of the job, especially those arising from the inability to have meaningful conversations with colleagues across the aisle. With four years of distance from that experience, it is easier now for me to acknowledge the conservative worldview that shapes the Republican positions on the budget, taxes, health care, and the invasion of Iraq. I also understand why many Americans fear the likely responses to climate change more than the risk to life on earth. Given the scientific information available to congressmen, the Republican caucus, in my opinion, understands the expert consensus but has adopted for political purposes a stance of denial or willful ignorance about our most difficult global challenge. Indeed, they can avoid discussing the science with *National Journal* reporters, but willful ignorance is still a basic dereliction of duty.

There is no greater long-term threat to life on earth than climate change, yet the American political system appears incapable of addressing it with the speed and on the scale it requires. The price of dysfunction on this matter is tragic; while the projected trends are alarming, we should be excited by the prospect of green technologies and services being the next big thing to lift our economy. Wind, solar, and tidal energy, more efficient batteries, improved emissions technologies, energy savings services, and more all provide opportunities for economic growth.

The Danes seized the opportunity to become world leaders in the manufacture of wind turbines and have a healthy business exporting to the United States. The Germans first, and now the Chinese, subsidized the manufacture of solar panels and built leading positions in an industry that could have been ours. But money matters more than science in our political system, and American fossil-fuel industries have plenty to spend to protect their interests.

There are, of course, multiple legitimate debates to be had over the pace and consequences of global warming, the costs of responding to it, and the costs of inaction, and the array of potential policies to cope with it. Productive discussions of those details cannot occur in a Congress in which climate change has become a zero-sum standoff, where any concession by either side is considered by others on that team to be betrayal, and where one team takes the position that there is nothing to discuss.

The place where I have been in closest touch with the earth and other living things is on the nineteenth-century farm where I spent summers as a child and now many weekends as an adult. This farm provides my primary source of reflection and renewal. From the hill behind the farmhouse I can see the White Mountains of New Hampshire, and the rest of country to the west I have seen from the air. Yet I have flown over Europe, the Middle East, Africa, China, and Japan, and looked down on lands inhabited by billions of human beings whose lives are increasingly inter-connected with our own.

Although we have given its parts multiple names, we still have only one ocean and one atmosphere to sustain life on earth. Both are at risk from greenhouse gas emissions. We have a responsibility to clean up the changes we have made in order to leave our children, grandchildren, and future generations with the life opportunities that we have known. For them at least, we must bridge the gulf between our competing worldviews and find common ground to protect the air we breathe, the water we drink, the land we inhabit, and the ocean that feeds us. There is no higher priority.

The Sources of Polarization

Morality binds and blinds.

—Jonathan Haidt

Twelve years in Congress. Daily conversations with Republican members of Congress. Bipartisan trips abroad with time to talk at length. Work on legislation of mutual interest with members across the aisle that I respected and admired. But those dozen years left me alarmed and frustrated by the inability of Republicans and Democrats to comprehend each other well enough to work together on our country's major challenges. We share the same titles and vote on the same legislation, but we see the world through dramatically different lenses.

It's those lenses that interest me most. To be sure, multiple other factors feed polarization and congressional gridlock. Cable TV 24/7 news has broadened coverage, but the scramble for ratings favors short segments with guests representing both ends of the political spectrum, not the middle. These days political campaigns never end; there is little breathing space for governing without looking toward the next election. Vast sums of money and highly organized groups create pressure on elected officials not to stray from the party line. House and Senate rules can be used for partisan purposes. Redistricting every decade creates chances for parties to draw lines that favor them for years. But in my experience our greatest challenge is first to understand and then to bridge the gap between the dominant but incompatible worldviews of the two parties.

Nothing I had learned about politics before my election prepared me for the intense polarization of contemporary congressional politics. When I first went to Washington to work for Sen. Ed Muskie in 1970, Republicans and Democrats debated public issues vigorously, but there was more genuine give and take, mutual respect, and the players did not treat politics as a blood sport. Six years on the Portland City Council taught me that most local issues could be resolved without petty or partisan combat.

Dwight Eisenhower accepted the major legislation of the New Deal. John Kennedy started the legislative push for a substantial tax cut. Lyndon Johnson came from a Senate known for working across the aisle. Richard Nixon signed clean water and clean air legislation. Ronald Reagan raised taxes many times to deal with mounting deficits created by his 1981 tax cut; George H. W. Bush did the same, to resounding criticism from the Right. Bill Clinton antagonized elements of his Democratic base by supporting a balanced federal budget, free trade, and welfare reform.

George W. Bush was different. His election in 2000 was, in hindsight, stage two of the Gingrich revolution. Senator Lincoln Chafee (R-RI) recalled, shortly after Bush's election, that Dick Cheney quickly laid out to a small group of moderate Senate Republicans, "a shockingly divisive political agenda for the new Bush administration, glossing over nearly every pledge the Republican ticket had made to the American voter."[1] In his first term, President Bush abandoned international treaties, invaded Afghanistan and Iraq, and drove through two massive tax cuts that primarily benefitted wealthy Americans.

Bush's 2004 reelection campaign employed "microtargeting" as a part of their successful strategy of mobilizing the Republican base instead of reaching out to the middle.[2] That political strategy was consistent with the Bush administration's style of governing and the way Gingrich and DeLay controlled Congress: drive through the most right-wing policy that the Republican caucus could support; only move legislation that has the support of a substantial majority of the majority party; take no prisoners.

As I listened over the years to baffling arguments in committee, on the House floor, or in private conversations, I lost hope in our capacity for bipartisan agreement on our major public policy challenges. On budgets, taxes, health care, and climate change the evidence that mattered to us made no difference to our Republican colleagues. What Democrats took as well-established fact, they understood as easily dismissed opinions. When we wondered, "Do these guys believe what they say?" our answer was usually no. But if the Republicans didn't believe the things they were saying, they were extraordinarily gifted performers on the House floor.

Our debates over particular budget and tax policies, health care, global warming, or Iraq were not driven by the details of the legislation. Differences over health-care reform became more about the role of government than the critical health-care trifecta of cost, coverage, and quality. To some, President Bush's decision to invade Iraq seemed grounded in family history—the failure of his father to "take out" Saddam Hussein. In addition, Secretary Rumsfeld stripped the military leadership of much of its desired invasion force and pushed for a rapid turnover of responsibility to Iraqis because he didn't want to create a "culture of dependency" among that population.

Taxes evoke intense emotions unrelated to their economic consequences. The Republican tax cuts were less connected to an established theory of economic growth than to convictions that tax cuts "pay for themselves" and the government is "too big." Moreover, the proponents believed that individuals know best how to spend "their own money"— even though individuals don't generally buy fighter jets or bridges, or spend their money on pensions or health care for people they don't know.

On economic issues, most Democrats accept mainstream Keynesian analysis about the federal government's capacity to reduce the adverse effects of recessions by stimulating aggregate demand (private and public) by a combination of spending increases and tax cuts. Republicans, on the other hand, are drifting with no coherent economic theory. The scientific consensus on global warming has been denied by the Right primarily because it is "an inconvenient truth" that would require Republicans to rethink the role and responsibility of the federal government.

Again, it's not the difference of opinions across party lines that matters but the inability to understand and value what the other side is saying. The ideological gridlock that plagues our government and politics now has multiple sources and is beyond the scope of this book. However, I believe that such an inquiry should start with the changes in the nature and reliability of work, particularly for American men, over the last four decades. Those changes are undermining the ability of individuals to control their own destiny. Yet economic dislocation and fear of change seem to be reinforcing attachment to the core American value of individualism and breeding hostility to collective action.

Whatever the socio-economic factors that feed our discontent, our system of government was designed by James Madison and the founders to foster sustained deliberation by representatives of the people who would be committed to acting in the "permanent and aggregate interests of the community." Too often, the Congress in which I served responds to the short-term interests of particular industries and groups. The Senate, once recognized as the "world's greatest deliberative body," hardly warrants that title today.

In short, although other explanations for our dysfunctional polarization abound, ideas do matter, especially when bundled into disparate worldviews. They have a power of their own that profoundly affects what politicians and the public say and how we act. Despite much of the press commentary, heated political rhetoric on major issues isn't all for show, or about pandering to voters, or gaining or retaining political power, or campaign contributions. Members of Congress are, in general, not that detached or disinterested in policy issues. They care, most of them, passionately, about the outcome of a debate, although less about the details than the direction the legislation represents.

Republican and Democratic weekly caucus meetings are not open to the press or public. But the arguments about legislation and strategy inside those rooms are typically passionate, vehement debates often as contentious as what happens on the House floor. Democrats argued forcefully to persuade their colleagues to support particular policies; I know the debates were just as intense in the Republican conference.

All too often the default analysis of a politician's position, argument, or action is self-serving. If he takes a position for or against a climate change cap-and-trade approach, it is to protect his political career back home. If she attacks an opponent over policy or blocks a bill from coming to the Senate floor, it is to gain some personal advantage. The simplest analysis of an action is to attack the actor's motives. These default analyses are not always wrong, but they are too simple to be always right. Personal political motivation is always an appropriate area of inquiry, but it is not the only one.

Democrats see Republicans as inattentive to evidence and expertise, unconcerned about Americans struggling to get by, and reflexively opposed to government action to deal with our collective challenges. On the other hand, Republicans see Democrats as the party of a government that routinely infringes on personal freedom, as creators of a "culture of dependency" among people who should stand on their own, and as promoters of change from traditional values that will leave us weaker than before.

These different perspectives drive congressional debates far more than the immediate subject before the House on any given day. Above all, the abiding clash between the view of government as a vehicle for the common good and the view of government as an obstacle to progress and personal freedom sits close to the center of our ideological gridlock. That's why I believe that Congress is best characterized as a forum for interest-group politics overlaid by worldview politics, and it's the latter struggle that contributes more to the dysfunctional nature of the institution.

In Budget Committee hearings and on the House floor, Republicans constantly disparaged "government" and "spending" without reference to particular agencies or programs. Their arguments, vague to us and principled to them, were faith-based—impossible to prove or disprove with data. Why did Democratic members of Congress not accept Republican rhetoric of hostility to government and taxes as a legitimate point of view? Because Democrats believe that government is a vehicle for advancing the common good. Why do Republicans seem so contemptuous about Democratic objections to "tax cuts for the rich?" Because they believe that more money for private sector "job creators" means more jobs for everyone.

To each side the positions of the other make no sense, and therefore, cannot be honestly held: "they" are lying; "they" will say anything to gain or hold political power; "they" are undermining America's strength and prosperity.

In short, what primarily drives us apart as politicians and Americans is not petty or even personal; the positions of the other side appear so extreme, so incomprehensible that they must be resisted. Both sides are engaged in a battle over what it means to be an American and what the lives of our children and grandchildren will be like far into the future. Republicans and Democrats today have incompatible worldviews about how we should relate to other human beings, what individuals can be expected to do alone, and what we should do together.

The principal reason for our polarization is the increasing incompatibility of Democratic and Republican ideas about individualism and community. The inability to compromise is primarily driven by the growing ideological rigidity of Republicans, which has become hostile to almost any form of government action across a wide range of disparate subjects.

The sources and power of that ideological rigidity are worth further examination. The set of ideas that led American conservatives into what is essentially a libertarian camp were not much in evidence for the twenty-five years after the end of World War II. Then they grew, promoted by thinkers like F. A. Hayek, Robert Nozick, and perhaps most significantly, Ayn Rand, whose two novels about heroic individuals captivated many Americans.

A second important factor was the organization and funding by wealthy American conservatives of right-wing think tanks, university chairs, and ultimately mass media, talk radio, and Fox News. The Fox News channel has captured a significant portion of the American public with its emotional, opinionated commentary, but it is frequently judged the least accurate news channel with the least well-informed audience.

Another factor was the explicit strategy developed by Newt Gingrich when he entered the House of Representatives in 1978—a strategy designed to win power for his party by portraying Congress as a corrupt institution not to be trusted by people outside of Washington. In his first term in Congress, Gingrich participated in a program of the American Enterprise Institute tracking members of Congress over several years. He had from the beginning a fully formed strategy for winning control of the House by intensifying "public hatred of Congress" so the voters would throw out the majority Democrats.[3] It was a remarkably successful political strategy but achieved at great social cost.

THE EVOLUTION OF REPUBLICAN DOGMA

By the time I was elected to Congress, the development and dissemination of theories of radical individualism had been accelerating for almost three decades. The turmoil of the late 1960s frightened many of America's business leaders who saw an emerging younger generation with little faith in the free enterprise system. In 1971 the U.S. Chamber of Commerce circulated a five-thousand-word "manifesto" by Lewis Powell: *Confidential Memorandum: Attack on the American Free Enterprise System*. Powell, who later served on the Supreme Court from 1972 to 1987, called for "careful long-range planning, . . . [and] a scale of financing available only through joint effort."[4]

In the 1970s, right-wing philanthropists and business leaders created or expanded the Heritage Foundation, the American Enterprise Institute, the Cato Institute, and the Business Round Table. Expansion into journals, talk radio, and cable television followed to drive the message that government was always the problem and free markets the solution. Over the next three decades, public confidence in government collapsed. The repeal of the "fairness doctrine" in 1986 opened the door to the vociferous media partisanship exemplified by Fox News and much of talk radio.

The election of George W. Bush in 2000 gave the right wing of the Republican Party unprecedented access to the White House. Grover Norquist, as head of Americans for Tax Reform, the leading anti-tax group in Washington, is the author of the "Taxpayer Protection Pledge," which

Republicans sign to promise never to raise taxes in any circumstances. He organizes weekly strategy sessions of Republican activist groups every Wednesday morning, which have been called the "Grand Central Station of the conservative movement."[5] The Wednesday meetings are attended by the National Rifle Association, the National Federation of Independent Business, and a variety of other right-wing groups, each with its own agenda. The rules are that participants have to stick to the group consensus even when a particular issue has no impact on them. I remember getting faxes from business organizations on issues that had no observable connection to that group's agenda.

With George W. Bush in the White House and Karl Rove attending the Wednesday strategy sessions, Norquist became an insider, not part of the GOP fringe. Rove and Norquist were in frequent, even daily, contact. Privatizing government functions, restraining government oversight of markets, and cutting taxes were the core principles—apparently regardless of evidence of the short- or long-term consequences.

For several decades federal spending has been mostly between 18 percent and 20 percent of GDP. Yet in November 2011 Grover Norquist told Steve Kroft of the CBS program *60 Minutes* that America had functioned "for a long time and quite well" with the federal government funded at 8 percent of GDP. Kroft pointed out that the 8 percent funding was early in the twentieth century before Social Security and Medicare; he asked Norquist if he believed the government has "any obligation to the poor or the elderly or the unemployed." Norquist replied, "It should stop stepping on them, kicking them and making their lives more difficult." In other words, if you are old, poor, or unemployed, you're on your own.[6]

Since Norquist had secured pledges from all but six Republican House members, their refusal in 2011 to agree to repeal some of the Bush tax cuts was a foregone conclusion. Why did Republican candidates and congressmen put themselves in thrall to a libertarian with such extreme views? I suspect because otherwise they would be likely to lose a primary election. How can Congress have a rational debate on tax reform if one side will never consider tax increases regardless of national need or circumstances? How can the country adapt to a changing economy or to changing demographics, like the aging of the Boomer generation with its attendant increase in the cost of Medicare and Social Security?

DUELING WORLDVIEWS: INDIVIDUALISM AND COMMUNITY

The fabric of our government was woven with certain threads in mind. James Madison warned that the new government could not merely be a forum for regulated competition among private interests: "the public good, the real welfare of the great body of the people, is the supreme object to be pursued; and . . . no form of government whatever has any other value than as it may be fitted for the attainment of this object."[7] The Founders also understood that self-interest was built into human beings, and needed to be checked and balanced by the structure and processes of government.

Abraham Lincoln, the first Republican president, used a simple principle to define the appropriate scope of government, which reflected his understanding of the common good. He wrote in 1854, "The legitimate object of government is to do for a community of people whatever they need to have done but cannot do at all, or cannot so well do, for themselves, in their separate and individual capacities."[8] President Richard Nixon could be described as operating on that principle when he approved legislation creating the Environmental Protection Agency and clean water and clean air programs.

But it is not always evident what we should be expected to do on our own and what we can accomplish better together. And that is the core of Republican and Democratic differences about the role of government.

For as long as I was in Congress, rank-and-file Democrats complained about the failure of our leaders to get our message right. But enormous amounts of time, energy, talent, and resources were spent on improving our communication with the public. Republicans did the same. Their advantage was that by portraying themselves as the party of individual responsibility, they were tapping into the most powerful strain of American culture. As a progressive party determined to make government work well, Democrats had to construct arguments in America's weaker second language of shared responsibility for each other.

Any anti-government party also has a structural advantage, because it is so much easier to block new legislation or regulation than it is to work through the extensive process of consultation and collaboration to put them in place. Democrats have to build broad-based communities before they can enact an agenda of change. Moreover, compared to parliamentary systems of government, our checked-and-balanced Senate, House, and presidency create an advantage for inaction. As Thomas Mann and Norman Ornstein have so carefully documented, our constitutional structure does not work well with ideologically polarized parties.[9]

The Democratic Party today has a broader constituency than the Republican Party, demographically and ideologically. Dick Gephardt used to say with pride that House Democrats were the only caucus of the two legislative bodies that "looked like America." We had about three-fourths of the women in the House, almost all of the Hispanics, and all of the African Americans during most of my tenure. The open struggles between liberal and moderate to conservative Democrats in the House and Senate reflect the diversity of the party. The "moderate" Republicans in the House and Senate are now a very small minority with limited influence.

If all this is true, why were Republicans in control of Congress and the White House for so long, why did they wield such influence in the minority, and why have they returned to the majority in the House? Democratic members of Congress are often puzzled by the political power of Republicans, who to them seem comparatively disengaged in public issues and overly attentive to the interests of the prosperous and powerful. I believe that the political strength of the Republican Party is the public's perception that they are the more articulate champions of the "first language" of American individualism that is central to the way we define ourselves.

As Americans, we all believe in working hard, pulling ourselves up by our bootstraps, and making our own way in the world. But if we alone are responsible for our own success, we alone are responsible for our failures.

The logical corollary is that those who fail in work or some other aspect of life have only themselves to blame. They are not our responsibility. That's the dark side of this profoundly American idea; it helps rationalize public policies that leave people on their own—without health care, an adequate education, or job opportunities.

The idea (in its purest form) that we control our economic destiny seems archaic in a globalizing world in which jobs can be moved overnight not to the next town but halfway across the planet. That idea can still be a powerful motivator for hard work and individual achievement. But its impact on American society depends on whether it is balanced with broader values about our mutual responsibility for others.

The resurgence of Republicans in the 2010 congressional elections, despite Republican responsibility for the continuing economic turmoil that had led to their epic losses in 2008, demonstrates a tragic irony: individualism is a powerful political message, but dressed in libertarian clothing it is a weak foundation for coping constructively with the intertwined, complicated challenges of the twenty-first century.

In American culture and politics, the defining tension between individualism and community need not be as divisive as it has become. As individuals, most of us value both self-reliance and support given to or received from others. Often, we promote the values of self-reliance even as we act, privately or publically, to help those who are less fortunate or to find other ways to strengthen our communities.

This core tension in American life and culture was captured by recruiting advertisements of the U.S. Army and the Army National Guard. A few years ago, on television and in print their empowering slogan was "An Army of One." Young Americans were urged to be, or belong to, that "Army of One." What does that mean? Could you be part of the ultimate team and still retain your individuality?

No other institution in American life but the military requires individuals to commit to making the ultimate sacrifice for a team, a group, the nation—a cause larger than themselves. But recruiting requires persuading young people that they will be personally empowered with new talents, including leadership skills, which will allow them to stand on their own in both worlds, civilian and military. An "Army of One" suggests both the power of a unified group in pursuit of common ends and the power of the trained individual prepared to cope with any contingency. In that sense it straddles the great divide in American culture and politics.

I spoke with a number of soldiers and marines who volunteered for multiple tours in Iraq; each one said he was re-upping to be with his "buddies." The bonds of caring and love that grow among men thrown together on the front lines of combat have been frequent subjects for writers of fiction and nonfiction, most recently Karl Marlantes's novel, *Matterhorn*, a powerful portrayal of the Viet Nam conflict. And the phrase "a band of brothers" goes back to Shakespeare's account of Henry V at Agincourt in 1415.

I have sought to explain congressional polarization and gridlock by arguing that Republicans have become so preoccupied with individual liberty that they cannot understand or work productively on major issues with Democrats who remain attached both to liberty and to the idea of a community of equally valued members. There are other lenses through which to view this subject. Here are some of them.

POLITICS AND PARENTING STYLES

George Lakoff, a cognitive linguist from Berkeley, California, has studied how Americans think about politics and the significant factors that influence their choices. Lakoff began his work by being puzzled by the disconnected provisions of the 1994 "Contract with America," and also by the ways his own, precisely opposite political views seemed equally disconnected from each other.[10] In his major work on this topic, *Moral Politics*, Lakoff argues that contemporary American politics is about competing worldviews.[11] The conservative worldview is grounded in a "Strict Father model," which emphasizes respect for and obedience to authority, self-control, self-discipline, and setting and following strict guidelines and behavioral norms. The liberal worldview is built upon a "Nurturant Parent model," which emphasizes empathy for others, nurturing of social ties, and becoming self-disciplined and self-reliant by being cared for and respected. He concludes that liberals naturally gravitate to the belief that government should help people, and conservatives lean toward the idea that government should require people to be self-sufficient.[12]

Lakoff also observes that although Strict Father morality and conservative politics are common in Europe and Asia, they do not include the uniquely American "resentment toward government that often borders on, or extends to, hatred."[13] That hostility has poisoned our politics and crippled pragmatic discussion of the appropriate purposes and priorities of government. Still, the conservative and liberal systems of morality that Lakoff describes help explain the partisan disagreement across many major issues. Studies have shown a clear correlation between traditional parenting practices—the "spare the rod, spoil the child" approach—and voting for President Bush in 2004. The states with citizens least likely to endorse spanking children, Massachusetts, Vermont, Rhode Island, and New York, voted heavily for Kerry.[14]

A Strict Father worldview seems evident in Donald Rumsfeld's stripped-down invasion force and plans for a rapid withdrawal from Iraq to avoid a "culture of dependency" by leaving the Iraqis on their own. Senator John Kyl's remark to Senator Hagel that the United States needed to "show these countries . . . that they cannot have these weapons [of mass destruction]" also reflects the conservative system of morality that Lakoff describes.

If Lakoff is right that Republican political ideas are woven together in a cognitive structure significantly different from Democratic ideas, and both are internally linked by different concepts of child-rearing, what should we do? Is change possible? Or are we locked in to different worldviews so deeply rooted that they are almost impossible to change?

POLITICS AND AUTHORITARIANISM

Similar questions are raised by other studies of political polarization among the American people and in Congress. Have our politics become so dependent on fundamentally different attitudes or world views that recovery of a more reasoned, pragmatic approach to public issues is beyond reach?

A study of the American electorate, *Authoritarianism and Polarization in American Politics* (2009) by Marc Hetherington and Jonathan Weiler, sheds new light on political views that are heavily influenced by whether people are more or less authoritarian. Those testing high in authoritarianism have a greater need for order and less tolerance for confusion or ambiguity than those scoring low on that scale. In addition, the more authoritarian tend to see the world in "black and white" while the less authoritarian are more comfortable with "shades of gray." The belief that "there is a right way and a wrong way to do almost everything" may lie, they argue, at the heart of the difference between authoritarians—who generally agree—and non-authoritarians—who don't.[15]

Authoritarianism can be viewed as a personality trait, an attitude, or an ideology, which forms the basis of "a set of beliefs and ideals that a person uses as a guide to interpret the world."[16] I am convinced that congressional debates on major issues are profoundly affected by the incompatible worldviews of the two parties. When my Republican colleagues argued and appeared to believe that tax cuts pay for themselves or that climate science is not proven, I was fairly sure that their convictions grew from something deeper than the writings of a rogue economist or scientist. The conservative worldview about government and personal freedom seemed far more important.

On issues that are "structured by" authoritarianism, people's opinions are correlated significantly with how they score on a scale of more to less authoritarian. Examples of such issues include (1) racial and ethnic differences; (2) crime, law and order, and civil liberties; (3) ERA/feminism/family structure; and (4) militarism vs. diplomacy. On these issues authoritarians and their opposites tend to have markedly different views. On others, like economic, health care, and environmental issues, the differences are not as wide and therefore not "structured by" authoritarianism.

Some groups of Americans test higher on a scale of authoritarianism than others; for example, evangelical Protestants test higher than other religious groups, southerners higher than those outside the South, and rural and less educated voters higher than urban and better educated people. Hetherington and Weiler conclude that polarization on issues structured by authoritarianism has become more pronounced over time because of choices made by Republican leaders to focus on those issues by emphasizing hot-button topics like immigration, the war on terror, and gay rights.[17]

Hetherington and Weiler make a convincing case that the American electorate has recently "sorted" itself into the two major parties based on cognitive styles reflecting greater or lesser authoritarian tendencies. They attribute that sorting process to the high profile or saliency of issues that are structured by authoritarianism. In the first three decades after World War II both parties were more diverse; conservative southern Democrats held powerful positions in Congress, and liberal Republicans from the Northeast were significant players as well. Today the regional decline of both groups has produced congressional parties more internally unified and more divided from each other on policy and worldview.

There remain two types of questions their research was not designed to address. First, why are members of Congress so much more polarized than the electorate? Republican congressmen do not share all of the characteristics of the typical citizen who tests high for authoritarianism. Given their relatively high educational backgrounds, congressmen should tend to be less authoritarian than the Republican electorate. On the other hand, since members on both sides of the aisle are expected to reflect the interests and perspectives of their constituents, perhaps congressional polarization flows naturally from the role of the representative. But is that enough to lead them to advocate positions for which evidence is slim to nonexistent?

Second, why are members of Congress, and much of the public, now so polarized over issues that are not structured by authoritarianism? Unlike the use of military force, traditional conservative preferences for the status quo, free markets, and smaller government are *not* structured by authoritarianism.[18] Why then are the parties so bitterly divided over the budget and taxes, health care, and climate change? How did the bill to increase the debt ceiling in 2011 bring the global economy to the brink of disaster over a vote routinely approved in the past, and over budget issues that used to be much easier to compromise? Why do Republican candidates for the presidency or the Senate in 2010 and 2012 apparently have to deny the human contribution to climate change to be competitive?

In addition, why is hostility, even hatred of government, more prevalent in the United States than in European and Asian democracies? Immigration to Europe from Islamic countries, an issue certain to be structured by authoritarianism, has given rise to right-wing anti-immigrant parties in those countries, but the anger on the right in America against government and taxes is much stronger than in Europe.

Part of the answer to these questions, I believe, is rooted in what Hetherington and Weiler set aside—the "issues" and "ideology" not seen to be structured by authoritarianism. In Congress, after listening to what is said and even not said clearly, I find it hard to overstate the influence of worldviews grounded in individualism and community. If taxes diminish human freedom and "new programs" mean added tyranny, then virtually all taxes and spending must be resisted. All issues become one. The conservative description of that issue, the "role of government," is too dry to evoke much passion unless the underlying struggle has profound emotional consequences. It does. We Americans have valued our independence, promoted self-reliance, and feared dependency for so long that change not of our making threatens our identity and well-being.

I find it hard to believe that the rigidity of the conservative worldview is not directly connected to the stagnation of the middle class over the past thirty years and the diminished economic opportunity this has meant for millions of Americans. When threatened, for example, in the aftermath of 9/11, non-authoritarians adopt more authoritarian attitudes. To the extent that includes a more black-and-white view of the world and less need for evidence, it plays into the conservative agenda. Thus, the economic quagmire for the middle class seems likely to have bred similar feelings of threat, frustration, and disillusionment.

Debates over budgets and taxes now have the same intensity as battles over abortion and gay marriage. Budget and tax debates are basically about what we should do together and what individuals should do for themselves. Health care in America triggers the same conflict over our mutual responsibilities. Climate-change issues raise uncomfortable questions about our responsibilities to future generations—a me vs. we conflict across decades and centuries. Even Iraq was, in the end, about forcing our will on that country and our allies, instead of continuing the less satisfying process of containment.

It wasn't just the Budget Committee that made me think I was working in "Wonderland." Across a wide spectrum of issues, the beginning of the chain of political reasoning for congressional Republicans was a worldview—individualism—that in America has become imbued with hostility to government, indifference to evidence, and rejection of mainstream economics and science. Those aspects of political individualism in its current form make its proponents appear to be engaged in "faith-based" (although not religious) political arguments.

The U.S. House of Representatives is the oldest directly elected legislative body in the history of the world. To those who are not devotees of Ayn Rand, it is bizarre and disheartening to hear America's democratic system of government attacked as if it were the seat of tyranny and as if taxes for public purposes were a crushing burden to individual advancement.

HEDGEHOGS AND FOXES

Another perspective on polarization is found in the work of the British philosopher Isaiah Berlin. In 1953 he wrote a short, influential book, *The Hedgehog and the Fox: An Essay on Tolstoy's View of History*. The title, he explained, was taken from a fragment of the Greek poet Archilochus: "The fox knows many things, but the hedgehog knows one big thing."

Whatever the meaning intended by Archilochus, Berlin used it as a metaphor to "mark one of the deepest differences which divide writers and thinkers, and, it may be, human beings in general." He argued:

[T]here exists a great chasm between those, on one side, who relate everything to a single central vision, one system less or more coherent or articulate, in terms of which they understand, think and feel . . . and . . . those who pursue many ends, often unrelated and even contradictory, connected, if at all, only in some *de facto* way, for some psychological or physiological cause, related by no [single] moral or aesthetic principle.[19]

Berlin concluded that Tolstoy was "by nature a fox, but believed in being a hedgehog." In other words, the greatest of Russian authors "saw the manifold objects and situations on earth in their full multiplicity . . . [but] longed for a universal explanatory principle."[20]

In the 1950s Berlin was writing in the shadow of the most destructive, all-encompassing ideologies of the twentieth century, Communism and Fascism. Clearly, the need for "a single central vision" is not characteristic of only the right or the left of the political spectrum.[21]

Today, however, nothing on the left in American politics comes close to a single unifying vision of the relation between people and our government. The guiding principle is closer to "whatever works" than "the government is right." Republican commentators sometimes argue that the goal of Democrats is to increase the power of government, but that thinking comes from the Republicans' own fixation on the subject. In fact, the obvious divisions among Democrats—even when they control the White House, Senate, and House of Representatives—make governing on major issues remarkably difficult.

The "single central vision" of Republicans at its core is about personal freedom, faith in free markets, and hostility to government action; therefore, government must be "smaller" and taxes "lower." That's it. A simple agenda uncomplicated by the multiple, often contradictory needs and desires of the people we represent. In the real world, most of our citizens certainly want lower taxes, but they also want good schools for their kids, clean air and water, affordable health care, Social Security, safe streets, solid infrastructure, fire protection, an effective national defense—and none of these and other governmental benefits are free.

PUTTING IT ALL TOGETHER

When focused solely on cognitive styles that contribute to political polarization, we see that competing worldviews can be described as related to different parenting styles (Lakoff), authoritarian and non-authoritarian characteristics (Hetherington and Weiler), or "hedgehogs and foxes" (Berlin). There is no need to sort out the differences, because each analysis in its own way suggests that our worldviews tend to shape our political philosophy and our positions on specific issues. In short, worldviews are near the beginning of the causal chain of our political reasoning. Politics, both on the surface and at its core, is about ideas and values in competition with each other. Yet those ideas and values are not easily covered by the media nor even discernible much of the time.

Again, the dominant Republican worldview has become defined by a radical individualism that is locked in place by a "single central vision" that includes hostility to government itself as a first principle. "Smaller government, lower taxes" is a succinct summary of the agenda. America's characteristic faith in self-reliance, the "first language" with we describe and understand our world, has been fiercely promoted to advance business interests in less government regulation, and by tactics and messages that have undermined the trust of the American people in their government. The irony is that a weaker government has, in reality, less capacity to provide a bulwark against economic downturns and less ability to provide the investment in human and physical infrastructure on which the private sector depends.

The dominant Democratic worldview is less clear because it values both self-reliance and working together, and assumes that collective action through governments can create opportunity and serve the common good. For me the definitive Democratic slogan was "Opportunity, Responsibility, Community" during the 1992 Clinton presidential campaign, but it leaves more blanks to be filled in than the perennial Republican counterpart. Those who want to make government work have the challenge of building broad coalitions for change in order to overcome the inherent inertia of the status quo. Community is both a value and an organizing necessity. Personal liberty in this view is intertwined with equality and justice.

Mitch Daniels, governor of Indiana and recognized budget guru, told David Leonhardt of the *New York Times* in January 2011, "I believe that there's a zero-sum relationship between government growth and freedom. . . . I think that the promotion and protection of liberty is the center of our project in this country." When Leonhardt demurred, Daniels said, "It's too broad a statement, I guess," adding that he said it without thinking it through. But Daniels then said, "Each time we take a tax dollar from a free citizen, we do diminish their freedom."[22] Daniels at the time may have been trying out rhetoric for a Republican presidential run, but his statement embodied the ideology stripped to its essentials: personal freedom is the primary object of American democracy and taxes always diminish individual freedom.

To many Democrats, the Republican Party seems to have become, in all but name, a libertarian party on the fringe of the American experience, a party hostile to the very idea of governing for the common good. In other words, government is placed in a box where the idea of human beings as social animals working, playing, and loving each other simply doesn't apply. Inside that box with its shriveled role for public leadership, there is no principled obstacle to using government to take care of your friends and contributors.

Democratic members of Congress also belong to a flawed party, but we do not have the ideological cohesion of the Republican Party today. During my years in Congress, activists on the Democratic left were most passionate about three particular policies: cutting off funding for the war in Iraq, enacting single-payer health care, and impeaching President Bush. None of those policies was ever adopted by a majority of Democrats in Congress or by our leadership. Moreover, those policies were not connected in the way that the "smaller government, lower taxes" mantra covers a broad range of issues for Republicans.

Democrats have, of course, contributed to the polarization and dysfunctional nature of the Congress. Like Republicans, we have used the procedures of the House at times to stifle the opinions of the minority. We too can be wary of needed financial reforms of key government insurance programs like Medicare and Social Security. Political campaigns by Democrats look a lot like Republican campaigns in the way the other side is portrayed. We have been resistant to reform that might adversely affect our core constituencies. Yet I don't believe that the back-and-forth procedural and political offenses that each side commits against the other are, in fact, important determinants of our polarization. Our competing worldviews are far more significant.

DIVERGENT MORAL MATRICES

Those worldviews have a moral component. In his recent book *The Righteous Mind: Why Good People Are Divided by Politics and Religion,* the moral psychologist Jonathan Haidt analyses the different "moral matrices" of American liberals, social conservatives, and libertarians. Haidt's research into group psychology led him to a "moral foundations" theory that highlights the variation in moral views by culture and economic class. The six core values (and their opposites) are care (harm), liberty (oppression), fairness (cheating), loyalty (betrayal), authority (subversion), and sanctity (degradation).[23] American liberals value care, liberty, and fairness in that order, but they lack strong attachment to the values of loyalty, authority, and sanctity. As an example, their comparative lack of attachment to sacred symbols is one reason why the Constitution and the American flag have more *symbolic* significance for conservatives than liberals.

Social conservatives (for Haidt, they are not identical to the Christian Right) in America respond to all six core values more or less equally. They are primarily attracted to the idea of preserving the institutions and traditions that sustain a moral community, whereas liberals are more open to change. Because liberals value care and compassion for the oppressed more than conservatives do, they are likely to conclude—incorrectly—that conservatives do not care at all about other people.[24] American libertarians, like liberals, score very low on valuing loyalty, authority, and sanctity but also rank lower than conservatives on care for others. Personal liberty and faith in free markets are by far their dominant values.

Despite the attention of the media for several decades to the Christian Right or "social conservatives," I am convinced that the Republican Party, both in Congress and among the population, has been evolving toward more rigid libertarianism—in the sense that personal liberty and free markets have become the dominant component of their political value system. Their intensifying hostility toward government action has pushed them to deny clear and compelling evidence rather than concede a role for government. In short, as Haidt observes, human beings are "deeply intuitive creatures whose gut feelings drive our strategic reasoning," which makes it "difficult—but not impossible—to connect with those who live in other [moral] matrices."[25]

The competing worldviews in American politics, whatever mix of personality type, attitude, ideology, or moral framework they may be, are shared by the voters and their representatives. Congress is more polarized than the public, but people are increasingly sorting themselves into the party that fits their worldview and less to the party that seeks to protect their economic interests.

Differences between worldviews, being much more deeply rooted, are more difficult to compromise than differences in economic interests. In fact, the notion of compromise seems hard to apply to competing worldviews. At least two factors are reinforcing the sorting of the electorate into competing camps. The first is media coverage of politics; the second is the increasing sophistication of candidates, pollsters, and media consultants in appealing to the emotions and attitudes of the public.

We will never return to the days when the evening news was considered a loss leader and a public contribution by the national networks. Today, though, 24/7 cable news coverage produces intense competition for audiences and ratings. Conflict and controversy sells. In general, short segments hold people better than longer interviews. Politicians and other guests learn that sound bites and a few short sentences fit the medium; nothing complicated can be covered in a matter of a couple of minutes. All of these factors mean that opinion is stronger than evidence, emotion more effective than reasoning, and clarity more easily absorbed than complexity. The result, on the whole, reinforces the differences between the parties and obscures opportunities for constructive dialogue.

After more than a decade with effective pollsters and media consultants, I am amazed by the sophistication of political advertising now produced for candidates and outside interest groups. Polling, focus groups, dial testing to get audience reactions to planned political ads, and a host of other techniques are used to fine-tune candidate messages and advertisements for maximum impact. Thirty-second ads are designed more to move voters than to inform them—which cannot be done easily in that time frame. Effective ads tap into the public's predispositions in order to move people toward or away from a particular candidate. Consequently, the most powerful vehicle for communicating with the public during elections, and often between elections by interest groups, is not capable of providing detailed information, and other sources, like newspapers, journals, and campaign materials, typically reach fewer people.

The rise of a powerful partisan media is both responding to and accentuating the polarization of the American electorate. In *Echo Chamber: Rush Limbaugh and the Conservative Media Establishment*, the authors Kathleen Hall Jamieson and Joseph Cappella rely on extensive media research to argue that "Rush Limbaugh, Fox News, and the opinion pages of the *Wall Street Journal* constitute a conservative media establishment" that has taken on what used to be political party functions, including vetting Republican candidates for president.[26] These three media outlets adopt two consistent strategic frames to advance the conservative cause: first, the mainstream media is "biased" in favor of liberal positions, and second, they provide "balance" by promoting conservative positions.[27]

The audience for Limbaugh, Fox News, and the editorial pages of the *Wall Street Journal* have the demographics of the core Republican base: middle-aged white men, churchgoers, and southerners."[28] Because of the sources of its information, that audience is becoming even more hostile to Democratic positions and candidates.

For the country the more troublesome impact of the conservative echo chamber is on Republican officeholders and candidates. The three principal conservative media outlets just mentioned have combined to validate true Republican principles and candidates from those considered less pure or reliable. That media pressure to conform to party orthodoxy has been reinforced by millions of dollars raised by conservative groups to attack Republicans in primary elections. The Club for Growth, Americans for Tax Reform, Americans for Prosperity, and emerging conservative Super PACS have driven congressional Republicans to the libertarian cause by openly opposing candidates and incumbents perceived to be insufficiently true to those groups' definition of party principles.

In short, partisan conservative media and its less influential imitators on the left are inviting their audiences to see the political world in black and white, conservative and liberal, good and bad, with the result that for the public and elected officials, it is harder to find common ground.

RELIGION AND POLITICS

Religion and politics are intertwined because our values and worldviews find expression in both realms. The founders determined that America would have no state-sponsored religion and that free expression would be protected. Centuries of religious wars in Europe drove them to their conclusion. Yet many political issues have religious components, and the religious faith of presidential candidates is a common topic in their campaigns.

Religious and political groups allow us to gather with people of like mind and to remain apart from those who think differently. In both, people have combined to pursue common ends and to define themselves in opposition to others. Even our habits of mind in political and spiritual matters can be aligned.

The major Abrahamic religions, Judaism, Christianity, and Islam, all include subgroups with diverse beliefs, rituals, and outlooks. In each group, some followers take the faith's central documents more literally than others. The result is a remarkable diversity of practices and understanding of what it means to be a member of a particular faith. The historian of religion Elaine Pagels has written about the difference among Christians between those for whom belief in the divinity of Jesus is the heart of the faith and those for whom what matters is the idea that "God's light shines not only in Jesus but, potentially at least, in everyone."[29] She suggests that the first idea makes it easier to create a church by gathering the like-minded together, while the latter does not. Yet the latter idea, that we are all God's children, whatever our conception of God, can help us treasure our common humanity rather than be alarmed by our differences and fear of "the other."

We build our churches in politics too, as the political parties and their multiple subgroups create a sense of common purpose among an in-group and differentiation from others outside it. On the left and the right I have seen firm adherence to doctrine or a set of convictions help build a committed group of the like-minded. But sometimes the most committed find it hard to work with others of different views. We accept an enormous variety of religious beliefs and activities because we believe they are—and should be—personal choices. In a democratic society, however, fixed convictions about political doctrine can undermine the effectiveness of governmental institutions.

In *American Grace: How Religion Divides and Unites Us,* Robert Putnam and David Campbell found that the more often people attend religious services, the more generous they become, not only to their own churches but also to other charitable organizations. Yet they found little correlation between charitable behavior and religious persuasion, daily prayer, or belief in hell. The critical factor was how enmeshed people were in relationships with their co-religionists, their friendships, and group activities. Putnam and Campbell concluded, "It is religious belongingness that matters for neighborliness, not religious believing."[30]

Jonathan Haidt takes that conclusion as further evidence for his proposition that human beings are "*Homo duplex,* [w]e are selfish and we are groupish." He argues that "religion played a crucial role in our evolutionary history—our religious minds co-evolved with our religious practices to create ever-larger moral communities, particularly after the advent of agriculture."[31] Morality, he suggests, binds human beings together in groups but blinds us to the values of others. In short, our minds were designed for "groupish righteousness," and that term explains much of the tension we endure in both religion and politics.

The Bible includes both a personal gospel of salvation and a social gospel of justice. We Americans spread ourselves across that spectrum, too.

The first looks inward, and the second looks out at the wider world. Some churches tend more to turn inward to serve and protect the flock; others encourage looking outward to act in the wider world in accordance with their beliefs. But the human connections built and nourished in communities of faith are central to helping make life meaningful for millions. The social gospel of the world's great religions is not unlike the civic republicanism (the "public virtue") that the Founders considered essential to the survival of the American democratic experiment. Political philosophies that strip away any sense of our mutual responsibility for each other will erode, to the extent they are accepted, the commitment to the common good that is vital to the preservation of democracy.

Churches and synagogues of every stripe are important to the peace and health of their congregations. Miracles of personal growth do happen in their midst. A democracy, however, makes other demands. Our two big-tent political parties can govern effectively only when they are more inclusive than exclusive. That means being open to diverse members and ideas. Perhaps more important, democracy requires participants—citizens—who are open-minded enough to engage in the give-and-take debate about public policy without assuming that their position must take control.

American politics on the right, including the 2012 presidential primaries, often appears to include matters of religious faith on specific issues like abortion, gay marriage, even contraception. The unfortunate consequence is to flood the public square with more zero-sum issues that widen the space between those with competing worldviews. Part of a path to recovering a more civil dialogue is to draw more deeply on what holds us together as Americans, even when we disagree.

DANGEROUS CONVICTIONS

Our convictions and worldviews limit our imagination and ability to act. I have argued that these explicit convictions—tax cuts pay for themselves, climate science isn't proven, government-run (or regulated) health care doesn't work, we'll be welcomed as liberators—grow out of a conservative worldview, which is individualistic, hostile to government, and able to wall off inconvenient truths. Whatever their sources, these convictions are dangerous—they deny the weight of credible evidence and expertise, and produce consequences adverse to any concept of the common good.

The budget failures of President George W. Bush's administration can be explained by the unresolved contradiction between its collective faith in "smaller government, lower taxes" and the enormous financial resources required to implement its Iraq policy and to offset the Bush tax cuts (which could not, in reality, "pay for themselves"). These signature foreign and domestic policies were matters of choice made without careful consideration of their costs. Two additional challenges were, in effect, forced upon the administration: the invasion of Afghanistan and the provision of some prescription drug coverage for seniors. Yet again, the Bush administration could not escape the contradiction between its core worldview and the pragmatic financial challenges that were thrust upon it. In short, its failures reflected the inability of the conservative worldview to deal with the complexities of the issues they faced and the associated budgetary consequences. The administration's successes, particularly the surge in Iraq and the bank bailouts in late 2008, came when preconceived convictions were set aside in favor of more pragmatic and flexible policies.

The last fifteen to twenty years of American politics have been marked by ideological conflict across a broad range of issues. The budgetary and environmental differences of the 1960s, 1970s, and even the 1980s, at least in retrospect, seem qualitatively different than the pitched battles of the Bush and Obama administrations. The Bush administration and current Republican candidates for high office appear more open to aggressive use of military force in Iraq and elsewhere, consistent with a constituency increasingly attracted to more authoritarian approaches to foreign policy. Budget and tax issues, health care, and climate change seem much more connected to the growing libertarian cast of the Republican Party. In that sense, these issues are structured by the competing worldviews I have described, the central components of which are preferences for the values of individualism or community. The extent to which those worldviews have penetrated the public can be seen in the research into the work of

Edward Maibach and his cohorts' "Global Warming's Six Americas" described in chapter 5.

The urge to explain the intensifying polarization and gridlock in Congress and throughout the United States has produced much more than a cottage industry of commentary. George Lakoff, Marc Hetherington and Jonathan Weiler, and Jonathan Haidt have all painted pictures of human beings driven by worldviews who use our capacity for reason more like lawyers than scientists—making arguments to lead to preconceived results. It would be easy to resign ourselves to the belief that such deep-seated differences cannot be overcome. Nevertheless, our capacity to reason together has not been lost and indeed is most effective when groups engaged in common endeavors work to bridge their differences. The capacity of Congress to deliberate across party lines is much diminished, but we can recover part of what we have lost *if* we understand how it happened. Money and sophisticated emotion-laden media have dumbed down our politics even as our challenges have grown more complex. The worldviews that shape our politics are not so ingrained at birth that we cannot reason about them as we seek to advance our democratic experiment. Understanding the deeper sources of ideas in conflict can, I hope, help us break the gridlock that handicaps America's prospects for the future.

Finding a Path to Recovery

One cannot be pessimistic about the West. This is the native home of hope. When it fully learns that cooperation, not rugged individualism, is the quality that most characterizes and preserves it, then it will have achieved itself and outlived its origins. Then it has a chance to create a society to match its scenery.

—WALLACE STEGNER, *The Sound of Mountain Water*

"What can we do? How can we get out of this mess?" It's actually easy to be pessimistic whenever America's polarized and dysfunctional politics comes up in conversation. There are no simple answers to a complex problem, but we must develop a clearer understanding of the forces that shape our political culture and the worldviews of those with whom we disagree.

America is in trouble not simply because we are too "polarized." To define the problem as the polarization of elected officials, and indeed the electorate, implies that the answer is more "bipartisanship," vaguely understood to mean working together. The primary question is *why* we are polarized; the answer will help set a path to overcome it. During my years in Congress, most commentators barely addressed that question. If they did, most tried to deal even-handedly with both parties; in other words, blame both or blame the "system," but don't blame one more than the other and don't blame the ideas of either. Take those as given. Commentators outside the mainstream media enjoyed the freedom to express overtly partisan views, to attack one party or the other for being in the pocket of special interests, or for being dishonest, or both.

Despite the 24/7 coverage of Congress, most reporting and commentary misses the conflict in worldviews that, beneath the surface of our debates, shapes our positions and intensifies polarization. As a result, the diagnosis is often "incivility," which is a symptom—not the disease. The remedy proposed usually contrasts past and present, highlights what we have lost, and suggests that we try to recapture the past. For example, in an earlier era members of Congress tended to live in Washington with their families and socialize across party lines on evenings and weekends. The ability of President Reagan and Speaker Tip O'Neill to enjoy each other's company is often seen as an example of how to make a divided federal government work. More senior members of Congress, when retiring, often lament that those days are gone.

But we are not going back. Members are expected to spend more time talking with constituents. Their spouses and children are less willing to be uprooted from their jobs, schools, and friends to move to Washington. Although stronger personal relationships help members work together, they cannot realistically be fostered by a return to the living and commuting patterns of an earlier era. Reviving greater mutual understanding would have to be a deliberate undertaking by those willing to reach out. Members need some safe space for private conversation and reflection about life and work in Congress.

Congressional delegations (CODELS) abroad are sustained learning experiences and often bring members closer to each other, but participation has declined since the parties started attacking each other for taking "junkets" claimed to have little value. A return to more frequent CODELS would require a political truce by the party leadership. Small bipartisan retreats, on weekends for perhaps three or four times a year, could serve a similar bonding function in an institution that has lost other opportunities for connection. The Faith and Politics reflection groups, like the one I attended for years, could help members on both sides of the aisle stay in touch with the inner vision that brought them to Congress and nourish the patience required to cope with the frustrations of service. However, the fundamental challenge is to understand and overcome our incompatible worldviews.

We need not try to parse the differences among cognitive analyses focused on parenting styles, authoritarianism, or a "hedgehogs and foxes" continuum. We can acknowledge that Jonathan Haidt's "moral foundations" theory improves our understanding of how we think about religion and politics. All of these cognitive lenses highlight ways in which our broader worldviews shape our reaction to specific political and religious issues.

People will always be divided among those who largely see the world in black and white and those who see it in shades of gray. Some will believe that there is a right way and a wrong way to do most everything, and others will disagree. Both lenses have more value at some times and less at others, but we can hardly expect people to change lenses that to them seem innate and true.

On the other hand, most of us value both self-reliance and working with others. However inarticulate we may be, we speak both our first language of individualism and our second language of community. These core aspects of the American psyche—the yin and yang of what it means to be an American—have been split apart by worldview politics. We are unlikely to recover a productive balance without an honest conversation about fundamental worldviews.

I am convinced now that the ideas and worldviews on both sides are honestly held, subject to the caveat that politicians learn to blend their ideas and their political interests until they seem indistinguishable. However, since today the views of one side cannot be understood by the other, each party assumes the worst about the motives or the integrity of the other.

For most Republicans in Congress today, the federal government is believed to infringe on personal liberty, undermine America's core value of self-reliance, and to carry out most of its activities with little competence or efficiency. Therefore, government is almost always part of the problem rather than part of a solution. In that worldview, domestic problems will probably be made worse by federal action, so they should be left alone or to others; if freedom is the central element of the American experience, restraint and regulation are its opposite; if self-reliance is the primal American virtue, dependency is the principal vice.

For most Democrats in Congress today, the federal government is one means of expanding opportunity and freedom of action to those who are willing and able to work. Americans share a collective responsibility to counteract accidents of birth and give the disadvantaged a chance to get ahead. Democrats also believe governmental leadership is essential to dealing with common challenges beyond the capacity or jurisdiction of the private sector or even national governments. In short, government by the people is not in itself a threat to our personal liberty.

Given the worldview of American conservatives, their reaction to a rapidly changing, increasingly interdependent world should be understandable. The American economy is more dependent on the health of other countries, our citizens have less economic security, and the federal government has broader responsibilities. There is and always will be an essential place in American politics for a conservative, pro-business, anti-regulation political party—unless in pursuit of those principles it refuses to acknowledge widely accepted evidence and expertise that bears upon the issues of the day.

The great paradox in American politics today is that the Republican Party has a significant political advantage: its dominant identity as the party of Americans' "first language," the language of individualism. But it also suffers a substantial policy weakness: its core principles of "smaller government, lower taxes" provide little guidance on the pressing problems of a globalizing world, which requires domestic public leadership and international collaboration. An inflexible belief that individual initiative is the only path to progress and that collective action through governments diminishes human freedom paralyzes efforts to develop policies to cope with the movement of American jobs overseas, our relative decline in educational achievement, the high cost and lack of health-care coverage for millions of Americans, and long-term strategies to deal with the threat of climate change. Those are not challenges that the "free market" will work out.

Those who believe that government is always the problem tend not to have a concept of a legitimate conservative government. The federal government isn't going away and is more likely to expand with the increasing complexity of issues and interdependence of nations. Without a defensible concept of what government should do for its citizens, Republican Party leaders default to "no" on controversial issues. To satisfy the growing libertarian/Tea Party element in their party, Mitt Romney, Paul Ryan, and other candidates for federal office present supply-side tax proposals, health reforms that shift costs to the public, and flat denial of the science of climate change. Those positions prevent discussions across the aisle from even beginning. On taxes and spending they have no stopping place on the downward slide to a federal government at Grover Norquist's 8 percent of GDP (see chap. 6).

The absence of a conservative concept of the legitimate functions of the federal government in the twenty-first century is a barrier to becoming an effective governing party. Elections can and will be won by being the champions of American individualism, but governing well is a matter of great complexity. I cannot articulate an effective set of conservative principles of governing for the Republican Party, but I also cannot imagine one that does not reject supply-side economics and accept the scientific consensus on climate change. Real-world problems cannot be wished away, and they have to be the responsibility of both parties. We will never get beyond our ideological polarization and congressional dysfunction without a Republican Party that has escaped the grip of the libertarian worldview and agrees that government can address problems beyond the capacity of the private sector.

FOUR NEGLECTED ESSENTIAL VIRTUES

No law, no commission, no national tragedy is likely to bridge the chasm between our two parties today. More responsible media coverage would help. A constitutional amendment to restore congressional authority to contain the influence of big money in politics would reduce the unbridled power of wealthy individuals and organizations. What else is needed to make American politics less dysfunctional? Changes in Senate and House rules would be on my list. Yet congressmen from both sides know that the rules will be used by the majority against the minority in the House and by the minority against the majority in the Senate. However, they are often appalled by the arguments of their opponents, and so polarization grows out of incredulity and distrust. We need to identify what's missing in our politics and try to fill the void.

It is easier to describe the changes we need than to explain how to make them. In an ideal future, reporters would press past sound bites and ask for evidence; citizens would demand more precise answers from candidates and officeholders; political leaders would speak to their base voters about the complexity of public issues rather than pander to their emotions; business leaders would treat Congress less as another profit center for their enterprises; and religious leaders would speak less of particular hot-button political issues and more of our common humanity.

Escaping our unproductive gridlock involves exposing the habits of thought that restrict our vision and separate us from each other. Congressional polarization is ultimately less about the defects of members of Congress than the beliefs and attitudes of the American people. We may long for more forceful, independent leaders, but active Democrats and Republicans and a vast array of organized interest groups vociferously demand that members of Congress not stray from the party or interest group path. We are the root of our distemper, driven by ideas and worldviews that fit awkwardly the times in which we live.

In our politics there are four neglected virtues that could light the path from where we are to where we ought to go: (1) respect for evidence, (2) tolerance of ambiguity, (3) caring about consequences, and (4) commitment to the common good. All are diminished by the ideology of radical individualism and neglected by much of the mainstream media. As our politics become more ideological, neglect of these four virtues in our political debates and media coverage exacerbates the polarization and gridlock in Congress. More attention to these tenets by the press and public would be a helpful antidote to our poisonous political culture.

First, our political polarization and dysfunctional public debate is largely driven by convictions and worldviews immune to contrary evidence and expertise. That is the most important thread that links the Bush administration failures in Iraq, health care, climate, and economic policies. Since that point has been made in preceding chapters, it may be enough to say that the press and public need more and better information about public issues. Both Democrats and Republicans could do better on this score, but the media would have to change the most.

Here's an example of how the media can skim the surface of even significant stories. In November 2011, Texas governor Rick Perry stated that if elected president, he would eliminate three federal agencies, but could remember only two. For a week or more the media obsessed over what his gaffe would do to his campaign. No commentator that I read or heard even attempted to discuss the consequences of eliminating the Departments of Commerce (including NOAA), Education (which funds 12 percent of K-12 costs), and Energy (which regulates exploration for oil and gas). Perry's proposal deserved more analysis than his flubbed sound bite.

Second, in a complex world, tolerance of ambiguity keeps human beings open to the perspectives and ideas of others. It is the opposite of a black/white, good/evil view of the world. The superficial comfort given by a leader of unshakeable conviction carries enormous risk that complexity will be ignored on matters of public consequence.

Former Treasury Secretary Paul O'Neill, after watching his boss, George W. Bush, confidently declare his rationale for the invasion of Iraq, mused to the author Ron Suskind: "Conviction is something you need in order to act, but your action needs to be proportional to the depth of evidence that underlies your conviction. . . . With his [Bush's] level of experience, I would not be able to support his level of conviction."[1]

I believe tolerance for ambiguity is a prerequisite for effective public leadership. But the coverage of our political campaigns, especially on television, effectively denigrates it by a laser-like concentration on any conflict between past votes or statements and current positions of candidates. As a nation we seem obsessed with getting absolute consistency from candidates for an office that will require great flexibility to deal with changing circumstances.

Tolerance of ambiguity is the opposite of Isaiah Berlin's "single central vision." It is an attitude that accepts, sometimes even revels in the diversity, confusion, and variety of the motivations, beliefs, and actions of human beings. It leads to pragmatic rather than ideological approaches to common problems. That's why we would be better off with a practice of evaluating the reasons *why* candidates have shifted positions rather than condemning their changes.

The third neglected virtue is caring about consequences: having elected representatives pay attention to the specific conditions in which their constituents live and work, and equal attention to the specific consequences of public policies. An ideological politics is likely to become absorbed in more abstract, remote factors like the culture of the country and the morality of its citizens, which cannot easily be compromised in any meaningful sense.

In general, members of Congress probably see and talk with more people of more varied circumstances than anyone else living in the districts they represent. Those who look will find an astonishing diversity of young and old, rich and poor, skilled and unskilled, competent and incompetent, fortunate and unfortunate, able and disabled, kind and selfish, honest and dishonest—the entire spectrum of human beings living and working in very different circumstances. Our political differences are exacerbated by the difficulty members of the public have imagining the lives of others. What we cannot imagine we interpret through our own experiences.

One trend has been obvious. Throughout my twelve years in Congress, alarming figures about the economic stagnation of middle- and lower-income Americans were readily available. The figures are worse today. From 1979 to 2005 the top 1 percent of American earners received more than one-third of all gains in national income, and the top one-tenth of 1 percent received over one-fifth of all after-tax income gains during that period. By contrast, the bottom 60 percent received only 13.5 percent of all gains in national income. As Hacker and Pierson point out in their *Winner-Take-All Politics:*

These mind-boggling differences have no precedent in the forty years of shared prosperity that marked the U.S. economy before the late 1970s. Nor do they have any real parallel elsewhere in the advanced industrial world.[2]

The authors argue that the distribution of income and wealth to a tiny group at the top has less to do with globalization, skill shifts, technological transformation, and economic change (which affected all developed countries) than it does with forty years of increased care and feeding of the interests of the very wealthy by American politicians on both sides of the aisle—though primarily by Republicans. If a democratic government is indifferent to such profoundly personal changes in economic opportunity and security, then members of the public can reasonably ask what its elected representatives are for. Failure to deal with the core economic issues of low- and middle-income families has eroded the public's trust in government, which is a fundamental precondition of a healthy democracy.

No member of Congress can avoid talking with seniors worried about whether their Social Security cost of living adjustment would be completely swallowed up by the increase in their Medicare Part B premium; with veterans denied services they felt they had earned; with students swamped with huge debts, frustrated by the lack of available jobs; with workers clinging to their disappearing manufacturing jobs; with small business owners worried about paying for health insurance and meeting payroll. And thousands more are not so easily categorized. Yet the circumstances of such Americans are hard to address unless first, elected officials understand what their constituents are going through, and second, believe that there is at least some appropriate role for government action even though not all individuals can be helped.

The fourth neglected virtue is a conception of the common good as the purpose of a democratic government. Too many Americans have concluded that organized interests are in control in Washington and ordinary people have been left behind. It is hard to imagine how public trust in the American government can be recovered without a sustained effort to breathe life into a concept of the common good.

Political and judicial "originalists" seeking conservative, timeless certainty in particular sections of the U.S. Constitution would do well to read again its mission statement:

WE THE PEOPLE OF THE UNITED STATES, in order to form a more perfect Union, establish Justice, insure domestic Tranquility, provide for the common defense, promote the general Welfare, and secure the Blessings of Liberty to ourselves and our Posterity, do ordain and establish this Constitution for the United States of America.

The Preamble to the Constitution is a succinct, elegant statement that the purpose of government is the common good. Yet it is hard today for people to believe that government is a principal forum for advancing the common good when money plays such a commanding role in American politics. A healthy democracy cannot survive in a swamp of distrust. Our political environment is poisoned by the split between a Democratic Party that still sees government as a vehicle for advancing the common good and a Republican/Libertarian coalition that sees it undermining the general welfare and impinging on personal freedom. We have lost a shared understanding of the purpose of democratic government.

James Madison, the most influential of our constitutional designers, labored to construct representative institutions that would encourage government officials to pursue the public interest instead of their own private interests. He wrote that "the public good, the real welfare of the body of the people is the supreme object to be pursued."[3]

Madison may be remembered most for his concern with "factions"—by which he meant "a number of citizens, whether amounting to a majority or minority of the whole, who are united and actuated by some common impulse or passion, or of interest, adverse to the rights of other citizens, or to the permanent and aggregate interests of the community."[4] Whether expressed as "the public good" or "the permanent and aggregate interests of the community," Madison understood that our Constitution and the institutions it created required a political culture that embodied the idea that government by the people was a collective undertaking for the common good, and not simply an arena for gaining private advantage—although men would try to make it so.

As Stephen Elkin points out, Madison's "crucial lesson" is that "in the absence of a widespread sense that there is a substantive public interest, we can expect nothing but rancor and dark suspicions that government is something to avoid."[5] One need only look around the world today to see that wherever governments are seen to be vehicles for private advancement, democracy does not flourish and is always at risk. Unbridled corruption is a plague for democratic governance, and its lesser cousin—manipulation of government for private advantage—a serious disease. That is our condition in America today; many if not most of our citizens believe that in Washington, money speaks louder than they, the people, do.

Judicial "originalists" like Justices Scalia and Thomas would confine the meaning of the Constitution to their perceived intent of the founders. But Madison understood, as they do not, that a constitution is not received, infallible wisdom for all time but a vehicle for ordering relations among people who seek to preserve a free democratic society for themselves and future generations.[6] The founders did not and could not specify the content of the public good because they believed it varies with time, place, and circumstance. Yet if the "common good" or the "permanent and aggregate interests of the community" are felt to be vague matters of opinion, then all are free to do what Madison abhorred—use government as an opportunity to advance their personal or group interests.

In fact, as the renowned historian Gordon Wood has observed, the authors of the Constitution in Philadelphia were appalled by the self-serving ambitions and actions of many of those elected in state legislatures. They bemoaned the decline of attention to the broader public interest and tried to create a constitution that would foster an alignment between the public good and the goals of those elected to federal office.[7]

These four virtues need nourishment to compete with their opposites: elevating opinion over evidence, interpreting the world in black and white, keeping an emotional distance from other people, and accepting interest group politics as an ideal. Outside of politics we promote virtues we neglect in politics. As an example, consider Rotary International's Four-Way Test, printed or recited at every Rotary meeting I attended:

Of the things we think, say or do

1. Is it the TRUTH?
2. Is it FAIR to all concerned?
3. Will it build GOODWILL and BETTER FRIENDSHIPS?
4. Will it be BENEFICIAL to all concerned?

We should promote in our politics the values we try to honor in our personal lives.

THE THREE-LEGGED STOOL

When I studied politics and government in graduate school, my first assignments were to answer three questions: What is Liberty, what is Equality, and what is Justice? Those are the three aspects of the core concept of a democratic society, a three-legged stool held together by their connecting braces. If we understand liberty to mean both freedom from legal or physical restraint and having enough resources to succeed in life, it blends into equality of opportunity. The idea that all men and women are created equal is rooted in recognition of our common humanity. Justice incorporates the idea of fairness, connected to equality by its emphasis on due process designed to treat equally individuals in similar circumstances. Abraham Lincoln and Martin Luther King Jr. may have been the most eloquent American political leaders on the three interwoven foundational concepts of our democracy. What is certain is that Ayn Rand, with her exclusive focus on liberty, is not of that group.

A year after 9/11, to demonstrate our respect and concern for the people of New York City, the Senate and House convened not far from

Ground Zero in Federal Hall, the site on which the first Congress met in 1789. On that solemn occasion I listened to Dennis Hastert, Speaker of the House, refer to America as a nation "conceived in liberty and dedicated to freedom." For Lincoln at Gettysburg, we were a "nation conceived in liberty and dedicated to the proposition that all men are created equal." Hastert's allusion to Lincoln's address while excluding the phrase "all men are created equal" spoke volumes about the libertarianism that has taken hold of the Republican Party today; for him it was better to mention liberty/freedom twice than equality at all. The loss of the Republican Party's original, more generous impulses has had a profound effect on our politics.

Ayn Rand's glorification of heroic individualists and her dismissal of "second handers" (who follow the ideas and values of others) re-emerge in conservative support of tax cuts for wealthy "job creators" and neglect of tens of millions of Americans without health insurance. In 2011 and 2012, Paul Ryan (R-WI), the House Budget Committee chairman and now nominee for vice president, was channeling Ayn Rand when he secured House passage of budgets that propose trillions in tax cuts to the wealthy and would strip trillions from services and tax breaks for the poor and middle class. As Ryan said in 2009 in one of his own campaign videos, "We are living in an Ayn Rand novel, metaphorically speaking. . . . Ayn Rand more than anyone else did a fantastic job of explaining the *morality* of capitalism, the *morality* of individualism and this to me is what matters most."[8] The House Republican whip Eric Cantor (R-VA), another opponent of tax increases, nevertheless suggested that Americans too poor to pay income taxes should pay some amount for income taxes in addition to the other taxes they pay today. These positions are not easily understood by Americans who believe that freedom, equality, and justice are all core democratic values and that the world's great religions ask us to care for each other.

In the real world liberty, equality, and justice cannot thrive alone. That's why Lincoln at Gettysburg trumps Hastert at Ground Zero, and why "Equal Justice Under Law" is engraved above the entrance to the Supreme Court. Mitch Daniels and the many conservatives who claim that liberty is the central American project have too narrow a vision of who we are.

RULE BY A DEMOCRATIC MAJORITY?

By 2006 I concluded that without hope of working across the aisle on major issues, the only path away from dysfunctional polarization was Democratic control. We would need a substantial majority in the House and Senate long enough to set a more pragmatic course for the country. As a six-term congressman from a small state, I had the recognition at home to make a credible run for the Senate. Senator Susan Collins (R-ME) was a popular incumbent with an approval rating well above 60 percent, but she had consistently sided with her party on close votes, and had supported President Bush's policies on Iraq and tax cuts for wealthy Americans.

During our campaign, Iraq receded as a political issue, and the economy went downhill. I lost my race, but Democrats won control of Congress long enough for passage of historic health-care reform, a major economic stimulus package, and legislation to regulate Wall Street. Democratic control lasted only two years, due to public opposition to the health-care plan, the worst economic collapse since the 1930s, the wall of Republican congressional opposition, and the rise of the Tea Party movement. In November 2010, the GOP made huge gains in both chambers. The intensity of America's political polarization had ratcheted up another notch. Forget political control by one party; we are back to what Dick Gephardt told our freshman congressional class at our first meeting—that legislation of lasting importance (almost always) requires bipartisan agreement. Ultimately, that makes more sense.

In this book I have written about what I perceive to be the most important, most neglected source of political polarization and congressional dysfunction—the incompatible worldviews held by most members of Congress and much of the public. There are many other contributors to our current gridlock, including the media, House and Senate rules, redistricting, bad practices by both parties, accentuating negativity, and perhaps even more than these—money.

THE MEDIA'S SINGLE LENS

Through the media's single-lens view of politics, Democrats and Republicans are arrayed along a one-dimensional spectrum from left to right. Yet that view misses the important ways in which we talk past each other. When Republicans attack government "spending" in the abstract and Democrats press to increase funding for education or job training, the two sides are talking on different planes about different subjects. The Republicans are concerned about a broad principle related to the size of government, while Democrats are focused on how to help people learn new skills. We talk past each other not because we are too far from each other on a left-right spectrum, but because we have different worldviews, one more abstract and the other more concrete.

One consequence of interpreting politics as a left-right spectrum is that commentators who seek to be above the fray tend to overvalue the "center" as a place not just where some political decisions get made but where better policy is made. That latter idea is often wrong, especially when the center becomes a place for political payoffs or policy confusion.

The mainstream media needs to ask both sides follow-up questions much more frequently, including "What is your evidence for that statement?" Revival of investigative reporting is essential; we have more than enough opinions from talk radio and cable TV. But even the failure of the *Washington Post* and the *New York Times* to embarrass Republican senators into investigating waste, fraud, and abuse by independent contractors in Iraq is an indication of how rare it is for mainstream print media to challenge its senatorial sources.

Independently funded investigative organizations like ProPublica may be part of the solution. Already, these independent newsrooms are uncovering or delving deeper into stories that the commercial mainstream media cannot investigate but are willing to publish. Among the groundbreaking stories from ProPublica are those uncovering tainted Chinese-made drywall; the risks of natural gas drilling; our nation's haphazard system of coroners and medical examiners; and vigilante justice in post–Hurricane Katrina New Orleans.

INSTITUTIONAL AND ELECTION REFORM

Congressional observers searching for remedies to our current polarization and dysfunction often concentrate on three categories: institutional reform, election reform, and campaign finance reform.

Norm Ornstein and Tom Mann are respected observers of the U.S. Congress, attached respectively to the American Enterprise Institute and the Brookings Institution. In their most recent book, *It's Even Worse Than It Looks,* they conclude that the debt ceiling debacle in 2011 that pushed the United States to the brink of default was "a template for all that is wrong with contemporary society and politics."[9] They perceive that the fundamental problem is "the mismatch between parliamentary-style political parties— ideologically polarized, internally unified, vehemently oppositional, and politically strategic—that has emerged in recent years and a separation-of-powers system that makes it extremely difficult for majorities to work their will."[10]

This mismatch is compounded by asymmetric polarization, specifically, by the Republican Party becoming an "insurgent outlier . . . ideologically extreme; . . . scornful of compromise; unpersuaded by conventional understanding of facts, evidence, and science; and dismissive of the legitimacy of its political opposition, all but declaring war on the government."[11] In order to draw more moderate voters to the polls, they recommend expanding the electorate by modernizing voter registration and moving Election Day to the weekend. They urge open primaries and alternatives to winner-take-all contests. Like other seasoned observers they decry the effect that filibusters and holds by a single senator have in undermining majority rule in the Senate.

Reducing opportunities for gerrymandering congressional districts is an oversold remedy for our polarized politics, but former Oklahoma congressman Mickey Edwards, among others, has suggested that redistricting of congressional districts should be turned over, in one way or another, to independent commissions, perhaps with judicial review.[12] The idea is anathema to both parties but could and should be implemented state by state if only to reduce the chances that incumbents can manipulate the results of their elections before they occur.

Tom DeLay's re-redistricting in Texas (after the state had been redistricted once after the 2000 census) because Republicans had won control of the State Legislature is only the worst of abuses in this area. Ten years later, after the 2010 census, the Texas redistricting process was resolved only after the dispute between the parties went all the way up to the Supreme Court. The convoluted shape of many congressional districts, made possible by computer programs that can determine likely voting patterns street by street, is clear evidence that parties and candidates have too many opportunities to choose their voters—instead of the reverse.

Political parties work to secure redistricting advantages for state legislative offices, but gerrymandering cannot affect races for governor or the U.S. Senate—and those campaigns appear just as polarized as races for the U.S. House of Representatives. It suggests that Americans, both politicians and the public, are polarized more by what they believe than the way legislative districts are delineated. The reform of redistricting practices cannot compensate for the movement of Americans into neighborhoods with like-minded people or the increasing ideological polarization of the public. There is no procedural mechanism that can overcome our ideological conflict. That we must deal with directly.

CAMPAIGN FINANCE REFORM: OVERTURNING CITIZENS UNITED

After I was elected to Congress in 1996, our freshman class made campaign finance reform a bipartisan priority. Since then, the amount and influence of money in politics has exploded beyond anything we could have imagined. The ever-increasing need for campaign contributions has a corrosive effect on Congress. First, every election cycle demands more time calling donors from the DCCC or RNCC cubicles; more fund-raising events in Washington and in the district; more time devoted to individuals and groups that are contributors. Members have less time for committee hearings, talking with constituents or staff, or attending to other official duties. Second, if you want a seat on a powerful committee, or a party caucus post, or a committee chair or leadership position, you must demonstrate solid fund-raising prowess and contribute to the party and individual candidates. Fund-raising prowess isn't the only criterion for leadership posts, but it is increasingly important. Third, members of Congress occasionally find themselves telling a committee chair or party leader, "I can't be with you on this." Both know this is code for, "Voting as you ask will cost me too much."

The way money is used to influence campaigns has changed. Independently financed attack ads were used in 1996, but by 2008 they were everywhere, subject to some late McCain-Feingold campaign limits. How will I ever forget the Photoshopped, mad-dog images of me accompanied by angry voice-overs plastered on TV screens night after night, thanks to big business's indignation over one of my votes? My opponent, Sen. Susan Collins, also had to contend with a slew of attack ads from groups that favored my candidacy.

Members rarely admit that campaign contributions influence their own behavior, but they are quick to point out the perceived effect on their opponents. The disgust of the public with Congress, as shown by numerous polls, is related to the perception that political money buys influence—which it does. But direct-to-candidate contributions constitute the most regulated, limited, and transparent money in politics today.

The gravest risk to government of the people arises from the vast sums that independent groups pour into defeating candidates who don't vote their way or will not if elected. By the time I left Congress, independent attack ads were pervasive and undeniably effective. Nevertheless, in a 5–4 decision in early 2010, *Citizens United v. Federal Elections Commission*, the Supreme Court declared unconstitutional central portions of the bipartisan campaign finance law that as a freshman I had worked so hard to enact. The law had limited the type of political ads that corporations and unions could run either sixty or ninety days before primary and general elections, respectively. The Court's decision unleashed corporate donors to pour millions more into political advertisements, often anonymously.

To reach its decision, the Court ignored the reality that money—especially big money—distorts elected officials' public policy decisions.

The justices' reasoning was myopic and tortured. First, they saw "corruption," the central justification for individual and corporate political spending restrictions, in a narrow, antiquated way. Only the quid pro quo variety mattered to them. Yet, as Justice John Paul Stevens noted in his dissent, "Corruption exists along a spectrum. . . . There are threats of corruption that are far more destructive to a democratic society than the odd bribe."

Then, having confined the concept of corruption to a narrow shed, the Court concluded that no harm would be done by allowing corporations to use unlimited amounts of corporate funds to support or attack candidates directly, as long as they did not "coordinate" their efforts with the candidates they support. In the two most obtuse sentences in the opinion, Justice Kennedy wrote:

> The appearance of influence or access, furthermore, will not cause the electorate to lose faith in our democracy. *By definition,* an independent expenditure is political speech presented to the electorate that is not coordinated with a candidate.[13] (emphasis added)

By definition, maybe, but clearly coordinated in the minds of most viewers and, too often, coordinated in fact one way or another, at the very least by signals from a campaign's own advertising about what the candidate wants from "independent" groups. The majority of the Court assumed that voters would perceive ads financed by "independent committees" (with patriotic made-for-TV names like "Citizens United") as not connected to the candidate that benefitted from them. Yet every member of Congress knows that constituents react to the content of the ads they see, not to the disclaimer. From countless conversations we also know that voters quickly get "sick of those TV ads."

The Court reached its conclusion by ignoring the ambiguity, messiness, and confusion of life. Rather than demanding reason grounded in evidence, even evidence about the impact of the legislation at issue, the majority preferred, as the dissent notes, "assertion over tradition, absolutism over empiricism, rhetoric over reality." The majority ignored the "mountains of evidence" of the corrupting influence of money in politics that Congress considered when the law was enacted. Because the constitutional issue was raised first by the Supreme Court itself, not the parties, the evidentiary record in *Citizens United* was barren of much data relevant to the decision. Yet the majority's astounding conclusion that the "appearance of influence or access . . . will not cause the electorate to lose faith in our democracy" was essentially a finding of fact. The majority's cavalier attitude toward data reflected the trademark approach of political conservatives in the other two branches of the federal government.

The majority of the Court did not understand that the more money in campaigns, the more negative the political climate will be. Early money is used by candidates to build the campaign infrastructure and promote the candidate; later money goes to buy television ads, more often negative than positive. Independent expenditures are far more weighted to negative television ads than to candidate expenditures. That's one reason why rapid increases in political spending do not lead to a more informed electorate. When it passed the McCain-Feingold law limiting independent expenditures during the two or three months before an election, Congress understood the threat that unlimited expenditures posed to our democracy. The Roberts Court preferred the comfort of a rule with the appearance of clarity—even though it would flood American political campaigns with huge amounts of additional money used by each side to attack the other.

Citizens United can be seen as the convergence of one line of Supreme Court cases in effect declaring "corporations are people" (by bestowing on the former some constitutional rights of the latter) and another line holding that "money is speech" (by rejecting congressional legislation to contain the corrupting influence of money in politics).[14]

The massive infusion of independent expenditures into American campaigns, which now seem to never end, is undermining our democracy, distorting our priorities, alienating our citizens, and turning Washington into another profit center for big business. However narrowly five members of the Supreme Court may define "corruption," we have a problem at the heart of our system of government, made worse by the Court's willful blindness to the consequences of its theories and by its inability to integrate concepts of equality with its attachment to liberty.

The Court's indifference to evidence of the impact of money in politics appears related to its preference for clear rules over actual consequences. In other words, a decision based on "free speech" can be grounded in a right that all citizens are believed to possess equally. Yet Americans generally want more than theoretical equality in democratic decision making. They do not expect equality of influence in public decisions, but most resent allowing billionaires to have vastly more influence than everyone else. The principle of majority rule, which is central to democratic societies, is grounded in a concept of equality of participation in elections; each citizen's vote counts the same. The Roberts Court failed to understand that *Citizens United* undermines how majority rule should work in practice. Senate rules and practices on "holds" and filibusters have a similar detrimental effect. They weaken majority rule and empower minorities far beyond the limited exceptions to majority decision making specified in the Constitution, which include overturning a presidential veto, approving a treaty, or impeaching a president.

Conservatives at the federal and state levels have repeatedly attempted and sometimes succeeded in establishing requirements for supermajorities to increase taxes, which effectively empowers future minorities to control the budgetary decision making of legislative bodies. The majority principle is necessary to maximize the chances of having government *by* the people, that is, as close as possible to government *by most of the people.* Although it cannot and is not meant to assure equality of influence, the majority principle remains a distinguishing feature of virtually all theories of democracy.[15]

Even our most basic values live in tension with each other. The irony of *Citizens United* is that the Court employed freedom of speech, an essential principle for any democracy, to weaken the voices of ordinary Americans and strengthen the power of corporate money in democratic elections. The trust of the American people in our democracy cannot be recovered if *Citizens United* remains the law of the land. Since the Court decision is grounded in the First Amendment to the Constitution, a constitutional amendment is required to reverse it. Proposed amendments have been introduced in both the House and Senate. Generating a political movement strong enough to succeed is a monumental task, since the decision serves some corporate and partisan interests so well. But overturning *Citizens United* is essential to the restoring public trust in American democratic institutions.

CONGRESSIONAL FAILURE: STRATEGIC DECISION MAKING

During my twelve years in Washington, Congress largely failed to make responsible long-term decisions across a wide range of issues. The Bush tax cuts, which were intended by supporters to be permanent, and the invasion and occupation of Iraq left the federal government in a fiscally weakened condition from which no bipartisan escape has proved possible. Congress did little to help the tens of millions of Americans without health insurance. The growing scientific consensus on the risks of climate change was attacked. In the four years since I left, Congress has descended to new lows of dysfunctional partisanship and vanishing public trust.

The debt ceiling debate of 2011 and the 2012 presidential campaign leave little hope that Republicans and Democrats in Congress can overcome their incompatible worldviews and make effective pragmatic strategic decisions about taxes and spending, health care and climate change. Republicans will insist that progress is driven by great individuals with initiative and talent, not by collective action, and certainly not by governments; that free markets are self-correcting and government regulation and taxes stifle growth; and that existing and additional government initiatives will stifle personal liberty. Democrats will continue to argue that Americans face complicated, intertwined challenges that require governmental leadership and investment to improve education, promote economic growth, insure citizens against the risks of illness and accident, and cope with the threat of a rapidly changing climate.

The last hope of many commentators is that the year-end 2012 crisis, with the expiration of the Bush tax cuts and the scheduled automatic spending cuts enacted by the Congress in 2011, will somehow force the two sides into a rational and sound compromise incorporating tax increases, spending reductions, and entitlement reform. There is little evidence to support that hope at this time.

With such different ideas of the tasks at hand, the two parties can barely find a common language to discuss our deteriorating physical infrastructure and the loss of our competitive advantage in education. How do we deal with periodic economic crises like the recent recession? The Obama administration helped keep General Motors and Chrysler in business when private capital was unavailable, but most Republican senators opposed the effort to protect more than a million jobs in the auto industry. The bank bailouts of the Bush and Obama administrations saved several million jobs but continue to arouse withering criticism from the Right.

"Size of government" and its focus on dependency and personal liberty are so abstract, so all encompassing, that they transform all political issues into one—a pitched battle over fundamental worldviews with all the inflexibility of issues like abortion rights and gay marriage. Slippery-slope arguments replace more pragmatic debate. Raising taxes by any amount becomes a step on the road to serfdom. Regulated competition among private health care insurers is seen as socialism. Acknowledging the challenges posed by global warming and ocean acidification is heresy. The conservative worldview has no concept of limited government flexible enough to be compatible with pragmatic debate on matters beyond the capacity of the private sector.

I understand and value the political passion for individualism that animates conservatives in America today. I respect those who argue in specific cases for a less intrusive government, for more support for business interests, for more authority for state and local governments, and for demanding more responsibility from individuals. I respect those opinions even when in particular circumstances I disagree with them, because they are an essential counterpoint to those who try to solve too many problems through government action.

This radical individualism of the last two decades is ill-suited to the twenty-first century, because our lives are intertwined as never before with billions of human beings around the world. Yet it still has political power in an America that cherishes, for good reasons, self-reliance. Many Americans, alarmed by our increasing global interdependence, resist acknowledging a responsibility for government to deal with matters beyond the capacity of the private sector. These convictions have proved to be dangerous: the same old mantras that tax cuts pay for themselves, we would be welcomed as liberators by the Iraqis, government-regulated health care doesn't work, and climate science is not proven. Once integrated into a libertarian worldview, they become immune to the reasoned deliberation that the Founders anticipated for the American Congress, and they produce consequences that are neither desired nor desirable.

We must revitalize America's second language—of community and the common good. It too is a central part of our heritage, grown out of two centuries of experimenting with self-government, an enormous variety of religious and secular organizations, and our personal life experiences. The tension between individualism and community, when properly balanced, is productive and healthy for a democratic society.

What mystified me about the claims of my Republican congressional colleagues makes more sense today. They do—generally—believe what they say. Moreover, their guiding value—individual initiative—is quintessentially American. The culmination of Newt Gingrich's strategy to win political power by attacking the institution of Congress has been largely successful because it tapped into Americans' first language of individualism and set up government itself as a threat to self-reliance. That worldview has become a "single central vision" so powerful that its adherents will fit evidence and expertise to the vision rather than open it to doubt. That's why disparate domestic issues like taxes and spending, health care, and climate change merge into one—driven by an emotional, sometimes bitter argument about whether government should act at all rather than what it should do.

Multiple political, social, and economic forces in contemporary society have split the American psyche in half. We have been unable to find a healthy balance between core values that together—only together—define who we are. The authors Mann and Ornstein see a mismatch between our parliamentary-style political parties and our checked-and-balanced system of government. I would add that the libertarian vision of the Republican Party is a poor fit for the interconnected, interdependent world in which we live. In addition, our democratic, representative structure for governing ourselves cannot be sustained without an accepted practice of deliberation about public issues in which evidence and expertise matter, and without a broad agreement that the intertwined values of liberty, equality, and justice inform our concept of democracy.

RECOVERING OUR BALANCE

We live in the "only superpower"—the "indispensable nation"—but we are not doing well. Something inside is draining our strength, our optimism, and undermining our core beliefs. America is being forced to adapt to a changing world and we are resisting, fighting, and denying change. We want to believe that our own economic success is within our control, but in a global economy, it isn't. We want to believe that our children can be anything they want to be, but upward mobility in America is decreasing as inequality grows. As individuals, we need, more than ever, help from others to succeed.

As the world we inhabit becomes more complicated and interdependent, many Americans long for the imagined clarity of a simpler time. The cultural and political shifts of the 1960s spawned a conservative reaction; the transformation of work by technology and instantaneous communication appears to have bred a renewed American hunger for structure and order. We have rebelled against the complexities of the twenty-first century instead of accepting and adapting to its opportunities.

Our peculiar national tragedy is that our signature idea—that opportunity for everyone here is as limitless as the frontier was once—has been used to establish a political dogma that is inconsistent with the forces shaping our world and now stops us from the collaborative, pragmatic decision making needed to thrive in this new environment.

Opportunity still abounds in America, but for most it is not a preexisting condition. It must be constantly re-created by family, friends, neighbors, groups, and governments. We have to help each other, even those we don't know and may not like, to get an education, find meaningful work, overcome the vicissitudes of life, and pursue happiness.

The world's longest surviving democracy cannot work well when so many Americans treat government with contempt—and do so at the instigation of one of our two major political parties. Breeding cynicism rots any sense of citizenship. Why should we participate in an ineffective, even corrupt activity? But look around the world. We don't do as well as some, but we do much better than most.

Our traditions of civic republicanism and community lack the emotional appeal of individualism in American culture, but they are still American traditions. I find it strange that high school commencement speeches are generally about serving others, that coaches at every level tell their players that "there is no 'I' in Team," that success in business is so often dependent on building a team committed to a shared mission, that our religious communities urge service to others, and yet in our politics one team takes the position that we are each on our own.

Collaboration is a way of life in America. As a congressman, I participated in hundreds of celebrations, openings, ribbon cuttings, and events to recognize the completion of a project, facility, or innovation. Virtually without exception, there were public, private, and charitable entities to thank. Often the list included federal government officials, state and municipal leaders, private companies, foundations, community organizations, and others. I attended events for new health-care clinics, hospital expansions, senior housing facilities, veterans services, drug treatment programs, bicycle trails, river restorations, conservation projects, abused and neglected children, ocean research, and other events far too numerous to mention. The operative word at all of these celebrations was "partnership." That's how I saw Maine people operating in the world. It was inspiring precisely because so much was accomplished not by heroic individualists but by ordinary people working together toward shared goals.

In the introduction, my quotation from Friedrich Nietzsche, "Convictions are more dangerous enemies of truth than lies," is the most important lesson I learned in Congress. That's not what I expected. I did, and still do, favor politicians with convictions—on both sides of the aisles—over those who always have a finger in the wind. But convictions impervious to evidence are dangerous.

The 2012 presidential election brought to the surface the individualistic and communitarian worldviews that have been shaping our politics in less explicit ways for more than two decades. As Mitt Romney and other Republicans doubled their bets on big tax cuts for the wealthy and big reductions in services for the disadvantaged and the middle class, President Obama preached that we all have a stake in each other's success or failure. Romney has the advantage of speaking the historic first language of American politics, and Obama the advantage of speaking the language required by the interconnected world of the twenty-first century. Although this book goes to press before the outcome of the election is known, worldview politics in the form described here will be with us for some time to come. The task of overcoming the gap of understanding remains.

Americans today are moving uncertainly into this globalized knowledge-based world. Our greatest asset—belief in individual initiative and self-reliance—has developed a dark side that has infected the body politic with the idea that government of the people, by the people, and for the people is by its nature an obstacle to personal freedom. When Americans arrive at that conclusion about our democracy, pessimism locks in. We all know at some level that we are not masters of our fate. The greatest challenges of our time must be met by the public and private sectors together. Take away public responsibility for our common challenges, and we are left without leadership of the necessary breadth.

Because the ideological sources of polarization are asymmetrical, the burden is greater on Republicans to rethink how a pragmatic conservatism might adapt to twenty-first-century complexities in a way that rigid hostility to government cannot. Their leaders have fed the anti-government tiger for so long that it has gained in weight and influence over them. They have ceded control of their identity to libertarians like Grover Norquist and the Koch brothers, and failed to challenge the more extreme stances of the Tea Party. The 2012 Republican primaries witnessed a rush to ideological conformity to satisfy core conservatives. With a few exceptions Republican members of Congress have been invisible in the development of policies for comprehensive health-care reform or to cope with climate change; they dare not stray from their arguments for supply-side economics. Without countervailing conservative principles, they slide farther and farther down the slippery slope of always smaller government, always lower taxes.

Democrats must gain a deeper understanding of America's archetypical individualism and look for opportunities to honor legitimate conservative concerns about heavy-handed government. The case for blending public leadership and private engagement is strong in many instances. Moreover, Democrats will have to accept cost containment reforms to Social Security, Medicare, and Medicaid. As believers in building community, Democrats will need to practice that art at the local level in addition to focusing on national politics. Ultimately, recovering a balance between individualism and community, our shared American values, is a task for all American citizens.

We must work to see the world as it is and find our place in it. Our place is defined by our relationships with others. Confronted by an increasingly complex, interconnected world, we have succumbed to emotional messages that promise simple answers. The modern media treasures conflict above collaboration. Political money is more effective in attacking than supporting candidates or their ideas. The dumbing down of our political discourse as our political challenges grow more complex erodes our confidence and undermines our collective capacity to thrive.

At the root of our anxiety and frustration is our failure to balance self-reliance and cooperation in our contemporary politics. Gary Cooper walking down Main Street in *High Noon* is no guide to the twenty-first century. Galt's Gulch in *Atlas Shrugged* is a fable. For our politics to catch up with the values of our businesses, churches, nonprofits, and athletic teams, we will need to remember Wallace Stegner's comment that cooperation rather than rugged individualism most "characterizes and preserves" the American West.

Most Republicans and Democrats come to Congress with hope that they can change America for the better. But our "reach exceeds our grasp," and the daunting complexity of the political and legislative process leaves lots of space and time and failure between significant achievements. We learn to cope with the experience of falling short of expectations.

In our Thursday morning reflection group, the conversation not infrequently turned to the question, "What are we doing here?" Sometimes we spoke of the personal frustration of not seeing our initiatives enacted. Sometimes we were appalled at the negative impact of our divisive behavior on the country and our constituents. We wanted to do more and be part of a more productive institution.

Sharing those frustrations with each other helped give us the strength to keep trying even when the chance of success was low. A reading from *The Irony of American History* by Reinhold Niebuhr sparked a discussion about our place and roles in bringing about the change we wanted to see:

> Nothing that is worth doing can be achieved in our lifetime; therefore, we must be saved by hope. Nothing which is true, or beautiful, or good, makes complete sense in any immediate context of history; therefore, we must be saved by faith. Nothing we do, however virtuous, can be accomplished alone; therefore, we are saved by love. No virtuous act is quite as virtuous from the standpoint of our friend or foe as it is from our standpoint. Therefore, we must be saved by the final form of love, which is forgiveness.[16]

How to make sense of it all—being part of the U.S. House of Representatives, the longest directly elected legislative body in history but mired now in confusing and often unproductive struggles over irreconcilable worldviews. We needed patience and commitment, renewed by reflection with others, to believe that there is available to everyone a generosity of spirit, which can draw us together despite our political differences.

I would have preferred to have been part of a moment in history when change rolls in on a tidal wave of popular support strong enough to move our checked-and-balanced federal government to make lasting improvements in the well-being of the American people. But my role was to stand in the fire, to make the case for change until reinforcements arrived. They came in 2006 and 2008—just in time to vote for unprecedented intervention to stop the slide to a depression, enact the most important health-care reform since Medicare, and change the financial rules governing Wall Street. That brief moment of productive legislative accomplishment was partisan, precisely because of the incompatibility of the disparate worldviews across the aisle. Consequently, it did little or nothing to restore the broader trust of the people in their government.

Hope, faith, love, forgiveness—we need them all to keep moving when completion of our purposes eludes us. For all my alarm at the frozen state of our political discourse, I still believe that by some not yet visible process we Americans will eventually find our way to more pragmatic public leadership inspired by a clearer commitment to the common good.

NOTES

INTRODUCTION

1. Friedrich Nietzsche, from *Human, All Too Human: Texts in the History of Philosophy,* trans. R. J. Hollingdale (Cambridge: Cambridge University Press, 1986, 1996). The aphorism "Convictions are more dangerous enemies of truth than lies," can be found in the text at S. 483.
2. Thomas E. Mann and Norman J. Ornstein, *The Broken Branch: How Congress Is Failing America and How to Get It Back on Track* (New York: Oxford University Press, 2006), 218.

CHAPTER 1

1. Anne Heller, *Ayn Rand and the World She Made* (New York: Nan A. Talese/Doubleday, 2009), xii.
2. Quoted in Jennifer Burns, *Goddess of the Market: Ayn Rand and the American Right* (New York: Oxford University Press, 2009), 43.
3. Ayn Rand, *Autobiographical Sketch,* 1936, quoted in Heller, *Ayn Rand,* 1.
4. Ibid., 300.
5. Ibid., 283.
6. Burns, *Goddess of the Market,* 43.
7. Mark Sanford, *Newsweek,* www.thedailybeast.com/newsweek/2009/10/21/atlas-hugged.print.html.
8. Ibid.
9. Robert Bellah et al., *Habits of the Heart: Individualism and Commitment in American Life* (Berkeley: University of California Press, 1985, 1996), 84.
10. Ibid., viii.
11. Ibid., 198.
12. Robert Putnam, *Bowling Alone: The Collapse and Revival of American Community* (New York: Simon and Schuster, 2000), see, e.g., 402–4.
13. Thomas Merton, *Essential Writings,* selected and with an Introduction by Christine M. Bochen (Maryknoll, NY: Orbis Books, 2000), 115. Preface to the Vietnamese edition of *No Man Is an Island.*

CHAPTER 2

1. Bruce Bartlett, *The Benefit and the Burden: Tax Reform—Why We Need It and What It Will Take* (New York: Simon and Schuster, 2012), 44–45.

2. David Stockman, *The Triumph of Politics: Why the Reagan Revolution Failed* (New York: Harper and Row, 1986), 174, 399–400.

3. Remarks of the president to the Greater Portland Chamber of Commerce, Portland, Maine, March 23, 2001, georgewbush-whitehouse.archives.gov/news/releases/2001/03/.

4. Paul Krugman, *Fuzzy Math: The Essential Guide to the Bush Tax Plan* (New York: W. W. Norton and Company, Inc. 2001), 8–9.

5. Ibid., 107.

6. Bill Thomas quoted in *New York Times*, March 22, 2001, http://www.nytimes.com/2001/03/22/us/republicans-consider-increasing-tax-cut-at-low-end.html?pagewanted=all&src=pm.

7. Mann and Ornstein, *Broken Branch*, 218.

8. Ibid., 219.

9. Clive Crook, "How to Take a Flawed Tax Bill and Turn It Into a Joke," *National Journal* 33, no. 23, June 9, 2001. Quoted in Mann and Ornstein, *Broken Branch*, 219.

10. Joel Friedman, Richard Kogan, and Robert Greenstein, "New Tax-cut Law Ultimately Costs as Much as Bush Plan; Gimmicks Used to Camouflage $4.1 Trillion Cost in Second Decade," *Center on Budget Policies and Priorities* Newsletter, June 27, 2001.

11. Ron Suskind, *The Price of Loyalty: George W. Bush, the White House, and the Education of Paul O'Neill* (New York: Simon and Schuster, 2004), 284.

12. Ibid., 291.

13. Ibid., 307.

14. House Budget Committee Transcript of Hearing, February 8, 2005, 3.

15. Ibid., 52.

16. Ibid., 21.

17. Ibid., 29 (emphasis added).

18. Ibid., 52.

19. House Budget Committee Transcript of Hearing, February 8, 2006, 39.

20. Ibid., 32.

21. House Budget Committee Transcript of Hearing, January 30, 2007, 24.

22. Ryan Lizza, "Fussbudget," *The New Yorker*, August 6, 2012, 27.

23. Gregory Mankiw, *Principles of Economics* (New York: Dryden, 1998), 29–30.

24. Mark Zandi, "Assessing President Bush's Fiscal Policies," Economy.com, Inc. July 2004, 4–7.

25. Philip G. Joyce, *The Congressional Budget Office: Honest Numbers, Power and Policymaking* (Washington, DC: Georgetown University Press, 2011), 56.

26. Ibid., 42.

27. Ibid., 81.

28. Bartlett, *Benefit and the Burden*, 43.

29. Jason Furman, "Treasury Dynamic Scoring Analysis Refutes Claims by Supporters of the Tax Cuts," Center on Budget and Policy Priorities paper, August 24, 2006.

30. Jonathan Chait, "Captives of the Supply Side," *New York Times,* October 9, 2007.
31. Quoted in Paul Krugman, "Redo That Voodoo," *New York Times,* July 15, 2010.
32. Ibid.
33. Bartlett, *Benefit and the Burden,* 45.
34. Ibid., 215.
35. Ibid., 49.
36. Ibid., 233.
37. Center on Budget Policies and Priorities, "CBPP Critics Still Wrong," June 28, 2010, 3.
38. Center on Budget Policies and Priorities, Media Briefing, March 10, 2010.
39. "Paul Ryan Discusses Budget Blueprint," *Washington Post,* March 20, 2012, video available at www.washingtonpost.com/politics/paul-ryan-discusses-budget-blueprint-133/2012/03/20gIQAGWMsPS_video.html.
40. Center on Budget and Policy Priorities, "Contrary to 'Entitlement Society' Rhetoric, Over Nine-Tenths of Entitlement Benefits Go to Elderly, Disabled or Working Households," February 10, 2012, 1.
41. Dana Milbank, "A Faith-based Lesson for Paul Ryan," *Washington Post,* April 27, 2012.
42. Ezra Klein, "The Danger of Being Wrong on Keynes," *Washington Post,* July 18, 2011.

CHAPTER 3

1. Colin Powell, *It Worked For Me: In Life and Leadership* (New York: HarperCollins, 2012), 217.
2. Tony Blair, "The Power of Community can Change the World," Speech to Labour Party Conference, Brighton, October 2, 2001.
3. George W. Bush, State of the Union Speech, January 29, 2002.
4. Scott McClellan, *What Happened: Inside the Bush White House and Washington's Culture of Deception* (New York: Public Affairs, 2008), 119–33.
5. House Armed Services Committee, transcript of hearing on September 26, 2002.
6. Stuart W. Bowen Jr., "Hard Lessons: The Iraq Reconstruction Experience," Report of the Special Inspector General for Iraq (Washington, DC: U.S. Government Printing Office, 2009), 3. This report has also been published as a paperback edition (USIAC) and a Google e-Book.
7. Ibid., 3.
8. Ibid., 8.
9. Remarks as delivered by Defense Secretary Donald Rumsfeld, "Beyond Nation Building," New York City, February 14, 2003, http://www.defense.gov/Speeches/Speech.aspx?SpeechID=337.
10. Ibid.
11. Thomas E. Ricks, *Fiasco: The American Military Adventure in Iraq* (New York: Penguin Press, 2006), 102–3.
12. Thomas E. Ricks, *The Gamble: General David Petraeus and the American Military Adventure in Iraq, 2006–2008* (New York: Penguin Press, 2009), 9.
13. Ibid., 159.

14. Ibid., 80, 38.
15. Ibid., 132.
16. Commission on Wartime Contracting in Iraq and Afghanistan, *Final Report to Congress, Transforming Wartime Contracting* (Washington, DC: U.S. Government Printing Office, August 2011), 2.
17. SIGIR Quarterly Report, January 2005.
18. David Pallister, "How the US Sent $12bn in Cash to Iraq. And Watched It Vanish," *Guardian,* February 7, 2007, available at http://www.guardian.co.uk/world/2007/feb/08/usa.iraq1.
19. All letters referred to between Senators Collins and Lautenberg in author's possession.
20. Tim Yehl interview with author.
21. Jonathan Mahler, "After the Imperial Presidency," *New York Times Magazine,* November 9, 2008.
22. David Nather, "Congress as Watchdog: Asleep on the Job?" *CQ Weekly,* May 22, 2004, 1196–97, www.fas.org/sgp/crs/misc/R41079.pdf.
23. Ibid., 1198–99.
24. Stuart Bowen, prepared testimony for hearing of the Committee on Homeland Security and Governmental Affairs, August 2, 2006, available at www.gpo.gov/fdsys/pkg/CHRG-109shrg2 at 45 (also at SIGIR 06-004T, 5).
25. Erik Eckholm, "Army Corps Agrees to Pay Whistle-Blower in Iraq Case," *New York Times,* July 28, 2011.
26. Byron L. Dorgan, *Reckless: How Debt, Deregulation, and Dark Money Nearly Bankrupted America (And How We Can Fix It!)* (New York: Thomas Dunne Books/St. Martin's Press, 2009), 149, 160–62.
27. Bowen, "Hard Lessons," 323.
28. Dov Zakheim, interview with Margaret Warner, PBS *Newshour,* September 1, 2011.
29. Commission on Wartime Contracting, *Final Report to Congress* (Washington, DC: U.S. Government Printing Office, August 2011), 6, 98–111.
30. Zakheim/Warner interview.

CHAPTER 4

1. Ron Brownstein, "Sebelius: 'What Is the Alternative,'" *National Journal,* September 25, 2010, 51.
2. *Newsweek,* May 8, 2000.
3. CBS, *60 Minutes,* October 17, 1999, interview by Mike Wallace, available at http://www.youtube.com/watch?v=uZGufvsxNeo.
4. Sherrod Brown, "Democracy Crumbles Under Cover of Darkness," *St. Louis Post-Dispatch,* December 11, 2003.
5. Gail Wilensky, "Developing a Center for Comparative Effectiveness Information," *Health Affairs* 25, no. 6 (November 2006).
6. See http://mediamatters.org/research/2011/03/22/a-history-of-death-panels-a-timeline/177776.
7. Stuart Butler, "Assuring Affordable Health Care for All Americans," Heritage Foundation, 1989, 1–2.
8. Ibid., 2.

9. Ibid., 6.

10. Dahlia Lithwick, *Slate,* Supreme Court Dispatches, March 27, 2012, available at http://www.slate.com/articles/news_and_politics/supreme_court_dispatches/2012/03/supreme_court_and_obamacare_why_the_conservatives_are_skeptical_of_the_affordable_care_act_.html.

11. Senator Mitch McConnell, interview by Chris Wallace, *Fox News Sunday,* July 1, 2012, reported by Greg Sargent, *Washington Post,* July 1, 2012.

CHAPTER 5

1. See NOAA materials on ocean acidification, including http://oceanservice.noaa.gov/education/yos/resource/01state_of_science.pdf.

2. Center for Climate and Energy Solutions, data available at http://www.c2es.org/facts-figures/trends/surface-temp; see also Richard Muller, "The Conversion of a Climate-Change Skeptic," *New York Times,* July 28, 2012. Muller was the leading scientific skeptic on global warming, yet his own research has confirmed the figures of others regarding the increase in global temperature in the last fifty years, as well as its correlation with greenhouse gas emissions.

3. For background on the Montreal Protocol see http://www.epa.gov/ozone/intpol/.

4. International Panel on Climate Change Reports, including the 2001 Third Assessment Report, are available at http://www.ipcc.ch/publications_and_data/publications_and_data_reports.shtml#1.

5. See http://www.arctic.noaa.gov/reportcard/exec_summary.html.

6. Coral Davenport, "Heads in the Sand," *National Journal* December 3, 2011, http://www.nationaljournal.com/magazine/heads-in-the-sand-20111201?mrefid=site_search&;page=1.

7. Seth Shulman, *Undermining Science: Suppression and Distortion in the Bush Administration,* 2nd ed. (Berkeley: University of California Press, 2006, 2008), 9.

8. See Oliver Burkeman, "Memo exposes Bush's new green strategy," *Guardian,* March 3, 2003, available at http://www.guardian.co.uk/environment/2003/mar/04/usnews.climatechange. Note: the memo is no longer available easily on the web; author's quotation taken from copy in his possession.

9. Frank Luntz, interview by Deborah Solomon ("The Wordsmith"), *New York Times Magazine,* May 24, 2009.

10. Shulman, *Undermining Science,* xiv.

11. Ibid., 22.

12. Ibid., 23–24.

13. Ron Suskind, "Faith, Certainty and the Presidency of George W. Bush," *New York Times Magazine,* October 17, 2004.

14. Ibid.

15. Suskind, *Price of Loyalty,* 155.

16. Davenport, "Heads in the Sand."

17. Andrew Revkin, "Industry Ignored Its Scientists on Climate," *New York Times,* April 23, 2009, available at http://www.nytimes.com/2009/04/24/science/earth/24deny.html?pagewanted=all.

18. Jane Mayer, *The New Yorker,* "Covert Operations: The Billionaire Brothers Who Are Waging a War Against Obama," August 20, 2010.

19. Ibid., 2, 11.
20. Davenport, "Heads in the Sand."
21. http://www.newyorker.com/reporting/2010/10/11/101011fa_fact_lizza?printable=true#ixzz1jWgTxAfh.
22. Neela Banerjee, *McClatchy Newspapers*, "Climate Change Skepticism Seeps into Science Classrooms," January 18, 2012.
23. See http://www.nsf.gov/news/news_summ.jsp?cntn_id=123324.
24. Eric Scigliano, *Crosscut*, "Rallying to Save the Souring Seas and the Northwest's Cherished Oyster Harvest," April 5, 2012, available at http://crosscut.com/2012/04/05/environment/22173/Rallying-save-souring-seas-Northwests-cherished-oy/.
25. Pew Oceans Commission, Report to the Nation, "America's Living Oceans: Charting a Course for Sea Change," May 2003, available at http://www.pewtrusts.org/uploadedFiles/wwwpewtrustsorg/Reports/Protecting_ocean_life/env_pew_oceans_final_report.pdf.
26. U.S. Commission on Ocean Policy, Final Report, September 20, 2004, "An Ocean Blueprint for the Twenty-first Century," available at http://www.oceancommission.gov/documents/welcome.html.
27. Riley E. Dunlap and Aaron M. McCright, "A Widening Gap: Republican and Democratic Views on Climate Change," *Environment Magazine*, September–October 2008.
28. Robert J. Brullee, Jason Carmichael, and J. Craig Jenkins, "Shifting Public Opinion on Climate Change: An Empirical Assessment of Factors Influencing Concern over Climate Change in the U.S., 2002–2012," *Climatic Change* 114, no. 2 (February 2012): 169–88.
29. Ibid.
30. Ibid.
31. E. Maibach, C. Roser-Renouf, and A. Leiserowitz, A. (2009) "Global Warming's Six Americas 2009: An Audience Segmentation Analysis" (Fairfax, VA: George Mason University Center for Climate Change Communication, 2009). Accessed from: http://climatechange.gmu.edu.
32. Ibid. Respondents were given "a great deal," "a moderate amount," "only a little," and "not at all" as choices, along with "don't know."
33. Ibid.
34. See http://environment.yale.edu/climate/files/Six-Americas-March-2012.pdf. The specific percentages described are taken from the "Six Americas 2009" of Maibach et al. The authors' continuing studies yield slightly different numbers but do not change the conclusions reached here.
35. D. M. Kahan, E. Peters, M. Wittlin, P. Slovic, L. L. Ouellette, D. Braman, and G. Mandel, "The Polarizing Impact of Science, Literacy, and Numeracy on Perceived Climate Change Risks," *Nature Climate Change*, online advance publication, http://www.nature.com/doifinder/10.1038/nclimate1547 (2012).

CHAPTER 6

1. Lincoln Chafee, *Against the Tide: How a Compliant Congress Empowered a Reckless President* (New York: Thomas Dunne Books, St. Martin's Press, 2008), 6.
2. See Douglas B. Sosnik, Matthew J. Dowd, and Ron Fournier, *Applebee's America: How Successful Political, Business, and Religious Leaders Connect with the New*

American Community (New York: Simon and Schuster, 2006), 11–61. The authors argue that "gut values" are what Americans want to see in a candidate "before they're even willing to consider their policies" (6). I would argue campaigns about values and worldviews rarely get to policies.

3. Thomas E. Mann and Norman J. Ornstein, *It's Even Worse Than It Looks: How the American Constitutional System Collided with the New Politics of Extremism* (New York: Basic Books, 2012), 33–34.

4. See Lewis Lapham, *Harper's Magazine*, September 2004; text of the Powell Manifesto available at http://reclaimdemocracy.org/corporate_accountability/powell_memo_lewis.html.

5. CBS News, *60 Minutes*, November 20, 2011.

6. Ibid.

7. James Madison, Alexander Hamilton, and John Jay, *The Federalist Papers*, No. 45 (London: Penguin Classics, 1987), 293.

8. Abraham Lincoln, fragment on government, *The Collected Works of Abraham Lincoln*, vol. 2, ed. Roy P. Basler (New Brunswick, NJ: Rutgers University Press, 1953), 220–21.

9. Mann and Ornstein, *It's Even Worse Than It Looks.*

10. George Lakoff, *Don't Think of an Elephant!: Know your Values and Frame the Debate* (White River Junction, VT: Chelsea Green Publishing Company, 2004), 5.

11. George Lakoff, *Moral Politics: How Liberals and Conservatives Think,* 2nd ed. (Chicago: University of Chicago Press, 1996, 2002), 3.

12. Ibid., 35–36.

13. Ibid., 271.

14. Marc J. Hetherington and Jonathan D. Weiler, *Authoritarianism and Polarization in American Politics* (New York: Cambridge University Press, 2009), 2–3.

15. Ibid., 34, 35.

16. Ibid., 36.

17. Ibid., 59, 64–65.

18. Ibid., 40.

19. Isaiah Berlin, *The Hedgehog and the Fox: An Essay on Tolstoy's View of History* (London: Weidenfeld and Nicolson Ltd., 1953, 1967), 1.

20. Ibid., 4, 36.

21. Berlin's concept of hedgehogs and foxes assumes that people are driven by some inner need to order the world around them to a greater or lesser extent. Others have used the metaphorical contrast differently and used the term "hedgehog" either to emphasize the importance of sustained focus on mission to achieve success in business or to describe a specialization of interest. See Jim Collins, *Good to Great: Why Some Companies Make the Leap . . . and Others Don't* (New York: Harper Business, 2001), 90–119; and Gordon Wood, *The Idea of America: Reflections on the Birth of the United States* (New York: Penguin, 2011), 10–11. Berlin's concept explains a good deal about Ayn Rand's thought in particular, and authoritarianism in general, because it includes the idea that some of us "by nature" need a structure through which to interpret the world.

22. David Leonhardt, "The Caucus," *New York Times,* January 5, 2011.

23. Jonathan Haidt, *The Righteous Mind: Why Good People are Divided by Politics and Religion* (New York: Pantheon Books, 2012), 181–84.

24. Ibid., 287.

25. Ibid., 318.

26. Kathleen Hall Jamieson and Joseph N. Cappella, *Echo Chamber: Rush Limbaugh and the Conservative Media Establishment* (New York: Oxford University Press, 2008), ix.

27. Ibid., 238.

28. Ibid., 239.

29. Elaine Pagels, *Beyond Belief: The Secret Gospel of Thomas* (New York: Vintage Books, 2003, 2004), 54.

30. Robert D. Putnam and David E. Campbell, *American Grace: How Religion Divides and Unites Us* (New York: Simon and Schuster, 2010), 473.

31. Haidt, *Righteous Mind*, 317.

CHAPTER 7

1. Suskind, *Price of Loyalty*, 325.

2. Jacob S. Hacker and Paul Pierson, *Winner-Take-All Politics: How Washington Made the Rich Richer—And Turned Its Back on the Middle Class* (New York: Simon and Schuster, 2010), 3.

3. *Federalist Papers*, No. 45.

4. *Federalist Papers*, No. 10.

5. Stephen L. Elkin, *Reconstructing the Commercial Republic: Constitutional Design after Madison* (Chicago: University of Chicago Press, 2006), 48.

6. Ibid., 9, 38.

7. Gordon Wood, *The Idea of America: Reflections on the Birth of the United States* (New York: Penguin, 2011), 134–38 of 446 (ebook).

8. See http://www.youtube.com/watch?v=WmW19uoyuO8.

9. Mann and Ornstein, *It's Even Worse Than It Looks*, 26.

10. Ibid., 102.

11. Ibid., 103.

12. Mickey Edwards, "How to Turn Republicans and Democrats into Americans," *National Journal*, June 15, 2011.

13. *Citizens United v. Federal Elections Commission*, 558 U.S. 50, 130 S.Ct. 876 (2010).

14. See generally Jeffrey D. Clements, *Corporations Are Not People: Why They Have More Rights Than You Do and What You Can Do About It* (San Francisco: Berrett-Koehler Publishers, Inc., 2012), especially 17–26.

15. See generally Elias Berg, *Democracy and the Majority Principle: A Study in Twelve Contemporary Political Theories* (Stockholm: Akademiförlaget, 1965), especially 157–59.

16. Reinhold Niebuhr, *The Irony of American History*, with a new introduction by Andrew J. Bacevich (Chicago: University of Chicago Press, 1952, 2008).

BIBLIOGRAPHY

Bartlett, Bruce. *The Benefit and the Burden: Tax Reform—Why We Need It and What It Will Take*. New York: Simon and Schuster, 2012.

Bellah, Robert, et al. *Habits of the Heart: Individualism and Commitment in American Life*. Berkeley: University of California Press, 1985, 1996.

Berg, Elias. *Democracy and the Majority Principle: A Study in Twelve Contemporary Political Theories*. Stockholm: Akademiförlaget, 1965.

Berlin, Isaiah. *The Hedgehog and the Fox: An Essay on Tolstoy's View of History*. London: Weidenfeld and Nicolson Ltd., 1953, 1967.

Bowen, Stuart W. Jr. "Hard Lessons: The Iraq Reconstruction Experience." Report of the Special Inspector General for Iraq. Washington, DC: U.S. Government Printing Office, 2009. This report has also been published as a paperback edition (USIAC) and a Google e-Book.

Brullee, Robert J., Jason Carmichael, and J. Craig Jenkins. "Shifting Public Opinion on Climate Change: An Empirical Assessment of Factors Influencing Concern over Climate Change in the U.S., 2002–2012," *Climatic Change* 114, no. 2 (February 2012).

Burns, Jennifer. *Goddess of the Market: Ayn Rand and the American Right*. New York: Oxford University Press, 2009.

Chafee, Lincoln. *Against the Tide: How a Compliant Congress Empowered a Reckless President*. New York: Thomas Dunne Books/St. Martin's Press, 2008.

Clements, Jeffrey D. *Corporations Are Not People: Why They Have More Rights Than You Do and What You Can Do About It*. San Francisco: Berrett-Koehler Publishers, Inc., 2012.

Collins, Jim. *Good to Great: Why Some Companies Make the Leap . . . and Others Don't*. New York: HarperBusiness, 2001.

Commission on Wartime Contracting in Iraq and Afghanistan. *Final Report to Congress*. Washington, DC: U.S. Government Printing Office, August 2011.

Dorgan, Byron L. *Reckless: How Debt, Deregulation, and Dark Money Nearly Bankrupted America (And How We Can Fix It!)*. New York: Thomas Dunne Books/St. Martin's Press, 2009.

Dunlap, Riley E., and Aaron M. McCright. "A Widening Gap: Republican and Democratic Views on Climate Change." *Environment Magazine*, September–October 2008.

Elkin, Stephen L. *Reconstructing the Commercial Republic: Constitutional Design after Madison*. Chicago: University of Chicago Press, 2006.

Hacker, Jacob S., and Paul Pierson. *Winner-Take-All Politics: How Washington Made the Rich Richer—And Turned Its Back on the Middle Class*. New York: Simon and Schuster, 2010.

Haidt, Jonathan. *The Righteous Mind: Why Good People Are Divided by Politics and Religion*. New York: Pantheon Books, 2012.

Heller, Anne. *Ayn Rand and the World She Made*. New York: Nan A. Talese/Doubleday, 2009.

Hetherington, Marc J., and Jonathan D. Weiler. *Authoritarianism and Polarization in American Politics*. New York: Cambridge University Press, 2009.

Jamieson, Kathleen Hall, and Joseph N. Cappella. *Echo Chamber: Rush Limbaugh and the Conservative Media Establishment*. New York: Oxford University Press, 2008.

Joyce, Philip G. *The Congressional Budget Office: Honest Numbers, Power and Policymaking*. Washington, DC: Georgetown University Press, 2011.

Kahan, D. M., E. Peters, M. Wittlin, P. Slovic, L. L. Ouellette, D. Braman, and G. Mandel. "The Polarizing Impact of Science, Literacy, and Numeracy on Perceived Climate Change Risks." *Nature Climate Change*, online advance publication, http://www.nature.com/doifinder/10.1038/nclimate1547 (2012).

Krugman, Paul. *Fuzzy Math: The Essential Guide to the Bush Tax Plan*. New York: W. W. Norton and Company, 2001.

Lakoff, George. *Don't Think of an Elephant!: Know Your Values and Frame the Debate*. White River Junction, VT: Chelsea Green Publishing Company, 2004.

Lakoff, George. *Moral Politics: How Liberals and Conservatives Think*, 2nd ed. Chicago: University of Chicago Press, 1996, 2002.

Maibach, E., C. Roser-Renouf, and A. Leiserowitz. "Global Warming's Six Americas 2009: An Audience Segmentation Analysis." Fairfax, VA: George Mason University Center for Climate Change Communication, 2009. Accessed from http://climatechange.gmu.edu.

Mann, Thomas E., and Norman J. Ornstein. *The Broken Branch: How Congress Is Failing America and How to Get It Back on Track*. New York: Oxford University Press, 2006.

Mann, Thomas E., and Norman J. Ornstein. *It's Even Worse Than It Looks: How the American Constitutional System Collided with the New Politics of Extremism*. New York: Basic Books, 2012.

Mankiw, Gregory. *Principles of Economics*. New York: Dryden, 1998.

McClellan, Scott. *What Happened: Inside the Bush White House and Washington's Culture of Deception*. New York: Public Affairs, 2008.

Merton, Thomas. *Introductions East & West: The Foreign Prefaces of Thomas Merton*. Greensboro, NC: Unicorn Press, 1981.

Pagels, Elaine. *Beyond Belief: The Secret Gospel of Thomas*. New York: Vintage Books, 2003, 2004.

Pew Oceans Commission, Report to the Nation. "America's Living Oceans: Charting a Course for Sea Change," May 2003, available at http://www.pewtrusts.org/uploaded-Files/wwwpewtrustsorg/Reports/Protecting_ocean_life/env_pew_oceans_final_report.pdf.

Powell, Colin, and Tony Kotz. *It Worked for Me: In Life and Leadership*. New York: HarperCollins, 2012.

Putnam, Robert. *Bowling Alone: The Collapse and Revival of American Community*. New York: Simon and Schuster, 2000.

Putnam, Robert D., and David E. Campbell. *American Grace: How Religion Divides and Unites Us*. New York: Simon and Schuster, 2010.

Ricks, Thomas E. *Fiasco: The American Military Adventure in Iraq*. New York: Penguin Press, 2006.

Ricks, Thomas E. *The Gamble: General David Petraeus and the American Military Adventure in Iraq, 2006–2008*. New York: Penguin Press, 2009.

Shulman, Seth. *Undermining Science: Suppression and Distortion in the Bush Administration*, 2nd ed. Berkeley: University of California Press, 2006, 2008.

Sosnik, Douglas B., Matthew J. Dowd, and Ron Fournier. *Applebee's America: How Successful Political, Business, and Religious Leaders Connect with the New American Community*. New York: Simon and Schuster, 2006.

Stockman, David. *The Triumph of Politics: Why the Reagan Revolution Failed*. New York: Harper and Row, 1986.

Suskind, Ron. *The Price of Loyalty: George W. Bush, the White House, and the Education of Paul O'Neill*. New York: Simon and Schuster, 2004.

U.S. Commission on Ocean Policy, Final Report, September 20, 2004. "An Ocean Blueprint for the Twenty-first Century," available at http://www.oceancommission.gov/documents/welcome.html.

Wood, Gordon. *The Idea of America: Reflections on the Birth of the United States*. New York: Penguin, 2011.

Note: Page numbers in *italics* indicate tables and figures.